THE
GREAT
GREAT
WALL

THE
GREAT
GREAT
WALL

ALONG THE BORDERS
OF HISTORY
FROM CHINA TO MEXICO

IAN VOLNER

ABRAMS PRESS, NEW YORK

Library of Congress Control Number: 2018936293

ISBN: 978-1-4197-3282-9
eISBN: 978-1-68335-530-4

Printed and bound in the United States
10 9 8 7 6 5 4 3 2 1

Abrams books are available at special discounts when purchased in quantity for premiums and promotions as well as fundraising or educational use. Special editions can also be created to specification. For details, contact specialsales@abramsbooks.com or the address below.

Abrams Press® is a registered trademark of Harry N. Abrams, Inc.

ABRAMS The Art of Books
195 Broadway, New York, NY 10007
abramsbooks.com

For Mildred

Life has to do with walls; we're continuously going in and out, back and forth, and through them. A wall is the quickest, the thinnest, the element we're always transgressing . . .

—John Hejduk, architect

CONTENTS

INTRODUCTION

Monument 252, Tijuana

The president of the United States knew little of the border, and less of any-thing beyond it. A northerner, he was hardly known (to the degree that he let anything of the sort be known) as an admirer of anyone's culture save his own; but for the course of political events, it is unlikely there would have been anything to connect him to Mexico or its frontier. In truth, the whole business never much interested him.

The subject had first crossed his desk in the form of a bulky portfolio, padded thick with maps and tables and photographic plates, arriving in the Oval Office less than two months after the incumbent had set up shop there. This was the *Report of the Boundary Commission*, the product of five years' arduous research on and around the southern border, conducted by a banner intergovernmental group of surveyors, engineers, and scientists.

Politically, the project was an orphan: The document had been left to lan-guish for months after being submitted under the previous administration. That administration hadn't commissioned it either, the diplomatic wheels having been set in motion by *its* predecessor. The report was long, and com-plicated, and the newly installed secretary of state, with whose perfunctory commendation it was transmitted to the president, was known to be hope-lessly senile. It is doubtful that the president even so much as glanced at it.

As a consequence, the president did not read about the life-threatening border climate that, as the group discovered, could cause perspiration at a rate of "7 quarts per day for the men and 20 gallons for the animals." He did not read about the recurrent and chillingly realistic mirages, one of them resembling "a city with all its buildings," another a palisade a hundred feet high, following the men for miles through a narrow valley; when at last it shimmered and vanished, the men discovered they had been traveling through a barren plain. The president did not read about the difficulties of getting and keeping the pack mules, the equipment, or the hired laborers who frequently quit once they'd had enough of the desert and its tricks. What the haze did not do (the commissioners reported) the human mind did, conspiring with the oppressive heat and the featureless expanses to produce fantastic distortions. "At times a jack rabbit would loom up on the desert with the apparent size of a cow," wrote the commissioners. "Occa-sionally the legs of animals would be so comically lengthened as to give them the appearance of being mounted on stilts."

The report recounted all this alongside an itinerary of injuries and acci-dents and endless searches for water in country that, even on the threshold of the twentieth century, was still more or less terra incognita. There were confounding encounters with desperately poor residents of a smattering of small towns, outside of which their year-round numbers amounted to no more than a hundred individuals in a region spanning some 24,000 square miles. There was ample evidence of the dead, small crops of gravestones clustered together in the desert, sometimes belonging to whole families who had perished of thirst and whose sun-blasted remains had not been found until the following rainy season. The commissioners did not see much evi-dence of the rainy season, since for the first two years of their sojourn the

Southwest was struck by a severe drought. They passed scores of dead cattle and forsaken ranches. They spotted evidence of disused dams, constructed (they speculated) by long-dead civilizations. The desert flowers, they noted, had no fragrance.

For all its privations, however, the work genuinely seemed enjoyable to those carrying it out, and the commissioners' chronicle is one of high adventure. What they were looking for was itself a variety of a hallucination. Although the border's cartographic location had been settled by a treaty following the Mexican-American War, no truly modern effort had yet been mounted to explore, and to permanently define, the whole border that divided the United States and Mexico between the Rio Grande and the Pacific. No one could even be quite sure where it was.

The border, with apologies to Robert Frost, was ours before we were the border's, and laying permanent claim to it was what the Boundary Commission was tasked with doing. They were not the first to try: An original attempt, the so-called Emory-Salazar survey, was completed in 1855 and had been if anything even more intrepid, but the crude markers it left behind had been undone by time, putting the boundary's precise location once again in doubt. Using the most sophisticated metrical techniques then available, the new expedition that set out in 1892 was to follow and document the frontier, demarcating it as precisely as possible using a series of small but sturdy monuments, purpose-built and distributed at intervals of no more than five miles beginning in El Paso, Texas. The monuments, fat obelisks of stone with placards bearing sequential numbers, stood about ten feet high, and the commission had immense difficulty (especially when the rain, at last, arrived) carting them into place and then rooting them in the shifting, sandy soil.

In all of these endeavors the group was aided by their opposite numbers on the Mexican side. The commission was a binational effort, and over and over the American group relied on the expertise of their Spanish-speaking counterparts—the region being, in the main, Hispanophone—to communicate with the locals and help guide them to wells and natural springs. In what seems now a grand geopolitical farce, this unlikely band of Mexicans and Americans spent five years wandering in the desert, trying to avoid dehydration, frequently crisscrossing the very border they were charged with delineating, exactly as though there were no border at all.

At times, it appeared that no one really cared. It was not a subject of pressing concern to anyone, least of all to President William McKinley, during whose term it just so happened that the US-Mexico border's real-world location was definitively established, and on whose desk the report landed. Except as an occasional cautionary tale about the dangers of silver coinage, Mexico was a nonissue in McKinley's rise to the presidency. The newly elected leader did not care about the commissioners' long hikes along parlous ridges, or their trudges into dark arroyos, or the final lines in their cover letter, extolling "our associates of the Mexican commission [who] have invariably shown a spirit of fairness and courtesy." The fleeting matter of the Boundary Commission was as much involvement as McKinley had with the border, until four years later, when his political manager made him go there.

Intended as a victory lap following his decisive reelection victory, McKinley made a nationwide tour in 1901 at the urging of his adroit handler Mark Hanna. In six weeks, the now twice-victorious candidate was to sweep across the map of the United States in a clockwise motion, beginning in the South and working his way to California before turning back east to upstate New York. Midway through, the presidential party arrived in El Paso. This was where, for a brief instant, McKinley nearly made history by becoming the first sitting president to visit Mexico.

Right within sight of Monument No. 1, McKinley gave a brief speech in the presence of Mexican and American officials. When he stepped down from the podium, the press reported, "the President expressed a desire to take a look over into Mexico and was driven down to the international bridge"—one of the crossings still operated today by the successor organization to the Boundary Commission. From there McKinley could look south, seeing "the old church of Guadalupe, over 300 years old, the Spanish prison and other interesting buildings in Juarez." If he had gone just a few steps farther, it would have marked two firsts, making McKinley not only the first president to cross the border but also the first to ever set foot in any foreign country while in office.

In the end, McKinley declined the gambit. Mrs. McKinley was invited to lunch in Juarez, but accounts differ as to whether she attended. Several weeks later, the first lady fell ill, forcing the couple's return to Washington and delaying the tour by several months while she convalesced. The president finally hit the road again in the fall, completing his journey in Buffalo, New York, at the Pan-American Exposition, where, in the auditorium of the Temple of Music, he was shot to death by an anarchist from Michigan. McKinley had recently completed a speech urging reciprocity in trade relations with America's hemispheric partners, a theme perfectly in tune with the fair's stated goal, the promotion of "commercial well-being and good understanding among the American Republics."

McKinley is long dead. Yet the Boundary Commission lives on, albeit more in body than in spirit. In addition to the border facilities still maintained by the latter-day agency, the monuments that the late-nineteenth-century team spread out through the southern desert are still visible, though increasingly difficult to find. I have seen one of them.

Monument No. 252 is located on the eastern fringes of Tijuana. It can best be viewed from the Mexican side by following a rugged dirt track, running parallel to the US-Mexico line past the looming tin sheds of the maquiladoras, the enormous factories that have sprung up in the wake of the North American Free Trade Agreement (NAFTA). The road, if one can call it that, serves as a back alley to the district of Escondido, a rough neighborhood of scrap heaps and cinderblock houses the backyards of which are like scrap heaps themselves, shaded in blue plastic tarps and filled with castoff machine parts. Women sit in the yards, doing piecework and yelling occasionally at stray dogs.

Opposite the houses, the upper stalk of No. 252 can be seen, half buried in rubble, but with the engraving in Spanish warding off would-be vandals still legible. There's a corresponding message in English on the other side, but when I first saw it, it was all but impossible to read. That is because the monument—part of the first coordinated attempt to impose some kind of manifest order, some eminent reason, on the geographical and conceptual wilderness of the border—was abutted on its northern face by a second attempt at the same object, a steel fence installed in the 1990s. To see them together, it struck me, was to see the border thickened in time, a dotted line made continuous.

The process hasn't stopped there. Just north of the first fence, no more than thirty yards away on the US side, I could see yet another fence, taller and with a sloped rampart at the top, built in the first decade of the twenty-first century. And, directly adjacent to that, easy enough to see by standing back from the stone monument and glancing eastward, were still other structures: tall slabs, varying in color from dun gray to russet pink, eight in all. Erected in the late summer of 2017, these were the prototype segments for the proposed border-length wall, a project that had, for more than two years, occupied the national conversation in the United States.

Four structures, spread across fifty yards and more than a century. The spaces in between them—what happens there, and why it happens over and over—that is where I would like to begin.

This is not a book about the land on which that line was drawn. I come as a stranger to the Mexican border region and will defer to others with regard to the character and culture of that particular borderland. Nor is this a book about borders as such, though most of the action will take place in those unquiet landscapes. This is a book about the artificial landscape, the built environment, as it has been impressed and is being impressed into the territory of borderlands everywhere. In its premier form, that man-made impression has taken the shape of a wall.

Inevitably, this book is also about *the* wall—*that* wall, the two-thousand-mile-long, multibillion-dollar elephant in the room of contemporary American life—the wall that the current occupant of the White House has repeatedly commanded (whom has he been addressing?) be built, turning the command into something like a spiritual affirmation for a dispirited wedge of the electorate. The proposed US-Mexico border wall, and its outsized role during the last national election, means that it lurks somewhere in every discussion about where our civilization is headed. The progress of the wall project, and the politics surrounding it, will be the metronome for what follows, setting the pace for everything else. But this is not *only* about the wall.

This is also a book about walls generally—though not all walls. For ten thousand years, since the end of the early Neolithic period, most human settlements have featured some kind of perimeter construction. To catalog them all would be impossible, not to mention boring; it would also be confusing, since a long and hazy adumbration of global walldom would quickly run afoul of a serious category mistake: What do we talk about when we talk about walls? Do we mean every kind of wall? What about the walls of houses? We would be tearing through the annals of history searching for anything that looked like one stone stacked atop another. The archaeological and conceptual waters are simply too deep.

They get deeper with every passing day. During the time in which I have researched, written, and edited this book, dozens of exhibitions and art projects, hundreds of films and radio podcasts, perhaps thousands of academic articles and news articles and opinion pieces have been published and screened and aired in the United States alone, all devoted to one or another aspect of borders, walls, and the current wall debate. Wherever I've gone looking for one wall, I've stumbled on a dozen others, and even when I wasn't looking for them they seemed to come unbidden. In Venice I saw crowds, equipped with champagne stems and tote bags, jamming into the American and German Pavilions at the city's architecture biennale to see wall-related installations. In Madrid for a foundation opening, I discovered our host had a section of the Berlin Wall in his backyard, and then listened as a Spanish guest talked about his own country's walls, separating the African outposts of Ceuta and Melilla from surrounding Morocco. While I was looking at border fencing in New Mexico, scholars from around the world were meeting in Montreal for a major conference about borders and walls. No one writer could account for all of this, and to even try would be hubris of a very high order. That way madness lies.

On the other hand, a little madness may be just what we need. As an historian and critic, my field is architecture: In principle at least, I am qualified to say more or less what a wall is, to expand at length on its meanings, manifestations, etc. There exists a vast body of scholarship about walls in theory, and about their individual histories, and I will turn to those sources frequently; many other sources from many other disciplines will be taken up as well, with further odds and ends in the endnotes and bibliography. But what I would also like to do, consonant with my secret life as a poet, is to talk about how walls *feel*. I have come to know a few of these structures, and with each one I have seen I have become more and more convinced that embedded deep in our fundamental makeup there is a pathology, a mysterious mania, expressed in the structures we build to keep each other out. To interrogate this condition, what I am aiming at here is a phantasmagoria—compounded of reportage and myth, of present and past—that might bring us closer to the sensation of walls in the mind and on the body. The object throughout is to convey something of the emotional import of these structures and the stories that surround them, seen as they really are and not as mere metaphors.

This is no easy thing, particularly given the insidious ways that walls have worked their way into language. Their figurative presence becomes harder to avoid the more you talk about them. The problem can drive you up the wall or push you up against one. Soon it will have you bouncing off them. You could be a fly or a flower, but eventually you'll run into one, be it of fire or of brick—and between you, me, and these four, it doesn't matter if you break the fourth or bang your head against it, because Pink Floyd's mother will always tell Mr. Gorbachev to walk through one or piss up another.

Let's hope we've gotten *that* out of our system. (I make no promises.)

Before we get underway in earnest, a little housekeeping.

It will be noted in the foregoing that I do not use a certain name. It is my intention throughout to use that name only sparingly. In part this is a matter of historiological scruple: Presidents don't build walls; societies do. But I will own to other scruples, perhaps more personal. When the Temple of Artemis at Ephesus was burned to the ground in the fourth century BCE, it was said that the arsonist did it so that his name would never be forgotten. In some art historical circles it is a tradition never to say the perpetrator's name in discussing the lost building. Methodology and morals do sometimes coincide.

At the time of writing, the status of the proposed southern border wall remains very much in flux. Any account of its development up to now will of necessity be fragmentary, ending in a cliffhanger. Future historians must finish this story. My role, as was once said of architecture critic Colin Rowe, is only as an historian of the "immediate past."

Of the more remote history I have chosen to look at those walls that interest me most, sticking to those intended as permanent installations, with an eye toward as much geographical and temporal diversity as I could manage while still being able to actually visit them. Their presentation will alternate with developments on the US-Mexico border, in accordance with a logic that I trust will be adduced by the reader; likewise, the parts of each story I choose to tell, the personal impressions I gathered, the incidents and coincidences that ensued—the way certain mountains suddenly turned into deserts or things became confused, started to resemble each other . . . They happen as they happened, and we will make these discoveries together. Again, this is not a definitive account, nor, I contend, would any such account be possible. This should be understood as a kind of cycle, like a frieze, or a mural in a long and twisting passage.

Ian Volner
Harlem, New York, January 2019

I

THE INVENTION
OF DIFFERENCE

JERICHO

Gog and Magog were in Egypt. Or perhaps Ethiopia. They might, in fact, have been in Libya, or somewhere on the far side of the Black Sea. They may have been two people or two places; they may have been one place and its king—Gog *of* Magog—or they might have been a single person— Gogmagog, a medieval giant so powerful he was said to have lifted up an oak tree and waved it around like a wand. In the Book of Revelation, it was foretold that at the time of Armageddon, the armies of Gog and Magog would encircle the city of Christ. Arrayed around the fortress of the saints, their numbers would be "as the sand of the sea."

This malevolent double entity is first named in the Book of Ezekiel, when God addresses the titular prophet and commands him to "set [his] face" against the foes of Israel. As with much of the Nevi'im—the second segment of the Hebrew Tanakh—Ezekiel was composed during and after the forced exile of the Jewish people in Babylon, when their traditions and language were in peril as never before. Gog and Magog were boogiemen (or, as the case may be, boogieman), a rhetorical effigy for God's chosen to burn as they sat in bondage waiting for the return to Zion.

But before they could lament their lost homeland, the Jews had to have a homeland to lament. In the traditional biblical chronology, Canaan, the country of their fathers, had been seized by the Twelve Tribes beginning around 1500 BCE following the death of Moses, seven hundred years prior to the Babylonian captivity. The record of its conquest is given in the Book of Joshua, written at the same time as Ezekiel and featuring some of the most harrowing passages in ancient literature. On that occasion, it was the Jews themselves who were the menacing outsider, sweeping across the Jordan River and into the basin north of the Dead Sea. For the Canaanites, the approaching Hebrew host was as horrible a specter as any Gog or Magog. So they dug in—at Jericho, their walled capital, where the Israelites first met them in battle.

Such, at any rate, is the story. Beginning in the 1950s, with the pioneering work of archaeologist Kathleen Kenyon, scholarship has fairly well debunked the biblical account, showing that no invasion occurred in the Jordan Valley at the time the Hebrews supposedly arrived there. But Jericho was no fiction, nor was its wall, as attested by Kenyon's discovery of ruins radiocarbon dated to as early as 8300 BCE, long predating the Israelites' arrival. The wall of Jericho was by most estimates the oldest of its kind in the world, the first urban fortification anywhere.

And this walled settlement, or its second-millennium BCE counterpart, is what the Israelites would claim to have attacked. "Now Jericho was straitly shut up," reads Joshua, "because of the children of Israel: none went out, and none came in." The Canaanites thought themselves secure behind their sloped barricade: The wall that most closely corresponds to the biblical period was covered in smooth plaster, making a seamless and apparently impregnable envelope around the city. But the Hebrews had an inside man. More precisely, they had an inside woman, a prostitute named Rahab.

Fearing the wrathful Adonai whom the Jews claimed as the one true god, Rahab hid a team of Hebrew scouts on their arrival in Jericho. As she lived atop the wall itself, she was able to let them down again by rope on their departure. In accordance with divine command, the Israelites then paraded around the walls of the town bearing before them the Ark of the Covenant—the gilded chest, decked with winged cherubim, that betokened their fealty to the Creator. On the seventh day, the walls of Jericho miraculously fell, and as the children of Israel overran the city they slaughtered every single man, woman, and child in it, sparing only Rahab and her kin.

The principle of herem, the holy ban placed on unbelievers in the Torah, is a subject little dwelt upon by modern Jews. The Canaanites, along with other vanished Semitic peoples (Jebusites, Hittites, Hivites) were prescribed for annihilation in the post-Mosaic settlement of the Promised Land, a program bearing a most discomfiting resemblance to what would now be known as ethnic cleansing. That the Hebrews could have carried out this agenda, considering their own predicament in Babylon (and later), is ironic enough. Even more so is that a history so laden with violence has been received, by the spiritual heirs of the Israelites, as a story of redemption.

Born of a people confined within walls, the Jericho story has long been used as an allegory for the triumph of justice over inequity, its unseemlier aspects—to say nothing of its archaeological improbability—all but ignored. In the early 1800s, slaves at work in the fields of the American South began to sing of Joshua, how he "fought the Battle of Jericho" and how "the walls came tumbling down." The spiritual would become, in the century that followed, an anthem of the civil rights movement and its latter-day admirers. On January 20, 2008, parishioners at Ebenezer Baptist Church of Atlanta, Georgia, formerly the home church of Dr. Martin Luther King Jr., heard a speech from a special guest about the wall of Jericho and its meaning. One year later to the day, Senator Barack Obama was sworn in as president of the United States.

Be it in songs and sermons, or in bricks and mortar, walls are sui generis among the artifacts of human culture. If not quite a precondition of culture as such, they must count among its first fruits, as elemental (or nearly so) as the sharpened stone and the roaring fire.

Prehistories of the built environment are notoriously shaky. Throughout the eighteenth and nineteenth centuries, the intellectual scene in Europe was riven by debates—led by now-obscure figures like the Frenchman Quatremère de Quincy and Germany's Gottfried Semper—about the origins of man-made structures: Were the first dwellings something like a Greek temple made out of wood sticks or more akin to a Bedouin tent? But those arguments tended to end in a mist of conjecture. To search for the beginnings of the wall-as-defense is to disappear into the same fog: The minute a house's wooden frame (or the fabric of a tent) is rendered sufficiently sturdy, that membrane might be considered a shield. Restrict the definition to freestanding walls, and one is still confronted by a structure so rudimentary that it is hard to imagine *not* imagining it. For all archaeologists have learned since the days of Semper and de Quincy, the best we can say is that walls have been with us as long as there has been an "us."

The proof is at Jericho—the real Jericho, not the storied place of the Bible but the historical site, known today as Tell es-Sultan (Hill of the Sultan), located in the modern-day West Bank in the Palestinian territories. Not only the oldest city wall known to us, the ninth-millennium site is also by most estimates the oldest city, full stop. The original settlement began at the foot of the Judaean Mountains next to a natural spring, doubtless the spot's initial attraction to roving nomads. Easily visible today from anywhere in the valley, today's tell (the archaeological term for such artificial hills) is the product of successive waves of construction in the area. Originally the town was not much higher than the riverbank a short journey to the east—though its situation on lightly sloping terrain did give it a slight prominence, the gradient acting as a glacis, a protective incline that any would-be attackers would have to ascend. In this sense, and like so many of its successors, the earliest wall at Jericho acted as a kind of accentuation of the terrain. Nature, as the old philosophes would have agreed, might be considered the template for architecture.

Tell es-Sultan (in the middle distance) and the Jordan River Valley, seen from the gondola lift to the Mount of Temptation

Freestanding walls do not, however, spring organically out of the rocks and hills. It would seem intuitive that warfare, or something like it, must provide the spur to their construction; yet Jericho demonstrates precisely the opposite. Not only is there no evidence of fighting in the area during the biblical period, there is also nothing to indicate any intense conflict in the ninth millennium BCE either. Excavations of burial sites from the period of the original wall's construction have shown that male longevity rates were comparatively high at the time, pointing to a period of relative peace. From this seeming paradox has arisen the theory that—contrary to the city's celebrated place in biblical lore—the original Jericho was something very different from an unwelcoming stronghold.

Nondefensive explanations for the city wall began to circulate in the 1980s, after anthropologist and archaeologist Ofer Bar-Yosef observed that the wall's pinnacle-like tower, a twenty-eight-foot structure located on the western flank of the original fortifications, was located *behind* the wall, not in front of it. Perhaps, Bar-Yosef speculated, it might have been meant as some kind of temple? In 2008, Tel Aviv–based researchers Ran Barkai and Roy Liran took this notion further, suggesting still broader "ideological reasons" for the city's mysterious armatures. Tracking the astrological and topographical relationship of the wall, the tower, and the landscape, the pair made a startling discovery: The tower was exactly placed so that when the sun set on the longest day of the year, the hills behind it made it appear as though the tower were casting a shadow precisely over the settlement, spreading from the tip of the lofty pinnacle to every house and hut in Jericho. Seen from the proper perspective, the tower would appear as a representation of the peak of the Quruntul—the highest point in the Judean Mountains, later renowned as the site of Christ's temptation—while the rest of the wall "could symbolize the ridge from which the Quruntul emerges." The wall and tower were indeed quoting the landscape, but solely for the purpose of creating a stirring spectacle. They were not, the scholars concluded, built to keep anyone out. They were built to impress them, and to invite them in.

While this "beacon" theory has made some headway in archaeological circles, it still leaves unexplained why exactly such a beacon should arise where it did, when it did. It would be natural to assume that if the people of Jericho were advertising something, it must have been some new kind of social and economic order, presumably of the farming-and-barter variety that usually forms the basis of city life. But this is not the case. As Barkai and Liran also note, both wall and city predate the adoption of a fully agrarian lifestyle by the people living inside it—the citizens remained primarily hunter-gatherers until well after the wall's construction. The city-dwellers were, in fact, almost indistinguishable from their nomadic cousins wandering through the valley below, looking up in awe at the wall. The only thing that separated them was the wall. The only thing it advertised was that the people of Jericho had built it.

It is a prospect that would have staggered the Enlightenment-era theorists. This wall, the earliest of its kind, may not have appeared for any particular reason; instead, it created its own rationale—*the idea itself of difference*—that there could be not only an "us," but a "them." Archaeology throws us back into the realm of ideology, and thence to myth, and we're right back in the company of the herem, Joshua, and Gog and Magog.

What philosopher Gaston Bachelard once observed about the invention of fire might also be said of wall-building. "Our theory would appear less daring," he wrote, if contemporary readers would "cease to imagine prehistoric man as being automatically subject to misfortune and necessity." Using the built environment as an instrument of separation was never the work of intellectual innocents seeking a purely practical means to a purely practical end. It was always and already a matter of ideology, an ideology born the instant the people of Jericho began stacking their undressed stones.

As compared to the significance of that act, the manner of the stacking is almost unremarkable. The initial wall of circa 8300 BCE, built shortly after the regular settlement was established, was nearly twelve feet high and six feet wide at the base. The town encircled by the wall, housing perhaps fewer than a thousand inhabitants, occupied about six acres in an ovular plan, with most of the dwellings built of loaf-shaped mud bricks—the indentations of bricklayers' thumbs are still visible on their tops. The wall, from its earliest incarnation, was already entirely of stone, brought to the site more or less as found in the surrounding hills and set up against an internal earthen bank with a flat top. Winnowing slightly in width at the upper end to lessen the vertical load, the wall was sloped back slightly, but other than that it did not sport any crenellations or other features that would enhance its defensive strength. It could not have been terribly effective as a barrier, not even against the occasional alluvial washes descending from the uplands, which appear to have progressively eroded it and required it to be periodically reinforced.

After several centuries of habitation, the community that had built the first wall disappeared from the area. Subsequent generations would return to the man-made hill and settle there again, building different types of houses and rebuilding the wall along different lines, blocking off the entrance to the old tower and its twenty-two internal steps. As each successive age built on the last, the city steadily rose into the man-made plateau one sees today; eventually the tower was subsumed altogether, and against its flanks the citizens buried their dead. Over six thousand years and more, different civilizations made different uses of the wall, suiting it to their own needs and culture. Finally, around 1500 BCE, the age of the Israelites arrived, and the wall of Jericho began its slow metamorphosis from a thing of stone and earth into an object of pure myth. A remarkable victory, it might be said, given that the Israelites probably never conquered Jericho at all.

Equally remarkable is that the popularity of the myth would eventually result in its being debunked. Most of this history of Tell es-Sultan comes from researchers who hoped to discover the wall discussed in scripture and prove that the story was true. They came above all from England, beginning in the nineteenth century, pioneers in the burgeoning field of biblical archaeology; full of piety and high ideals, few of them truly knew what they were doing, and most of them may have done more harm than good. It was not until the 1930s that any of them even succeeded in positively identifying Tell es-Sultan as the remains of Jericho.

At last one arrived who did know what she was doing, and then some. Dame Kathleen Kenyon—K to her associates, the Great *Sitt* ("Lady") to her Arabic-speaking workers—first came to Tell es-Sultan in earnest in the dig season of 1952. No less a believing Christian than those who came before, she was of a far more exacting disposition, and, while she professed interest in verifying the Book of Joshua, she refused in any way to be blinkered by her convictions. Cutting a deep trench into the tell on its western side, Kenyon peeled back the soil layer after layer in five-meter squares, meticulously sifting and sorting every potsherd and castoff artifact. Her mostly untrained local labor (many of them the displaced and dispossessed of the recently concluded First Arab-Israeli War) were transformed into expert field hands by the redoubtable K, who stalked around the dig with a cigarette in one hand, often giving off a strong smell of gin. So precise, so careful were the methods deployed by her and her team that they were able to detect and preserve the most delicate traces: the skin of an evaporated fluid on a stone surface, the trail of a white ant across the remains of an ancient reed mat.

Kenyon's conclusion—that not only was there no wall for Joshua to bring down in the second millennium, but probably no town at that particular moment either—was a definitive rebuttal to the Joshua legend. She was coy in announcing it, as she had to be: Her expedition, intended to last a single season, grew into a six-year-long effort and financing it required institutional support that was more easily sustained by stirring up the press back home with stories echoing the biblical tale. Bearish as she could be, Kenyon was also capable of great tact, a birthright of her immensely privileged upbringing: Her father, Sir Frederick Kenyon, had been director of the British Museum, and she was raised in a house that was effectively built into the museum itself. For her entire life she moved in a rarified circle of elite academics, aristocrats, and government officials. She knew how to play the game and would occasionally let slip to the British papers some tantalizingly conjectural remark about how a piece of pottery might have been left behind by "a frightened Canaanite housewife fleeing her kitchen in the face of Joshua's assault."

Further than that, she would not go. In the past—the French in Egypt, the Germans in Turkey—archaeologists had gone shoveling their way carelessly through what might have been invaluable historical material, trying desperately to reach what they wanted to believe was there, be it gold-filled tombs or the ruins of Troy. But K was no more interested in the fifteenth-century BCE layers—the period that notionally overlapped with Joshua—than she was in all the rest that Tell es-Sultan had to offer. In a private letter sent from the site, she declared that she "hadn't seen a sign of Joshua," and most of the specialists who came after, figures like Bar-Yosef and Barkai and Liran, have tended to follow her lead. Kenyon declared of the pseudobiblical period in the town's life that it was "not spectacular."

That assessment did not satisfy some hearers then, and still does not now. Since Kenyon's death in 1978, there have been many scholarly revisions of her discoveries, some of them making the assertion—gladly seized on by the press—that Kenyon was wrong, that the site was occupied at the time of Joshua, and that the Canaanites really were routed by an invading Hebrew force sometime around 1400 BCE. Since 1990, Dr. Bryant G. Wood, an archaeologist then affiliated with the University of Toronto, has claimed that evidence from Kenyon's finds points to a major destructive event at Jericho during the second millennium, more or less the estimated date of the Hebrew arrival. (Wood, an avowed creationist and editor of the journal *Bible and Spade*, admits that radiocarbon dating does not support his theory, but finds fault instead with the dating system itself.) Other advocates of the biblical version have pointed to fire damage on roughly contemporaneous sections of wall, as well as the frequency of earthquakes in the area, which could easily have caused the wall to collapse at some time after the Israelites began to settle in Canaan. Even if the Bible story isn't completely accurate, they contend, it still reflects a truthful event, a natural disaster that could readily be interpreted as an act of God.

Such interpretations have not been enough to spur major new digs at the site, and few archaeologists have returned there since Kenyon removed its sentimental scriptural halo. For forty years, Rome's Sapienza University has been the only major Western institution with a continued presence in and around Jericho, working with the Palestinian Authority, under whose jurisdiction it now falls, carrying out preservation and research projects in collaboration with local university students and scholars. There are no known plans for another large-scale expedition anytime in the near future, and the continued political instability of the region makes such a development less and less likely. Though Tell es-Sultan is frequented by religious tourists, it is mostly an afterthought even for them, a place to stop en route from the Mount of Temptation to the Baptismal Site of Christ on the Jordan. If there is any magic left to the place for the nonbeliever, it would be difficult to say what it is. So I decided to go find out.

Down the eastern hills from Amman, into the rift valley, to the banks of the Jordan River was no more than an hour's drive. Getting through security took twice that time, even after accepting the Jordanian government's proffer of an "express service" that in principle entitled the buyer to a quicker ride over the often traffic-clogged Allenby Bridge, but whose main privilege appeared to be a cup of tea in a waiting room choked with cigarette smoke. Arriving after much travail on the Palestinian side, I arranged for a driver at the reception desk of the Oasis Hotel on the outskirts of modern Jericho. The city of today is a dingy if bustling town slightly to the east and south of its ancient forebear, and the driver who took me through it and up to Tell es-Sultan cost nearly as much as the entire journey so far. He was fast, however, and at least reasonably safe.

Past the tourist bazaar and the parking lot there stands a tiled fountain, the remains of the spring that first brought settlers to Jericho and, beyond that, the path leading up to the mesa of Tell es-Sultan. When I reached the top of the archaeological site there was a large American tourist group, most of them standing on a metal platform that had been placed over a deep crevice in the sandy hill. Equipped with earpieces, the group was listening to a headset-wearing professional guide as she explained Kathleen Kenyon's excavation techniques, how she and her team had cut the wedges into the ground, how they'd combed meticulously through the soil, how the building techniques of the ancients had changed from millennium to millennium, from the earliest crude mud bricks to the stones of the Iron Age. Most of the Americans nodded appreciatively, squinting down at the narrow artificial ravine—all except for two young women, who stood off to one side.

A group of eight or so Palestinian children had gathered around the pair, none of them more than ten or eleven years old, some of them in prim school uniforms. The women were taking snapshots with the children, and the children were playing along gladly, jumping up and down, trying with mingled success to formulate questions in rudimentary English. Eventually the group began to move on and the two women said their good-byes to their young friends, who waved at them frantically as the women rejoined the group and slowly made their way down the hill, vanishing out of view.

Once they had gone, there was no one else on the hill. The area around the tell today is a genuinely desolate spot, and what remains of the dig site is not such as to cheer the heart. La Sapienza's improvement efforts have come to naught, consisting mostly of faded interpretive signs with second-rate English translations. Few of these remain intact: The plates with the text and photos have been prized off most of the standards, leaving behind only bare metal sheets, dented and pockmarked.

Stopping to read one of the less damaged ones, I tried once more to understand the history that was packed thick and deep into the ground below, an eon in every inch. There beneath the metal platform was the prehistoric tower, the beacon of Liran and Barkai's theory, looking more like a dirty well but with its internal steps still clearly visible. The wall adjoining it at the base of the pit had to be the ninth-millennium wall, the first wall . . . or was that only bedrock I was seeing? The discolored images on the sign hardly helped—any more than Kenyon's drawings in her book, which betrayed her unfortunate lack of talent as a draftswoman. And which were the fifteenth-century walls, the ones claimed as Joshua's by the biblical literalists? One sooty deposit looked so much like the next.

Ten thousand years of human habitation is difficult for the mind to accept. It stymies the innate desire to imagine what a ruin "originally" looked like, to create a mental restoration: On the one hand, the imprecision of the archaeological record makes it pure guesswork; on the other, there is simply the inadequacy of our idea of an "original," of a definitive version of the past. This place, like all places, was in flux every year, every month, perhaps every day of its long existence. Jericho was falling down from the moment it was built—and then it was rebuilt, and rebuilt again. It was finally reconstituted one last time, albeit in a radically different way, in the form of a dig site, with its gridded-off sectors and stratigraphic markers. Now even that was lost, a victim not to arms and plunder but to wind and rain and neglect.

I stood in the middle of it, reading the text on the sign, when suddenly there came a loud metallic *pang*. I didn't think anything of it, but an instant later there came another and then another. Something was striking the sign from the far side. I looked around it, over to the northern side of the site. There, no more than thirty feet away, were the children from before, lined up now like crows on a fence, silent and half-smiling. Each one had a rock in his or her hand.

The barrage that ensued lasted half a minute, maybe a shade more. Many of the rocks were small, pebbles really; even if they'd struck me, it's unlikely they would have done any harm. In the event, none of them made contact, most of them clattering against the steel signboard, to which I drew closer, using it as a shield. The metal sheet might have been their intended target all along—though a couple of the kids had remarkably good throwing arms, and a few stones arced over the sign and got within inches of my head. I shouted at them to stop, to no effect, and I grew increasingly concerned that one or more of them might go a step farther and come close enough to get around the sign. If, that is, they really meant to hit me in the first place.

I never had a chance to find out. In the far distance, as much as a hundred yards or more, a man on a bulldozer started shouting in Arabic. Whether he was shouting at the children, or could even see them, was unclear. Whatever the case, he succeeded in frightening them. The bolder among them lingered for a second longer, but most of them started to jog backward toward the dusty hills. Presently the whole group broke into a run.

When I got back to the Oasis Hotel that evening, I reported what had happened to the friends I had been staying with back in Amman. One of them, Palestinian by birth but raised in the United States, responded quickly by text message: *I'm so sorry*, he wrote. *Everyone over there has shaken baby syndrome.* I appreciated the attempt at dark humor, and the empathy, though it hardly seemed an explanation. But maybe there was no explanation.

Is tribalism hardwired into the human animal? It might not be. A 2008 study led by the University of Sheffield in England revealed that babies do not demonstrate any marked preference for faces of their own race at birth, acquiring it only over the course of the first few months of life. In the well-publicized Robbers Cave experiment from 1954, named after the Oklahoma State Park where it was conducted, researchers randomly divided sixth-grade boys into two groups, separated the groups and gave them a week to bond (and name themselves), then brought them together for a series of competitions. Shaping up, at first, like a true-life *Lord of the Flies*, the scenario took an abrupt turn when the children had to cooperate to accomplish common goals like food-gathering. After three weeks both sides insisted on returning home on the same bus. Scholars in the emerging field of cultural cognition have argued that, despite our predilection for group-think and ideological prejudice, we may be more susceptible to reason than our polarized politics would have us believe. "The fog of cultural conflict," as Yale's Dan Kahan has termed it, could yet be dispelled through "effective communication strategies"—the fault lies not in our stars, but in our discourse. Whether or not one finds this prescription convincing, it might still be best to not always assume the worst. Sometimes a wall is just a wall: In probing the illusion of difference, one has to be on guard not to fall for it oneself, however convincing and disorienting its effects.

The embarrassed excitement of the children at Tell es-Sultan as they took to their heels suggested that it had all been high sport, a game, with no real-world stakes that they could grasp. The long tradition of Palestinian rock-throwing—variously interpreted as a form of self-defense, as symbolic resistance, and as racial violence—is impossibly fraught, and to young minds it might easily have been divorced from any real political significance. A bunch of ten-year-olds could not likely have guessed that the visitor cowering behind the metal sign was Jewish, still less that he was American (at least until I started yelling at them to stop). Kids throw stones: When I was eleven, the police were called to a birthday party after a schoolmate hurled a paver at a passing car. Only in Palestine does the act come to look like a part of something else, a vast and heartbreaking scheme in which anyone can quickly become complicit, as I did, hiding behind my own makeshift wall. Doubtless the children never gave any thought to the bizarre historical synchrony, that this tribal dumbshow had occurred at the birthplace of tribalism. I only thought of it later, and the realization made me shudder.

It wasn't the first time, or the last. What I encountered in Jericho was only an especially potent version of a phenomenon I had already seen, and would see again, in various forms in borderlands all over the world. I found it in the dry swamp beds around the Rio Grande and on the flats surrounding the Tijuana estuary. Something similar pervades the air in northern China, its outline reflected in the surface of frozen lakes; it appears again in England, and in France, and in Germany. How it came to be in the West Bank—the forces that have created that hothouse environment—would only become clearer to me later, in looking at one last wall, very close to Tell es-Sultan but separated from it by ten thousand years. In that space of time, as we will see, what was born at Jericho became a perennial global pandemic, passing through countless different places at different times before returning to the land of faith. And then it moved on, once again, to the land of the free.

CONQUEST

Physical walls like that at Jericho are not so prevalent in the New World as they are in the Old. If, as Daniel Webster wrote, "the principle of free governments adheres to the American soil," defensive walls are a nonnative species, one that has thrived in the Western Hemisphere but that was originally, like the peach and the dandelion, imported.

Invasion came first to the south. Camped in a small village in Central Mexico, a group of Spanish soldiers listened as a local chieftain, garlanded in turquoise and obsidian, explained for the first time how the cities of his people were built. "All the houses have flat roofs," he told the Europeans, "which by raising breastworks when they are needed can be turned into fortresses." The Spanish learned that the capital of this exotic empire was on an island in an enormous lake, only approachable by lengthy causeways: The ruler could cut off routes in or out of the city at will, obviating the need for further bulwarks against external threat. The visitors were duly impressed by this wall-less wonder, and while they demanded their interlocutor leave off human sacrifice and accept the yoke of Spain, they must have sensed themselves at a disadvantage. But the Aztec cacique also made what seems, with the hindsight of four hundred years, a grave strategic error—he told the group about the "great store of gold and silver" kept by his emperor. The Spaniards pressed on (they had little choice, their leader Hernán Cortés having ordered them to burn their boats behind them) and by the end of 1519 they had taken the island city of Tenochtitlán. The native chieftains and high priests were dressed by their new masters in white Christian robes, their hair still dark and matted with sacral blood.

Few Pre-Columbian cities could boast so well-wrought or novel a defensive network as that of Tenochtitlán, by some estimates the largest city in the world at the time. Yet most indigenous people in the New World found no more recourse to wall-building than the Aztecs. Though urbanization in Central and South America was firmly established when the conquistadores arrived, it had followed a wildly different pattern from the European model: The closest thing to city walls that predates Spanish conquest would be the citadels of the Andean peoples, such as Sacsayhuamán near the ancient Incan capital of Cusco, Peru, the gigantic stone remains of which are still present today.

In North America, where cities were thinner on the ground, walls were fewer still. The Mississippian culture that flowered in the late first millennium favored large conurbations with mound-like platforms for religious and civic functions. But the Mississippians mysteriously vanished, and excavations have revealed only the occasional wooden enclosure around a smattering of sites. Some nineteenth-century researchers, amazed that even this was within the reach of mere Natives, insisted that the mounds were the work of one of the so-called Lost Tribes of Israel, supposed to have wandered out of the Middle East at some period between Jericho and Babylon, making themselves at home on the banks of the Big Muddy.

Save for in a few select quarters (among them the Church of Latter-Day Saints, where it is still technically a point of dogma), the Lost Tribe idea has fallen out of fashion. Anthropologists now recognize that building permanent walls was not much beyond the capacity of North American tribes, but that their habits of life rendered them pointless. The rites of many indigenous people included ritual warfare, brief, usually seasonal skirmishes between forces of roughly coequal strength that did not entail the besieging of settlements or the construction of elaborate systems to repel attack. That kind of warfare came only with arrival of the new god, and with those who considered themselves the god's new Israelites—like the people who sought to build a new Jerusalem on Massachusetts Bay.

The North American adventure in wall-building opened with high drama. Arrows in a snakeskin quiver—a coded threat from a hostile sachem—had lately arrived by messenger when, in November 1621, the residents of the faltering Plymouth Colony decided to take action. They had been in North America scarcely a year, and relations with segments of the native population had already begun to sour; weak and outnumbered, the colonists thought it prudent to erect the village's first palisade, a line of sharpened stakes set in a square formation half a mile long, constructed under the supervision of Plymouth's designated defender, Myles Standish.

Standish had trained as a military engineer in the Netherlands before embarking to the New World with the Puritan cohort. Though he was among them, he was not of them: A man of action, not a man of god, the phlegmatic Standish had already seized the initiative against problematic local tribesmen, dispatching a few of them during a daring midnight raid. On receiving the symbolic threat from the chief of the nearby Narragansetts, the English captain responded by sending the snakeskin back, this time packed with powder and musket balls.

Once the fortifications were in place, Standish formed his fifty-some men into four brigades, assigning one to each side of the perimeter. The ten-foot-high wooden posts stood flush against one another and were joined together by lateral logs; behind them were a series of elevated platforms (and eventually a central fort) allowing the militiamen to see over the wall and take aim at incoming marauders. Day and night, Standish drilled his tiny band, instructing them how to keep the watch, marching them back and forth along the parapet's lofted planks, turning the trembling pilgrims into a company of proficient soldiers.

Standish's palisade was not the first such structure built by Europeans in the Americas. Cortés's compatriots erected several walls around Spanish port cities like Lima and Cartagena—mostly to defend against other Europeans, the English first and foremost. The English responded in kind, constructing a stone bulwark around Jamestown, Virginia, topped by cannons to discourage the Spanish. But the case of the Puritan pickets was of much greater consequence, an augur of things to come.

Only a month after the wall's completion, Standish led a detachment of his newly trained guard on an expedition against the Massachusett people to the north. Inviting their chief to negotiate over supper, Standish had his men shut the door to the house, took his guest's knife, and stabbed him repeatedly in the chest. On their captain's orders, the English then executed two other Massachusett warriors, skirmishing with others in the surrounding forest before returning to Plymouth bearing their enemies' heads.

Terrified, many Indian communities fled the area following the incident, leaving the colony without the trading partners upon which it depended. But the threat of invasion was gone. The wall—which was expanded and repaired in the 1630s—never operated in a truly defensive role. Yet it served a critical purpose. Within a generation, the Massachusetts and the Narragansetts had all but disappeared, and the whole of New England lay open for European settlement. The wall taught the watchmen of Plymouth that faith alone would not bring about their new Zion in the wilderness.

The descendants of Myles Standish and the descendants of Hernan Cortés remained at considerable physical remove for more than a century, both preoccupied with the heirs of the Massachusetts and the Aztecs who peopled most of the land between them. Mexico, then called New Spain, technically became an ally of the nascent United States during the Revolutionary War, when its ruling empire declared itself in alliance with France against Britain. With American independence established, the upper-class Mexican *peninsulares* shortly became anxious for their own independence project, even more so when their mother country was overrun by the French during Napoleon's romp through Western Europe. By the time the Bourbon dynasty had been restored to the throne, there was little chance of reconciliation between Spain and its largest colony. In 1821, "the political bands which connected them," in Thomas Jefferson's phrase, were dissolved.

Typical of the noninterventionist stance of the United States at the time, the country had not seen fit to assist the Mexicans in casting off their imperial thraldom. George Washington's injunction against "foreign entanglements" still echoed in American ears, though it wouldn't for long: In 1823, President James Monroe formulated the doctrine that bears his name, announcing that the United States would at least passively campaign for republican causes in the Americas against domination from European powers and that any interference by the latter on this side of the Atlantic would be read as a "manifestation of an unfriendly disposition toward the United

States." With almost no navy and no standing army at all, the Americans were in no real position to enforce this heady declaration. But at least they aspired. What happened in Mexico City would now be of official interest in Washington, D.C.

Interest found its way into policy when, in 1825, the first official American minister was dispatched to the Mexican capital. The representative's instructions, crafted by the recently inaugurated President John Quincy Adams, were strictly limited, confined to advocating for American commercial interests and acting as a faithful ombudsman of democracy, ready at all events "to explain the practical operation and the very great advantages which appertain to our system." In short order, these seemingly narrow directives would expand into a mission of far greater scope.

The man responsible was one to whom millions of Americans do faithful homage every Christmas. Very few of them know they do so; fewer still would be pleased if they did, given his connection to three issues that tend to make Americans, for various reasons, distinctly uneasy—the eradication of Native Americans, slavery, and relations between the United States and Mexico. Though largely forgotten, his memorial is everywhere, year in and year out, in the bright red flowers that sprout from every centerpiece and mantelpiece not otherwise decked with holly and mistletoe. This plant, originally known as *flor de Nochebuena* (the good-night flower) had been prized among the Aztecs for its use in dyes and as a fever reducer; north of the border, it is known as poinsettia, after its American popularizer, Joel Roberts Poinsett.

Poinsett introduced the species to the United States in the 1820s after he made his first brief visit to the newly liberated Mexico. An avid traveler, sometime congressman, and amateur botanist, the South Carolinian thought the plant would make a fine ornament to his plantation back home, where he kept nearly fifty men and women as slaves. Notwithstanding the states-rights sentiments of many of his fellow Southerners, Poinsett was unfailingly loyal to the federal government and most of his travels were undertaken in its service, including his five difficult years in Mexico.

By the time Poinsett returned there as minister in 1825, the short-lived Empire of Mexico had passed from the scene to be replaced by the First

Mexican Republic, an unstable regime teetering precariously toward political disarray. Poinsett was charged with trying to keep it in the republican column—but the task was never as straightforward as that. The expansion of American values and American trade was understood from the start as indissoluble from the expansion of America itself. A generation earlier, the United States had taken advantage of the global Napoleonic disorder to snap up the better part of the North American interior, buying from the French land that had lately belonged to Spain; with a few emendations, the original border between Mexico and the United States was that border, a zigzag line running from East Texas to the Oregon Territory. Shifting that line south and westward once again, via a similar cash transaction, was a tacit American objective. Poinsett knew this.

So did his new hosts, and they were not much taken with the idea. The Mexican president to whom Poinsett first presented his credentials, General Guadalupe Victoria, espoused the view that Americans were an "ambitious people, always ready to encroach [upon their neighbors] without a spark of good faith." In any case, Mexico had already made arrangements to secure her own interests. In their pursuit of independence, the country's leaders had looked to England, not to the United States, for support, and they had found His Majesty's government most forthcoming. This automatically placed Mexico somewhat at odds with America's new hemispheric policy, and it put Poinsett in a tight spot from the moment he arrived.

Though he entertained high hopes for Mexican democracy, these did not necessarily translate into high esteem for the Mexicans as individuals. Years later, Poinsett would advise President Martin Van Buren that it would be in error "to compare [Mexicans] with the free and civilized nations of America and Europe in the Nineteenth Century." As Poinsett explained, the Mexicans were a rough, uncultured people, albeit through no fault of their own, having been held in peonage under their European masters for so long. The Spanish crown, and its successors among the Mexican nobility, had cut the country off from the world, barring "all intercourse with foreigners as well as the introduction of all works which could enlighten their minds." The only cure for Mexico's inconvenient otherness, Poinsett maintained, was for the country to open itself up, specifically to America.

Once that was done, the Mexicans were bound to be more amenable to a real estate deal.

Hoping to show them the light, Pointsett began taking measures that arguably exceeded his mandate. His ministerial headquarters—a fine villa at the heart of the capital, centered on a courtyard fronted by an iron gate—soon became a hub for those who did not share Victoria's dim view of the United States, but who considered the Catholic Church, wealthy landowners, and the military establishment as the foremost threats to a liberal and prosperous Mexico. In touch with these elements shortly after his arrival, Poinsett hosted them to a dinner where he encouraged them to become an organized faction: the Yorkino, a fraternal political club similar in structure and doctrine to the Masonic lodges that had produced much of the early political leadership of the United States (including Poinsett himself). Swearing oaths and raising toasts, the Yorkinos committed themselves to liberty and progress; in other houses, in other streets, their enemies the Escoceses, also a Masonic faction but firmly pro-clerical and anti-American, pledged themselves to God and country. A partisan standoff was brewing.

The American was not the sort to shrink from the conflict. Later in his career, Poinsett would become Van Buren's secretary of war, directing with considerable zeal the final stages in the forced removal of Native Americans from their ancestral homelands in the southeastern United States. Later still, despite his retirement, he made spirited pleas to his fellow Southerners against disunion—on the grounds that slavery enjoyed more protection under the Constitution than it would in the event of secession. (Not an entirely inaccurate view, as it happened.) Studied neutrality was not Poinsett's way, and when the internecine conflict in Mexico began to boil over in the winter of 1828, the diplomat did not feel any compunctions about behaving a little undiplomatically.

His friends in the Yorkino movement had been sorely disappointed during the national election that year by the failure of their candidate to triumph over his conservative opponent. In their late-night conclaves, Poinsett had always interceded with the liberals to abide by the rule of law and the will of the electorate. This time, sensing a turning point was at hand, he gave at least unspoken endorsement to an antigovernment plot.

In December, shots rang out in the plazas and back alleys of Mexico City, the warring factions battling it out from house to house and neighborhood to neighborhood. Already the target of conservative ire, Poinsett managed to make himself, and his official residence, a lightning rod for the populist group as well, giving sanctuary there to a group of aristocratic Spanish citizens. When an angry mob gathered in front of the gate, Poinsett's theatricality did not fail him. He appeared on the balcony overlooking the street, holding aloft a giant American flag and waving it at the intruders.

The move worked: The crowds dispersed. The liberals carried the day, and the American (restored again to their good graces) put himself front and center yet again, inviting several of the victorious rebels to another celebratory supper at his handsome urban mansion. But backing the winning side would avail Poinsett little in the long run—and it would avail Mexico even less. Earlier in 1828, Poinsett had concluded the first-ever territorial treaty between the two nations; but it only reaffirmed the initial border agreed upon with Spain, and when a new president, Andrew Jackson, asked the minister to try again to move the frontier, Poinsett rebuffed him, stating that any further negotiations were now impossible. The late-night goings-on at the *casa* Poinsett had backfired, and America's first overture across the border ended up reinforcing the divisions, both physical and political, between north and south.

It would hardly seem credible that two peoples, so alike in politics and promise, should suffer such an early rupture. Yet when the rupture came, it proved not only profound but practically irreversible as well, the beginnings of a fault line that still runs down the border today.

Following the flag episode, even Poinsett's Mexico City friends would be demanding his recall, tired of his meddling and increasingly wary of his country's intentions. The gallant American returned home, not quite in disgrace, but leaving behind a legacy precisely the opposite of the one he had intended to fashion for himself. The insurrection he'd helped foment would set a precedent from which Mexican democracy took decades to recover. As junta followed strongman, the one constant would be a firm opposition to *poinsettismo*, a byword for American interference and territo-rial wheeler-dealing.

The perceived threat from the "colossus to the north," as the United States would often be described, brought about a steady calcification in Mexico's outlook over the 1830s. Instead of pursuing an opening with the States, the increasingly autocratic leader General Antonio López de Santa Anna (himself a former liberal and a sometime friend of Poinsett's) sought to reassert his authority over the ever-rising volume of Anglo immigrants moving into the farthermost reaches of their territory, especially modern-day Texas, where English-speaking settlers were becomingly increasingly restive. Spearheading Santa Anna's efforts against the Texians—as the Amer-ican settlers called themselves—the Mexican army sought to strengthen its position on the far side of the Rio Grande, consolidating troops, clearing supply lines, preparing fortifications. Having so little to build with in the vast wastes of South Texas, the Mexicans repurposed existing buildings for military use, turning everything from homes to storefronts into impromptu barracks. They even commandeered a half-abandoned Catholic church compound, the Misión San Antonio de Valero, shortly to become better known under a different name.

From the start, the building that the Texians referred to as the Alamo has loomed far larger in American memory than was ever warranted—certainly far larger than the actual building, which was even smaller than I expected when I first saw it, one early San Antonio morning. The cur-rent Texas official in charge of it (a member of the Bush family no less) has conceded that it is "one of the most disappointing landmarks in our nation," and I found I did not disagree, although the gardens are lovely and the rooms well kept. Passing through the chapel, courtyard, and outbuild-ings, the visitor can see where, in 1836, three hundred Texians set up a gar-rison after rashly declaring their independence, only to be confronted on February 23 by Santa Anna at the head of over a thousand troops. In spots marked by informative placards, I saw where the Mexicans finally breached the compound, pursuing the Texians until all were either stabbed or shot, after which Santa Anna "ordered every one of the Americans to be dragged

The Alamo, San Antonio

out and burnt," according to one eyewitness. When news of the slaughter reached the American public, it caused a sensation, turning the Alamo into an instant symbol and, eventually, a monument.

Today that monument makes special note, through signage and wall text, of the many Alamo defenders who were not themselves American: men like Damacio Jiménez, Juan Badillo, and Toribio Losoya, pro-independence Mexicans who gave their lives alongside Davy Crockett and Daniel Boone. At the time, however, these heroic figures were upstaged by Santa Anna, who presented a compelling new image to American audiences—a Mexican villain, brutish yet hapless. Before the siege had begun, the general had hoisted high a blood-red flag, signaling his intention to take no prisoners; he maintained this policy after the siege, leading to still another massacre a few miles away at Goliad. And yet, within days, Santa Anna's fortunes had collapsed. After a disastrous skirmish at San Jacinto, the Mexican army was put to rout, never to challenge the Texians again. The retreating general was apprehended hiding in the tall grass of the nearby prairie, "disguised in a blue cottonade round-jacket and pants," pretending to be an ordinary private. To Americans sympathetic to the Texian cause, Santa Anna's combination of cruelty and ineptitude quickly turned him into a patriotic punching bag. The general, according to one American newspaper, was "that savage fiend"; his capture, claimed another, had seen him "tumble headlong from a lofty throne" to "a chained slave at the feet" of the Texians. It was rumored he had to take laudanum to calm his nerves after his capture.

His failure vindicated (at least partially) the fallen of the Alamo. What it did not do was concede to the Texians the desired location of the border between their newly independent republic and Mexico, an issue that remained a matter of intense dispute. The agreement the general had signed under duress staked the line at the Rio Grande; to Mexicans, this referred to a river well to the north, known today as the Nueces River, not to the waterway still known in Spanish as the Rio Bravo del Norte. But for the emboldened Anglos of Texas—as for their American allies, eager to annex the republic and turn it into a new state—this hardly mattered. It was their convinced opinion that the border was theirs to determine. The Mexicans, in the person of Santa Anna, had proven themselves unworthy to do so.

All through the late 1830s and into the 1840s, as the border and annexation questions stoked tensions between the two countries, the picture of the Mexican national character that had first emerged in San Antonio became fixed in the American mind. "The Mexicans," declared the New Orleans *Times-Picayune* after the war, were "too lazy to advance and too grovelling a nature to entertain a solitary ennobling aspiration." In Detroit, a correspondent for the *Democratic Free Press* concurred, claiming that "not the slightest reliance can be placed on the professions and promises of the Mexicans." During the runup to the 1844 election that would ultimately make James K. Polk the country's youngest president to date, political speeches frequently featured rhetoric about the "wicked barbarians" to the south: "These Mexican savages must be whipt into civilization," declared one New York clergyman to his congregation, a responsibility that enjoined the Anglo to take not just Texas but the whole of continent from these "reptiles in the path of progress." In fairness to Joel Roberts Poinsett, his caricature of Mexican backwardness was always tempered with a belief in Mexican potential. His countrymen embraced the former, but neglected the latter.

Polk pushed for war, and when it finally arrived in 1846 the little Spanish mission in San Antonio served as part of the country's psychological casus belli. Remembering "the Spartan-like defense of the Alamo," Americans flocked to the southwest; as they marched through Texas under General Winfield Scott, newly conscripted soldiers from around the country were regaled by locals with stories of the Texian revolt, and young infantrymen waiting in San Antonio to be sent to the front visited the old mission building, fueling their ire at the shrine to their slain countrymen. (Apparently it wasn't so disappointing to *them*.) In a convenient twist, the Mexican government obliged the would-be Alamo avengers by restoring the exiled Santa Anna to his former command, reviving anew the memory of "the soulless butcheries of Goliad and the Alamo," as one American military man called them. Filled with revanchist fervor, the Americans advanced rapidly through the desert, then invaded by sea, overwhelming Santa Anna's defenses en route to the capital, where they quickly triumphed after an hourlong siege of the Castle of Chapultepec.

With that, the last drive toward Manifest Destiny was complete. The Treaty of Guadalupe Hidalgo, signed in February 1848, ended the Mexican-American War and achieved the aims of Polk and his partisans, establishing a border (on paper at least) that would now be formed by the Rio Grande as the Texians intended it and then extend due west to the Pacific Ocean along an irregular path partially defined by the Gila River. Not Texas alone, but *all* of the former Mexican territory north of the line—encompassing all or part of Arizona, California, Nevada, Wyoming, Utah, New Mexico, and Colorado—was henceforth ceded to the United States; this would be augmented in 1854 by the Gadsden Purchase, the procurement of a further sliver of territory in Arizona and New Mexico for a southern transcontinental railroad, finalizing the national boundary as it stands today. Between the two acquisitions, the United States absorbed some 560,000 square miles of land. And more than land: Thousands of Mexican residents of the territory remained in what was now the United States, all of them granted citizenship and guaranteed property rights under the treaty. "Wicked barbarians" no more, these first Mexican-Americans joined the Mexican martyrs of the Alamo—woven, sometimes invisibly, into the fabric of the American West.

Around San Antonio, they all but *are* the fabric: Most of the crowds at the Alamo appeared to be Latino families and, though not outwardly more impressed by it than anyone else, their very presence seemed somewhat incongruous in view of the narrative that was inaugurated there. "American blood," Polk declared, had been "spilled on American soil"; in the United States, the victory over Mexico was tantamount to the victory of right over wrong, with the old mission standing as the symbol of outraged Anglo dignity. Like Myles Standish's stakes in the ground at Plymouth, the Alamo might more be more properly considered the emblem of a new kind of belligerence—but then symbols, architectural symbols especially, are often elastic in this way, stretching to accommodate any ideology. They are also highly fungible, capable of crossing over from one culture to the next. "From the halls of Montezuma," declares the anthem of the United States Marines: A reference to Chapultepec, the line ignores the fact that the Aztec kings never dwelled in the castle, casting the Americans back two hundred years earlier into the role of Cortés and his men, crossing the gangway to the city in the heart of the lake.

II

BORDER AS FORGE

HADRIAN

Few illusions about borders are more persistent, and more pernicious, than their ostensible linearity. We customarily think of them as they appear on maps, as lines, real and verifiable locations. In truth, as philosopher Thomas Nail has put it, "the border is in between": It exists not as a place, but as the two-dimensional seam at the meeting of two places. No person, and certainly no wall, can be truly "on" the border, but only on one side or the other; even where marked by natural features—which are, after all, subject to change—boundaries remain mere abstractions.

Besides making borders appear more substantial than they are (intimating, in a way, the presence of a wall that could run along the same path), the illusion of the border-as-line obscures another, still more important fact. Beyond the surveyor's fiction of the border lies the reality of the borderlands—a territory straddling the line, where people live and meet and produce a culture reflective of their peculiar condition. A more accurate map might represent this by drawing the borderlands as a thick gradient, fading steadily outward from the border itself. Even that would only capture part of the reality, since the culture that emerges at the border can stretch out almost indefinitely, suffusing all that surrounds it.

The bigger the border, the bigger the borderlands and the more culture radiating out of them. And the political order that boasts the biggest borders—and consequently the type most subject to their influence—has a name: Empire, a title that first appears in history in connection with the fractious, nebulous, confounding supranational entity known as the Roman Empire. Lasting in one form or another for more than a thousand years, Rome took into its geographical compass an astonishing amount of territory, stretching at its greatest extent from the deserts of the Sahara to northern Europe and from the Atlantic Ocean clear to the nearer shores of the Caspian Sea. This created one of the largest borders ever known to civilization, and with it one of the most intense cultural dynamics to emerge from any of the world's sundry borderlands.

Beginning around 100 AD, the Romans embarked on the most aggressive period in their expansionist enterprise. Under Emperor Trajan, the empire swelled to include most of modern Jordan, with fingers reaching northeast and southeast down the Arabian Peninsula, while in Europe it swallowed up first the whole of what is now Romania, then surged eastward into the Caucasus. Trajan was a product of the Roman military, with extensive service around the known world and a string of victories that made him a popular figure in the army. In addition to his tactical and strategic skill, he also understood that conquest was as good a guarantor of political security as any would-be emperor was likely to have. The previous wearer of the imperial purple, Nerva, was viewed as too old and temperamentally unwarlike, and he faced dissent from his restless legions throughout his brief tenure.

Trajan's victories brought new revenue into the Roman treasury while bucking up his own stature among the senate and people in the imperial capital. But it also came at a price. During his nineteen-year reign the empire stretched to include many more inhabitants unacclimated to Roman rule and boasted an even longer external boundary than ever before. Conflicts emerged on both sides of its borders, in particular in Asia Minor: first among the Parthians in Mesopotamia, and then, in far more dramatic fashion, the Jews of the empire's eastern provinces, who objected to infringements on their religious prerogatives. Subduing these revolts consumed most of Trajan's final years, and he died in 117 AD while still campaigning in the Near East.

His successor appeared at first likely to continue the process of imperial aggrandizement. Publius Aelius Hadrianus Augustus—Hadrian, as he was universally known—had been a loyal administrative lieutenant to Trajan in his military tours, as well as his adopted son and the husband of his grand-niece. By some accounts Trajan received the news of his ascent to the emperorship from Hadrian personally, and as the years went by the younger man played court to his patron's retainers and family members, binding himself further to the imperial household. At the time of Trajan's death, Hadrian had been in Syria continuing the fight against the Jewish uprising. He would go on fighting it even after he was declared the new emperor, subduing the rebellion completely before returning to Rome to shore up his support in the Senate.

Yet for all of Hadrian's fealty to Trajan's legacy, there was always something in him that seemed at odds with his predecessor—or indeed any of his predecessors in the one-hundred-plus years since Augustus first took the title *primus inter pares*, first among equals. In his youth Hadrian had been more inclined toward reading and hunting than was thought becoming for a serious-minded Roman aristocrat. These cultured pursuits were considered indelibly Greek, and Hadrian had even acquired a nickname, Graeculus—the little Greek—poking fun at his Hellenic pretensions. While romantic relationships between men were common enough among the elite of Rome, Hadrian may have been exclusively homosexual: His marriage was known to be an unhappy one, and he famously remained in perpetual mourning for his lover Antinous after the young man drowned in Egypt. Where Trajan had been prosaic, martial, and Italocentric, Hadrian was poetic, pacific (if not quite pacifistic), and cosmopolitan.

A man for his time, it might be said, as the empire he had inherited was already a multicultural hotchpotch of breathtaking proportions. The Berber tribes of North Africa, the Germanic tribes north of the Danube, the Iranian tribes of the Pontic Steppes—the Romans had been steadily incorporating an ever-richer medley of races and religions and languages since the turn of the millennium. Hadrian himself was a provincial by birth, a native of southern Spain; so was Trajan, the first emperor not born in Italy (though both he and Hadrian belonged to ancient Roman families). Full citizenship had been granted to residents of most of the major provinces by Julius Caesar, but the Jewish rebellions had shown how poorly some of the empire's newer elements had taken to their subject status. Discontent could well up at any moment among the communities nearest the borders, only adding to the perils that awaited beyond them.

Facing the new emperor from the instant he donned the laurel crown was a border some three thousand miles long, on the other side of which waited potential enemies both known and unknown. Tribes who had been ill-used or beaten in previous battle, or who harbored grudges against immigrants from their own lands, or who simply sought plunder from the Roman border colonies, all posed a constant danger, and the ballooning of the empire meant there were more of them than ever. Hadrian could have done as previous emperors had, relying on additional conquests to push the border farther away from Rome, forestalling the danger at least for the time being. He had the authority, he had the legions, and, despite some dissent in the senatorial ranks, he had the backing of the broader Roman public, as well as of most of the elites who furnished the generals and governors that kept the empire ticking. Instead, Hadrian had a vision, and the world changed overnight.

Compared to many of the world's most ancient walls, the one that Hadrian built in the north of England is a walk in the park to visit. This is not merely a figure of speech. The British have enshrined their most prominent piece of Roman architecture (and the world's: It is the largest remaining pre-served Roman artifact anywhere) as a national treasure, embedding it in the sprawling Northumberland National Park. Regional authorities have fur-nished the most scenic sections of the park with a comprehensive bus route, giving it the cheeky designation "AD122"—the year work on Hadrian's Wall was begun—and equipping the vehicles with automated messages about local points of interest, noting for example that Northumberland boasts "England's darkest skies." This is meant to highlight its qualities as a star-gazing destination; it could, however, refer to daylight conditions, which can turn dreary even on a sparkling morning in late May. The clouds and occasional downpours do nothing to deter the seasonal visitors, rushing in from all over the UK and beyond, all of them coming to see what local signage portentously bills as "The Edge of Empire."

Today, Hadrian's Wall marks the edge of a few sheep pastures and the B6318 highway. But it was, more or less, the absolute limit of Roman civilization at the time that Hadrian conceived it. How he did so was first revealed in a parish church in Jarrow, just east of Newcastle-upon-Tyne, when an inscribed stone, or stele, was found there in the eighteenth century. The Saxon builders of the church had placed the stone facedown and cut a chunk out of it, but translators were able to reconstruct most of the original message:

> Son of all the deified emperors, the Emperor Caesar Trajan Hadrian Augustus, after the necessity of keeping the empire within its limits had been laid upon him by divine precept ... thrice consul ... : after the barbarians had been dispersed and the province of Britain had been recovered, he added a frontier-line between either shore of the Ocean for 80 miles.

It would be interesting to know how precisely this "divine precept" was "laid upon" the emperor. The phrase smacks suspiciously of revelation, as though the wall had appeared to him in a dream.

He might simply have made it up in the heat of the moment, an inspired improvisation that could well have occurred at the site of the wall, speaking to the men who were charged with building and then defending it. Hadrian is believed to have toured the Roman province of Britannia in the year that wall construction began, part of a continental sweep that saw him become perhaps the best-traveled emperor to date. From Spain in the west to Asia Minor in the east, the "explorer of all things interesting," as one near contemporary would call Hadrian, witnessed firsthand the social and military state of play in the far-flung extremities of his domain. Lacking Trajan's soldierly background, it served him well to ingratiate himself with the troops. The report of the divine precept, if delivered in person, might have served as a clever motivational strategy, a rallying cry for a unique military mission.

Such motivation would have been much needed. The troops whom Hadrian might have addressed found themselves in a land of terrors and wonders. The northernmost peoples of the British Isles were known to the Romans as Caledonians and were described by Roman writers as "wild," with "reddish hair" and "large but flaccid bodies"; the people were said to dwell naked with their sheep in "wattled huts." Not the most daunting or organized foe the empire's troops had faced—yet they feared them. The Caledonians, according to Roman historians, were believed to consume a secret compound that allowed them to go without food and water for days and to run through the marshes submerged in mud "up to the waist." They painted fantastic animals on their bodies, their only apparel being iron, which they valued as the Romans did gold and which they fashioned into elaborate adornments or beat into the swords they carried slung over their shoulders. The country they lived in, later Roman writers would claim, was a miasmic wasteland, populated chiefly by lizards and snakes, its air so pestilential that the Caledonians alone could breathe it.

The hostile and enigmatic North—ultima Thule, the island at the end of the earth, believed to lay just beyond the Scottish Highlands—had loomed large in the Roman imagination since before Julius Caesar's first tentative forays across the English Channel in the first century BC. Even after subsequent emperors had made Britain a Roman province, its farthest limits remained shrouded in myth and mystery. And now Hadrian's men had built a bulwark against that unknown, spanning the entire width of the island at one of its narrowest points between the Irish Sea and the River Tyne. They did it in just six years, a fact made the more astounding for how much of it still stands nearly nineteen hundred years later.

From atop the rampart, anywhere on the central stretch, the walker today can stand where the soldiers once manned the watch and endured the damp and chilly weather in little more than the *lorica segmentata*, strips of metal body armor hung together by rope, worn over a knee-length tunic, with the thin leather boots called *caligae* tied up over woolen batting to keep out the cold. Great numbers of these garments have been recovered during excavations at the wall, along with the ovular shields used by the auxiliary troops who were stationed in Britain; the shields had a metallic boss at the center, and, though reasonably light, they were bulky, as much as three and half feet high. Lugging them along, together with their swords and their iron helmets (the only full galea headgear ever found was recovered by Hadrian's Wall), the men would patrol the length of the wall by night, under the sparkling firmament of what is now advertised as "England's darkest skies."

Sycamore Gap at Hadrian's Wall, Northumberland

The romance of the wall is undeniable—and it is definitely the aspect most thoroughly plumped by the British today for the benefit of the AD122 crowd. At the Roman Army Museum, in the aptly named Walltown, twenty-first-century wall-goers are treated to an "Edge of Empire" video (in 3D, no less) portraying the harrowing business of soldiery in the woods and wilds of second-century Northumberland. The digitally rendered landscape is repopulated with trees, and actors in sandal-epic drag stare out from a sound-stage rampart, worrying about the barbarians waiting in the dark as an eagle surveys the scene from above. The narration, by acclaimed Scottish actor Brian Cox, extols the courage and fortitude of Hadrian's legionnaires in this far-flung outpost. "And I was their symbol," says Cox: The narrator, it is revealed, *is* the eagle.

The English have been energetic in finding novel ways to capitalize upon their archaeological assets, and everyone seems to get in on the act. On my way to the wall, heading into the heart of Northumberland National Park, I passed Hadrian Healthcare, Hadrian House Care Home, Hadrian's Electrical Engineering, and Hadrian Architectural Glazing Systems, Ltd.

Closer to the wall itself, there's the Hadrian Lodge, not to be confused with the Hadrian Hotel—which is in the town of Wall, not to be confused with nearby Walltown. It is a cottage industry, with actual cottages, and I did wonder what the late emperor might have made of one local business, which claimed that "Hadrian can offer anything from a quick wash to full vehicle detailing."

Delighted though he might have been by the Wall's endurance, there is every reason to believe that the emperor's consternation would have been fairly acute. At the very least, he might have hoped that his name would not be so closely associated with this *one* wall or that posterity might consider it more than an "edge" of the Roman world.

Assuming that Jupiter did not, in fact, intervene to command its construction, Hadrian's reasons for building his most famous structure seem plain enough. He was faced with a practical conundrum: The empire's expansion meant there was simply too much space to defend and not enough resources, human or material, to defend it with. Given the rebellions and incursions that had broken out in Trajan's time, it would be easy to see how Hadrian might have concluded that Rome had gone far enough and that it was time for gains to be consolidated.

That would account for much of the strategy that Hadrian adopted, and not just in northern England. The wall that bears the emperor's name was only one component (if an especially impressive one) in a vast scheme of strategic entrenchment that saw the Roman military dig in and hold their ground in almost every corner of the empire. In modern-day Algeria and Tunisia, also under Hadrian's orders, the army constructed the Fossatum Africae, a series of ditches to slow the advance of the desert peoples who threatened Rome's coastal cities in the southern Mediterranean; south of the Carpathian Mountains, in modern-day Romania, he built another series of earthworks and wooden fortifications. In Central Europe, the empire strengthened its position along the Limes Germanicus (the German frontier), a network of mostly wooden towers and palisades that had been in place in various locations since Augustus. Further enhanced by Hadrian's successors, these fortifications would form a nearly unbroken line running clear down the Rhine and then cutting east in parallel with the Danube nearly as far as the modern-day Czech Republic. The British wall is by far the best known and best preserved, but the vision of Hadrian's Wall was by no means limited to Britain.

The Northumberland wall is of special importance, however, as it lays bare a peculiar feature of Hadrian's strategy. As far as archaeologists can determine, the dreaded Caledonians—those supposedly poison-breathing savages—spent most of their time minding their sheep, staging only sporadic raids. Their population was sparse during Hadrian's reign and separated into multiple tribes that were often hostile to one another and only occasionally capable of coordinated action. Against this divided host stood as many as ten thousand Roman auxiliary troops, a minimum of five hundred in every one of the wall's fifteen-odd forts, and thousands more in the garrisoned cities nearby and in a smattering of advanced-position forts in Scotland built for scouting and reconnaissance. The effort to construct and maintain all of this, at so much expense and so much risk: How could it possibly have been worthwhile to hold back a ragtag band of proto-Scots?

Fear needs no reasons, of course. But the Romans, for all their fever dreams about swamp-dwellers, were never overly fearful of foreigners as such. The same liberality that had made provincials into citizens was extended even to people from beyond the frontiers. Greek orator and author Aelius Aristedes, who had grown up and been educated during Hadrian's reign, would later extol the extraordinary largesse that the Romans had visited on the sundry nations absorbed into their empire; writing to Hadrian's successor, he would praise the many achievements of the emperor before turning to the one that "deserves as much attention and admiration now as all the rest together":

> I mean your magnificent citizenship with its grand conception, because there is nothing like it in the records of all mankind . . . You have everywhere appointed to your citizenship . . . the better part of the world's talent, courage, and leadership, while the rest you recognized as a league under your hegemony. Neither sea nor intervening continent are bars to

citizenship, nor are Asia and Europe divided in their treatment
here. In your empire all paths are open to all.

At the time that he said it, this was almost true. Entering Roman territory
with relative ease (in small enough groups at least; larger ones would have
been regarded by the Roman army as potential raiding parties), immigrants
were free to conduct whatever business they cared to do in the empire, for
as long as they liked, with the understanding that if they took up residence
they would become subject to the empire's rules. They then received the
classification of peregrinus ("one from abroad"), the lowest rung on Rome's
social ladder, not citizens but not without rights either.

Citizenship's extension to the newer peoples of the empire was highly
qualified, with only limited privileges conferred upon immigrant popula-
tions. Jealous of their historical prerogatives, the heirs of the Latins kept the
franchise tightly controlled, along with public benefits like the *alimenta*,
a free food allotment to the poor available only on the Italian peninsula.
The ability to vote, exemption from the imperial poll tax, the inheritance of
property—all were reserved exclusively for full citizens. The peregrini, on
the other hand, while deprived of any sure legal recourse against citizens,
nonetheless enjoyed considerable advantages: they could settle in their own
communities; they could largely manage their own affairs; and they had
access to all the appurtenances and amenities that made Roman urban life
so very attractive, the baths and libraries and marketplaces, and the grand
places of worship. Peregrini would not be compelled to honor the Roman
gods, and the empire even accommodated its subject peoples by incorporating their gods into the Roman pantheon. For the immigrant content to
live a marginalized, if unmolested life, it was easy enough to do.

For those who wanted something more, there was an option, and
Hadrian's Wall was part of it. Discovered at one of the best-preserved wall
sites, the document known as the Chesters diploma bears the signature of
a later *pontifex maximus* conferring upon a group of infantry and cavalry-
men in Britain "who have served twenty-five years and have been hon-
orably discharged . . . Roman citizenship to those who do not possess it."
This was the recipe for full enfranchisement—two-and-a-half decades of

faithful military service would make any barbarian into a Roman citizen, along with all of his immediate family. It was not an easy choice to make: At a time when life expectancy beyond infancy usually hovered around six decades, it meant giving up half of one's life to the army. Once mustered, the non-Roman would have little to look forward to except a meager ration of grain, as well as incredibly strict discipline in which punishment for serious infractions could include being stoned to death by one's own comrades. Training was arduous and was not complete until troops had proven they were able to march nearly twenty miles in a single day bearing all their gear on their bodies; after that, there were all the hazards of warfare, to say nothing of the perils posed by the borderlands themselves, where one could die of heatstroke in the deserts of the south or malaria in the damp forests of the north. Nevertheless for countless thousands of men, the lure of citizenship was enough. The military was Rome's great equalizer: It was a machine for making more Romans.

And it was in this process that the empire's walls, Hadrian's Wall among them, were essential cogs. The military did not just turn its constituent ethnicities, its Assyrians and Dalmatians and Iberians and Gauls and Scythians, into loyal subjects by a wave of its legal wand; it made them into an integral part of the empire by sending them into each other's territory. Hadrian's Wall was exclusively manned by these auxiliary, foreign-born units, and along the wall have been found standards and other paraphernalia pointing to the presence of units from as far afield as today's Spain, Croatia, and beyond. Near the former Aballava fort, one third-century inscription listing local dignitaries includes mention of the "*Maurorum Aurelianorum*"— the Aurelian Moors, troops recruited from Morocco and suspected to have remained in Britain even after being disbanded. At Housesteads, the unit that garrisoned the fort there for two centuries was the "Cohors I Tungrorum," members of a Belgian tribe; while there, they might have worshiped at the fort's temple to the god Mithras, whose cult was popular in the Roman army but originally imported from modern-day Iran. Pulled out of their homelands, sent to the opposite ends of the empire, these very different peoples became part of something larger, thrust together on the Emperor's wall.

And not just thrust together with one another: Others were there as well, making life at the wall somewhat less daunting than portrayed in the Walltown video. Near the wall, archaeologists have uncovered a second-century tombstone dedicated by Barates of Palmyra, a Syrian soldier, "to the spirits of the departed [and to] Regina, his freedwoman and wife, a Catuvellaunian"—the name of one of the local Britannic tribes. Close to the wall, in small communities directly on its southward side, there lived native Britons, the descendants and near-cousins of the Gaelic-speaking peoples with whom the Romans had first made contact in Julius Caesar's time. Half-Latinized, these wall-bound communities lived cheek-by-jowl with the soldiers, buying and trading with most of them, and even marrying some of them, as Regina did. Their presence is attested everywhere around the remains of the wall today—in the ruins of the small settlements (*vici*) near the wall forts, and in the ancient votive altar stones and trinkets on display in the museum, found in and round the legionary barracks but bearing the names of Britannia's local deities—Cocidius, the hunter god, or Belatucadros, "the fair slayer," god of war. The granaries and stables and bathhouses around the wall, all still visible in bare stone outlines today, are testaments to the genius of Rome's military engineers. But they also speak to the countless non-Romans who were part of the northern borderlands, the people who harvested and threshed the soldiers' grain, who groomed their horses and stoked their furnaces.

This was common to all of Hadrian's walls, not just the English one. Wherever the Romans established their borders, there were always people from either side who flocked to them, some seeking asylum from internecine conflict, some wanting to trade, others simply attracted by what they had seen or heard of the Roman way of life, the aqueducts with fresh flowing water and the homes with heated floors. Living in the Roman borderlands these people could, in principle, become a part of the same mechanism that turned the auxiliary troops from foreigners into fully fledged members of the Roman *civitas*. The wall, with all its economic and social appendages, represented a thin but durable deposit of Romanism laid down in the soil of Britain, upon which other layers could slowly accrete. Beyond the Jarrow stele, we have no sure notion of what exactly Hadrian was thinking when he commissioned his barriers. But it is not so farfetched to suggest that all his walls, including his namesake one, were intended less as a break from his forebears' mission of imperial expansion, than an attempt to achieve the same end by other means.

Seventy miles long, most of it in stone stacked fifteen feet high and ten thick; the forts, spaced at distances of approximately six miles, containing the basic amenities to support **the men who** guarded them; 80 castles and 158 towers located between every pair of forts; additional outbuildings; roads; a giant ditch, the *vallum* (the word that forms the origin English word *wall*), running parallel on the south side: Hadrian's Wall was nothing if not ambitious. Yet the Romans weren't done yet. Only fourteen years after Hadrian's was completed, they started to build a second wall a hundred miles away in the Scottish Lowlands.

Weighed against its sister fortification to the south, the wall known as the Antonine—after Antoninus Pius, Hadrian's successor and adopted son—might better be described as the wall that wasn't. Though its builders evidently intended it to be as imposing as Hadrian's, they never got further than a stone substrate and a few ramparts projecting from some of the fort structures. For the most part it remained nothing more than an earthen heap with a long ditch, thirty-nine miles across, from the North Sea to the Irish Sea, in front of it. The Roman army occupied it for less than a decade before retreating back to the earlier wall. What remains of their presence in Scotland is almost negligible.

The sharp contrast with Hadrian's is the more striking if one sees the two walls in quick succession, as I did, banking by train off the west coast of England and then heading north to the hills just outside Glasgow. There, walking through what are essentially suburban backyards (long gone is the snake-bedeviled wasteland of the Roman imagination), I spent much of the time wallowing in the dugout that was once the Antonine, wondering if a thistle patch was about to render the route unpassable. Compare that to Hadrian's, where I had to step heel to toe along the spine of the Great Whin Sill—the geological ridge that the wall largely follows—looking down sheer drops to sheep paddocks fifty feet below. The nerve of the whole undertaking is still so very palpable, the wall vanishing at the horizon point in both directions, the footprints of the forts so well preserved that I could wander through the chambers of the bathhouses, from sauna to cold pool to steam room, as easily as if the buildings were still there. This, the imminent presence of history, is what has drawn people to the wall ever since it was first uncovered in the seventeenth century, and perhaps no other wall in the world has beckoned so many people to walk the entire length of it—or to write about their adventures while doing so. The bibliography of Hadrian's walkers is deep; few such treatments have been accorded its poor cousin to the north.

And yet the very existence of the Antonine Wall points up a thorny problem. Whatever Hadrian meant for his British wall to do, it does not appear to have done it to the satisfaction of his successors. Their abortive attempt to build one within Caledonia itself was meant to be an improvement, and it might have seemed that way at first: Occupying a narrower band of Britain, the Antonine is less than half the length of Hadrian's, making it cheaper to man and maintain. But it was no more successful than its Northumbrian counterpart at stopping the periodic Caledonian raids, which continued till the day the Romans departed Britain. Hadrian's Wall, as even most of its walker-admirers will confess, was a military dud.

In its other, subtler capacity—as a cultural catalyst—it may have been more effective, though probably not in the way Hadrian would have hoped. In the centuries that followed the completion of the wall, the British-Roman borderlands remained remarkably static; imperial chroniclers wrote little about northern England through most of late antiquity. But in those same years, the empire at large changed dramatically, turning into something radically different from the thriving if ungainly creature it had been in Hadrian's time. Emperor followed emperor with accelerating speed, while bouts of civil strife and armed rebellions broke out on a regular basis, some from within the ranks of the Roman army. By the fourth century, a new religion—itself the product of a different Roman borderland—had become the official imperial faith, and the center of the empire's political gravity shifted eastward. The emperor who effected both of these changes, Constantine the Great, visited the frosty northern backwater beyond the seas and deemed himself to have reconquered it, assuming the sobriquet Britannicus Maximus. Following Constantine's death, one late-Roman writer would claim that "the Romans could no longer regain Britain, but it remained under usurpers from that time."

This overstated matters, or at least preempted them. Only a few years later, Britain was visited by Constantine's son Constans; a contemporary recounted his reliance upon a group of specialized wall soldiers called *arcani*, semi-secret agents whose duty it was "to hasten about hither and thither over long spaces, to give information to our generals of the clashes of rebellion among the neighboring peoples." These *arcani* served as middlemen between the Roman administration and the guardians of the wall, and they helped keep Britain nominally Roman. At least, that is, until they fomented a revolt of their own.

The year 367 witnessed a large-scale mutiny of the troops of Hadrian's Wall, with parts of its garrison joining the growing disorder of Roman Britain on the side of the people they had supposedly been sent there to control. The Great Conspiracy, as the event became known, lasted a year and saw once-loyal troops fighting side by side with the Caledonians and other local tribes, both beyond the wall and within it. With the *arcani*'s extensive knowledge of the disposition of Roman forces, their complicity may have given the conspirators—who would eventually include fighters from Germany and Ireland, making coordinated landings by sea—an insuperable advantage as they tore through the English countryside, attacking Roman cities and setting the whole social and political structure of the island to riot.

Reinforcements from the continent would eventually cross the channel, disband the *arcani*, and restore some semblance of order. But the damage was done, and there was no turning back. Over the decades that followed, Britain would produce its own claimants to the imperial throne, usurpers backed by local troops who no longer felt any loyalty to the far-away capital. The changes that had been wrought in the heart of the empire had rendered it less and less capable of maintaining not just its military authority, but its cultural sway in a place as far away as Northumberland. The wall was now part of a different milieu: In the 400s, an indigenous British auxiliary unit, the Cohors I Cornoviorum, had come to serve on the wall, rather than being dispatched abroad as in the past; inscriptions in the stone in several sections, dating to the same period, testify to the non-military British tribesmen—the Dumnonii, the Durotriges—who had been enlisted to help repair the wall, work previously reserved for auxiliary troops. Britain had always been, during the period of Roman occupation, less a single nation under foreign rule than a concatenation of ethnic groups held together by an uneasy Roman truce. By the time the Romano-British guardians of the wall decided to throw in their lot with the locals, the decision may not have been all that difficult to make: They *were* the locals, just another tribe like the rest. There was little else for them to identify with, least of all back in Rome.

Hadrian had perhaps not calculated that the threat posed by the untamed imperial borderlands would be as grave as the threats of corruption and political atrophy that waited in Rome itself. The memory of the Roman presence was so quickly effaced that by 731, the historian Bede was incapable of pinpointing when the wall had been built, believing that it had been a last-minute endowment of the fleeing Romans to the British allies "whom they were forced to abandon." Four hundred years of the wall had left no durable cultural legacy, but instead an object lesson in the limits of empire-building: Without something to back it up—some prospect of acceptance, of membership in a society still worth believing in; without something not just to defend, but to represent—a wall may not be worth the stones it's built with. An empire too sclerotic to keep pace with the culture of its borderlands risks alienating those who live there—confining them to "spaces of non-existence," to use anthropologist Susan Bibler Coutin's term—a condition from which no army and no building can retrieve them.

"To ravage, to slaughter, to usurp under false titles, they call empire; and where they make a desert, they call it peace." The famous declaration of the Caledonian leader Calgacus was probably never made by him (it was more likely an invention of the historian Tacitus), though by the time the Romans quit Britain they could hardly claim that their empire, or their peace, held much more allure than that, least of all for the inhabitants of their former borderlands. No sooner had the soldiers decamped from Hadrian's Wall than the locals set about demolishing it piecemeal, putting it to the uses of the new order they created to supplant the defunct Provincia Britannia. Until its rediscovery and subsequent elevation to a national icon centuries later, farmers all around Northumberland pillaged the stones of the walls to build their farmhouses and churches, establishing the emerging pastoral economy that replaced the Roman town model. The people responsible for this slow-motion plunder—the same who had taken the Jarrow stele from the wall and carved a cross on its back—were a new one under the British sun, though the wall had helped them get there, in a roundabout way. The Germanic participants in the Great Conspiracy, supposed to have been in league with the perfidious *arcani*, were known as Angles and Saxons. Their political rise would eventually give them title over England, and, with a little racial mythmaking, their self-proclaimed progeny would extend that dominion to the Americas.

Notably, for all their success, the original Anglo-Saxons didn't stop the Caledonians (eventually the Scots) from raiding either. Instead of redeploying the wall for their church floors and (much later) farm enclosures, they might have put it to the use—or uses—that Hadrian intended. But their relations with their northern neighbors were already too intimate for that, their culture too interconnected; in time, their empire would be a shared one. They could also just as easily look along the Great Whin Sill, at the stony outcroppings and the stream-carved dips, and see that there would always be some way to get across, to go over or around.

EMPIRE

"Let there be a desert between strength and weakness." So said President Sebastián Lerdo de Tejada, the last authentic democratic reformer to reach high office in Mexico in the nineteenth century. Long after the conclusion of the Mexican-American War with the Treaty of Guadalupe Hidalgo in 1848, no railroads, few bridges, and fewer thoroughfares connected the former belligerents. In Tejada's view, and the view of many of his Mexican contemporaries, the relative amity between the two nations was best preserved by a respectful distance, one conveniently facilitated by the landscape.

It wouldn't last. Through the latter part of the nineteenth century and into the twentieth, economic and political ties increased at a rapid clip, the growing relationship between the two nations punctuated by regular crises.

Trouble started even before the US Civil War was over, when Ulysses S. Grant—in an almost Pointsettian mood—dispatched a subordinate to the border to provide moral support to Mexican militias resisting a recent Austro-French invasion. Grant at least kept his troops on the American side of the Rio Grande; subsequent US military commanders would not be so beholden to scruple, crossing the border on policing errands against various raiders no fewer than twenty-three times between 1873 and 1882. These regular incursions were not undertaken with the advisement, much less the consent, of the Mexican government, and they landed as repeated body blows on Mexico's national pride. "Every Mexican schoolboy could recite them," noted one regional historian. "Most United States citizens never heard of them."

Despite these campaigns, cross-border brigandage—mostly consisting of Indian raids, including the final exploits of Geronimo's former band— continued well after the turn of the century, deepening Americans' doubts about the Mexican capacity for self-government. There were superficial improvements in relations, though these too reflected underlying anxieties: In 1909, President William Howard Taft finally took the step McKinley had not, staging an historic summit in both El Paso and Juarez with Mexico's president-for-life Porfirio Díaz; while successful, the meeting was mainly undertaken to secure American financial interests south of the border (and the two were nearly assassinated, their would-be killer disarmed by a Texas Ranger). Only a year later, American distrust seemed validated when the Mexican people overthrew Díaz. In the chaos that ensued, the United States found an excuse to mount its largest incursion yet.

"It is almost too much to hope that our own border can be protected by American troops," complained the *Washington Post* in 1915. The feeling that the United States had to do something—anything—to keep its unruly neighbors in check had already led to the temporary American seizure of the Mexican port of Veracruz a few months prior, nearly precipitating a second war. That adventure did nothing to diffuse the roiling disorder that followed Díaz's departure, and in 1916 the revolutionary leader in the north, Pancho Villa, in need of money and materiel, staged a cross-border raid on the community of Columbus, New Mexico, burning the settlement and killing more than a dozen civilians. For this violent enterprise Villa achieved almost nothing except to goad the American government into another hasty action. The administration of President Woodrow Wilson dispatched General John J. Pershing into northern Mexico with an expeditionary force that would eventually grow to include ten thousand men, the better part of America's standing army at the time.

The Villa expedition, like the ones that preceded it, was of a piece with a broader pattern: Though not yet embroiled in World War I, the United States was then engaged in multiple punitive interventions around the world, with American flags popping up in Cuba, Puerto Rico, Haiti, and the South Pacific. (Pershing himself had served in the Philippines.) But alongside this global enterprise was a countervailing trend in domestic politics, one with which the Mexican misadventure would collide head-on.

For most of United States history, few if any laws governed the admission of immigrants. Anti-immigrant movements there had been—most notably the short-lived American Party, the "No Nothings" of the antebellum years—but they had come and gone with little impact on public policy. That changed abruptly in 1882 with the passage of the Chinese Exclusion Act, a response to increasing labor unrest in the American West. The measure was intended as provisional, a move to stem what was imagined as a passing crisis; this was a misreading of the demographic tea leaves, as the numbers of foreign-born workers soared nationwide. Between 1890 and 1924, no fewer than ten pieces of immigration legislation received presidential signatures, each building upon the last to tighten restrictions and strengthen enforcement. The economic motives were paired with less material concerns: Without proper measures, "alien immigration . . . will tend to produce an inferior rather than a superior American race," one prominent advocate of restrictions on immigration warned. Implemented in 1924, the country's first immigration quota system ensured that visas were issued solely in proportion to the presence of nationalities in the United States as of the 1890 census. The intent was to slow, if not halt, any change in the country's ethnic complexion.

Racial panics came and went during this period. But, at least as a legal matter, Mexican Americans were not the object of undue persecution. The 1924 legislation imposed no quotas on immigrants from Spanish-speaking countries, including Mexico, thanks to a peculiar kink of American racial theory: Indians who had intermarried with whites in the United States were deemed white; Latin Americans, likewise the descendants of Native Americans and Europeans, were also classed as white, and, accordingly, no restrictions whatsoever were levied on Mexicans. In the event, the numbers of Mexicans who *wanted* admission was low, topping out at around twenty thousand legally admitted persons annually in the 1910s. A small number of others, it may be presumed, simply walked in unchecked. Until the end of the decade, America's border patrol was a rump organization of just a few dozen mounted officers whose primary objective was to inhibit Chinese, not Mexicans, from entering the United States. America's real border defense—the army—simply had far more important things to worry about—namely, Pancho Villa.

The US commitment in Mexico lasted more than a year, into the early months of 1917. Though Villa never again sought northern plunder, he did evade capture, dealing a serious setback to America's military prestige at the very moment a continentwide war in Europe was threatening to draw America into it. And Villa produced another embarrassment as well, however accidentally. For by the time Pershing and his men, bowed if not quite broken, trudged back across the desert into Arizona, the army had been saddled with a novel and somewhat inconvenient cargo: 427 Chinese-Mexicans, who had flocked to the American columns for protection and who now marched in their train.

Attitudes among native-born Mexicans regarding the local Asian population were not necessarily more enlightened than those held by their Anglo counterparts. The Chinese had done little to improve relations by assisting the American invaders. "At any truck concentration point . . . one Chinese at least appeared," relates the only definitive chronicle of the encounter, composed thirty years after Pershing's expedition. "Pies, doughnuts, candy, tobacco, matches and fruit were stock items that these desert merchants offered for sale. The soldiers bought on sight." Under the circumstances, Villa found it convenient to stir up anti-Chinese feeling, leaving the immigrants even more vulnerable.

Pershing, meanwhile, was an agnostic when it came to race. He had begun his service as the commander of the 10th Cavalry Regiment, one of the first all-African American, Buffalo Soldier, fighting units to serve in the western territories. The general's willingness to lead these supposedly "undesirable" elements earned him his nickname, "Black Jack" Pershing. While chasing Villa, Pershing continued to make considerable use of the Buffalo Soldiers, whose outstanding horsemanship proved invaluable in the desert. "I cannot commend too highly the spirit shown among the colored combat troops," he later declared. Pershing demonstrated a similar lack of prejudice with regard to the beleaguered Chinese community in Mexico. He extended US protection during the incursion, and then insisted they accompany him back across the border when the expedition drew to a close.

Others came with them—nearly three thousand refugees in all, including a number of American-born Mormons—but the Chinese presented a special problem. As per the most recent iteration of the Exclusion Act, none of them were permitted to stay indefinitely and were expected to return to Mexico in time. They were encamped in military quarters, first in Columbus, later in San Antonio, staying only a short distance from the Alamo; there they remained for the duration of World War I, where their minders quickly put them to work reshaping the landscape of their new borderlands home. Camp Travis, named for one of the Alamo heroes, was built on land to the northeast of downtown as a training facility for American soldiers bound for Europe. Setting down rail lines, laying out streets, and clearing thousands of cactus-covered acres to make way for camp's tents and depots was expected to take as much as four months. The Chinese refugees did it in five weeks, working until near midnight at twenty cents an hour, hewing a miniature military city out of the Texas brush.

The facility (now a part of Fort Sam Houston) continued to be of use to the army long after the war was over; the men who labored to put it there were another matter. By 1920, the War Department had no money left to support its adopted Chinese, but it also recognized that they could not be safely returned to Mexico. Instead, against heavy political headwinds, an effort was launched to cut through the bureaucratic red tape and have them admitted to the United States on a permanent basis. Advocates for the Chinese went all the way to the top: They turned again to Black Jack Pershing, who had not only recovered from the ignominy of the Villa fiasco but been elevated to secular sainthood through his leadership in the Great War. Urging the House of Representatives to act, Pershing transmitted his "kind remembrances to all refugees" and begged that relief be extended to "these deserving men." At last, after waiting patiently for two years in increasingly dire conditions, the community by then known as "Pershing's Chinese" became the first legally sanctioned Asian mass immigrant group in the state of Texas. Many of their descendants remain in the area today, some within only a few miles of the military installation their ancestors helped build, their unique border odyssey only a dim memory passed down in family

lore—and occasionally in names. In honor of the community's great champion, one descendant reportedly gave his child the name "Blackjack Wong."

Fences, typically meager ones of metal, had cropped up in a number of
border cities during the early twentieth century. Often aimed at corralling
wayward livestock, they were cooperative endeavors between neighboring
communities on either side—the people of the borderlands molding the
territory to their own ends, undisturbed by any national political debate
about Mexicans and Latino immigrants. That debate had yet to take shape,
though its contours were already discernible by midcentury.

In the early morning hours of July 15, 1948, in the middle of a miser-
ably hot Philadelphia summer, Harry S. Truman took the podium at the
Democratic National Convention, speaking to a packed audience of men in
shirtsleeves fanning themselves with printed broadsides. At the time, Truman had been president for more than three years, but he was a first-time
presidential nominee, having assumed the office on the death of Franklin
Delano Roosevelt. Truman was not much liked by the left wing of his party
(he would face a third-party challenge from FDR's previous vice president
and his own former Commerce Secretary, Henry Wallace), and, in a bid to
prove his liberal bona fides, Truman and his backers had begun to court
segments of the Democratic base whose support and patience during the
war years it now seemed prudent to reward.

Congress had given him a golden opportunity to follow through with
one group in particular: immigrants. Only a month earlier, the legislative
branch had passed a bill nominally addressing the postwar refugee crisis, but without removing the prewar quotas, making the bill worse than
useless. Sawing at the air in front of the grandstand, Truman made a firm
promise: "I shall ask for adequate and decent laws for displaced persons
in place of this anti-Semitic, anti-Catholic law which this 80th Congress
passed." The audience in Philadelphia erupted in cheers.

Following his improbable victory, Truman would follow through on his
pro-immigration stance, vetoing an attempt in 1952 to continue the 1920s
quota system that he lambasted as "the dead hand of the past." Already

his administration had made simultaneous inroads with other minorities, backing a Jewish state in Palestine and throwing support behind civil rights for African Americans. Standing up for immigrant rights was an extension of the same logic: Jews, Italians, and other "white ethnics" in northern cities could complain equally about discrimination under the quotas. But throwing his weight behind the anti-quota movement was also a political leap of faith for Truman. Excluded groups—as Pershing's Chinese could easily attest—had few friends in American politics, for the simple reason that they had not been admitted in sufficient numbers to constitute a voting block. Exclusion based on race, Truman would later declare, was "unworthy of our traditions and our ideals." But traditions and ideals did not vote. Congress overrode his veto, and the quotas lived on.

Of all the electoral aims Democrats might have hoped to fulfill through their new immigration plank, winning over Mexican Americans was near the bottom of the list. Not only had people of Mexican origin never been subject to quotas, but the Democratic Party did not make a convincing savior from the day-to-day discrimination that they did face. All-white Democratic primaries were still common throughout the South, and, though primarily aimed at excluding blacks, they also, in a border state like Texas, locked out even larger numbers of Latinos. Truman's civil rights position might have been some token of his earnestness among minorities like Mexican Americans—but the Republicans had long since beaten the president to the punch, having had similar language in their platform for decades. Although the labor policies of the 1930s had drawn many Latinos into the New Deal coalition, there was no guarantee they'd stay there.

Indeed, in the wake of the Second World War, it was Republicans, not Democrats, who offered themselves as the strongest proxy for Latin American immigrants, and the Grand Old Party now moved to capitalize on that advantage and steal Truman's pro-immigrant thunder. In 1952, the Democrats faced a still more formidable challenge from Dwight D. Eisenhower, formerly the Commander of Allied Forces in Europe. His overwhelming popularity notwithstanding, Eisenhower's team took no chances; they began looking for supporters among traditionally Democratic voters, drafting public relations agent John A. Flores to head up *Latinos con Eisenhower*, an organization with offices in Washington, D.C., and Arizona. The latter state, where 17 percent of residents had Spanish last names, had already been made a laboratory for Republican outreach: In 1950, J. Howard Pyle was the first Republican to be elected as governor since 1929, thanks in part to energetic outreach among Mexican Americans—efforts orchestrated by a canny young Arizona conservative named Barry Goldwater. Flores's group picked up where Goldwater left off, making Eisenhower's 1952 campaign the first in American history to print buttons in Spanish. "*Yo Quiero Ike*," read some; others, "*Me Gusta Ike*." Neither translation quite has the music of "I Like Ike," but the intention was clear.

Not satisfied with sloganeering, Flores and company adopted a cunning strategy, focusing their efforts on a handful of states like Florida and New York where they hoped to sway voters with a message similar to the one Goldwater had brought to Arizona: that Democrats' top-heavy bureaucratic governance was ultimately hurting the working people they claimed to help, Latinos included. With the overwhelming Republican victory, it appeared that Flores's labors had borne fruit, and for Eisenhower's reelection bid four years later the GOP doubled down on the same approach. In California alone, the campaign's special Latin American Division established 173 local support groups, with express appeals to immigrant groups from the incumbent himself. While data on ethnic voting patterns is thin, it appears likely that the Eisenhower-Nixon ticket fared well among Mexican Americans. Their two-time opponent, Adlai Stevenson, mounted no organized effort to appeal to Mexican Americans at all.

Sunny PR aside, all was not well on the border during the Eisenhower years, and more recent immigrants faced a less than hearty welcome from federal officialdom. Since 1942, hundreds of thousands of Mexicans had been moving into the States as far north as Oregon to participate in the Bracero Program, a national effort to recruit agricultural workers from across the border for temporary employment in the fields and orchards of the West. ("*Bracero*" means manual laborer.) Intended to alleviate World War II-era labor shortages, the program was poorly regulated and led to many migrant workers settling illegally in the United States. Labor and community groups were riled by the sudden presence of so many low-wage farmhands in their midst, and they were not alone—the Mexican government was also dis-tressed at this exodus of their would-be workforce. Desirous of having them back, it asked America to return them, only to have the Americans respond in 1954 with rather more energy than might have been hoped: The administration stepped up an enforcement regime that would result in the deportation of 1.25 million individuals in its first two years of operation. The initiative, Operation Wetback, took its title from a derogatory term for Mexican immigrants that had entered the American lexicon in the 1920s, a reference to migrants swimming across the Rio Grande to find work in the United States; the name tells us something of the flavor of the program, which was marked by abuses and overreach. During a subsequent congres-sional investigation, one official described a cargo vessel by which immi-grants were returned to Mexico as a "penal hell ship."

Despite the excesses of Operation Wetback, the policy did not sig-nal a meaningful change in the political disposition of the Republican Party toward Mexican migrants, immigrants, or their naturalized cousins. "Republican conscience and Republican policy require that the annual number of immigrants we accept be at least doubled," read the party's offi-cial platform for the 1960 campaign year. As the right wing began to gather momentum against the more moderate Eisenhower faction, it seemed likely the GOP would only become more welcoming to Latinos, not less. Emerging from the deserts of Arizona, capital-C Conservatism was a true product of the borderlands, and Goldwater's fellow travelers embraced the influx of foreign labor as all-American capitalism at its best—as another prominent Arizona conservative declared, initiatives like the Bracero Pro-gram had been "beneficial both to the Mexican nationals who come out of this country and to the consumers of the United States." Goldwater's ulti-mate vision of the border was spelled out in a 1962 article he wrote for the *Tucson Daily Citizen*, in which he looked ahead sixty years to the Arizona of the future. "Our ties with Mexico," he wrote,

> will be much more firmly established in 2012 because some-time within the next 50 years the Mexican border will become as the Canadian border, a free one, with the formalities and

red tape of ingress and egress cut to a minimum so that the
residents of both countries can travel back and forth across the
line as if it were not there.

As the lifelong Arizonan imagined it, the ensuing prosperity would give rise
to a future borderlands environment of booming suburbs, its cities sprawling yet still surrounded by the desert's "pastel paradise," nature and man
together in a boundless, fenceless idyll.

On the other side of the aisle, there was no comparable vision. The
elite of the Democratic Party, increasingly concentrated in the Northeast,
was less vitally connected to the border region and had little understanding of its culture and economy. Eisenhower's successor, John F. Kennedy,
under whom Operation Wetback would continue at a slightly reduced pace,
had devoted less than a couple paragraphs to Mexican Americans in his
1958 book *A Nation of Immigrants*. By contrast, the man intent on being his
challenger in the 1964 election was a member of Lodge 129 of the Alianza
Hispanic Americans Club and had even been featured on the cover of its
magazine: Barry Goldwater, April 1953's "Brother of the Month."

The comet of conservatism, Goldwater came streaking out of the Southwest
to announce the new political faith, only to burn out on the national scene
just as quickly. His loss in 1964 to Lyndon Johnson—by the largest share of
the popular vote in US history up to that point—appeared for a brief while
to extinguish his movement altogether. It would be reborn just a few short
years later, though by then tectonic changes would reshape the policy landscape surrounding immigration, along with the very physical landscape of
the borderlands.

After his sweeping victory, Johnson used his political capital to finally
make good on the promise of Truman's 1948 declaration, ending the quota
system for good. Johnson was one of a vanishing breed among high-ranking
Democrats, not just as a Texan but as one with an intimate knowledge
of immigrant life among Mexican Americans. He had been a not-quite-
conversant Spanish speaker since at least the 1920s, when he worked as a
teacher in Cotulla, Texas, mostly with the children of Latino farmhands.

Most of their families had come to the country as part of the Bracero Program, though doubtless many had entered without proper processing or long overstayed their official welcome. "It never even occurred to me in my fondest dreams that I might have the chance to help the sons and daughters of those students," Johnson said; now, as president, "I do have that chance and . . . I mean to use it."

The reforms LBJ initiated weren't quite aimed at the immigrant community he knew best—and in an unexpected turn they may have done Mexican Americans more harm than good. "The day is not far off when the population explosion in Latin American countries will exert great pressures upon those people to emigrate to the United States," said Senator Robert Byrd, a conservative Democrat from West Virginia. Johnson, an ace parliamentary horse-trader since his days in the Senate, had lassoed the votes of Byrd and other reluctant members of his own party by promising them that visa quotas would be raised on some groups, even as they were eliminated for others. The Hart-Celler Act, which went into effect in 1965, reduced the number of visas allotted to residents of the Western Hemisphere by half. Mexicans, to whom the quota system had never applied, were now suddenly targeted, while Byrd and his allies believed they had secured a less-Latino future.

Fretting about demographics was always part of the political repertoire for conservatives of Byrd's stripe. But LBJ and his allies had little reason to push back against it. On the whole there seemed no reason for immediate concern about Mexico: While the relative weakness and strength of the two nations remained as it always had been, material and political conditions in Mexico had improved immeasurably after the dust of the Revolution had settled. Under the mixed-economic strategy of the long-ruling Partido Revolucionario Institucional (PRI), industrial development had proceeded apace, obliging the United States to deal with its neighbor not as a hopeless truant but as a genuine hemispheric partner. At the same time, American leadership now faced a far more serious global challenge than it had a half-century earlier. With the Soviet Union threatening US interests on multiple fronts, the Mexicans, it was reasoned, could be valuable allies in the struggle against Communism, and the border could be used to entice them.

In a textbook example of border-theory meeting border-reality, the course of the Rio Grande had suffered various changes due to wind, weather, and human intervention over the course of the preceding century. The most dramatic of these shifts had occurred between El Paso and Juarez: As far back as the 1860s, during a series of storms, one resident on the Mexican side recalled the banks collapsing with a noise "like the boom of a cannon"; when the citizens awoke, they found the river had changed course during the night. Similar events steadily pushed the waterway northward until it formed a long, slow-moving oxbow, and to stop the consequent flooding the two governments (through the International Boundary and Water Commission) agreed in 1899 to shift the route southward again. The result, however, was to maroon a significant slice of Mexico on the American side of the border, some six hundred acres, creating even more trouble than before—known as the Chamizal, the territory was claimed by both sides. Tensions surrounding its ownership were a factor in the ill-starred Taft/Diaz summit of 1909, which took place on the Chamizal itself and nearly ended in tragedy without producing any resolution to the issue. Now, with the Cold War at hand, the Johnson administration put the matter to rest by simply conceding most of the land to Mexico and rechanneling the river. The process of peaceful cooperation, which would be repeated elsewhere on the border, was commemorated in El Paso with a park and museum, the Chamizal National Memorial, located on the formerly disputed floodplain, with a sister facility sitting on the Mexican side.

The American memorial would be completed by LBJ's Republican successor, another border-state native who labored with equal diligence toward improved relations between the neighboring nations. Though not much admired for his cultural sensitivity, Richard Nixon, like Johnson, had known Mexicans all through his hardscrabble upbringing in Southern California, and he had a rough appreciation for them as people. ("They have a heritage," the Watergate tapes reveal him as saying, "At the present time they steal . . . [but] they do have some concept of family life. They don't live like a bunch of dogs.") Not a Spanish speaker himself, Nixon did profess a love of Mexican cuisine, to the degree that he persuaded the Adobe de Capistrano Restaurant near his San Clemente home to devote its menu exclusively to regional fare. (The establishment still maintains a plaque and portrait at Nixon's favorite seat.) A more emphatic, more durable expression of Nixon's admiration was the construction, under his administration, of Friendship Park, a binational public space on the border between San Diego and Tijuana completed in 1971.

Only steps from the beach—atop a hill featuring the westernmost border marker of 1855, one of the few still standing—the park was built to facilitate reunions between families and friends from the United States and Mexico, who could meet and mingle there freely under official supervision. With no fencing to separate the two nations at the time, such encounters were always more or less tolerated; the park simply provided an infinitely more attractive and more formal setting, with sweeping views of the Pacific Ocean from the top of Monument Mesa. The first lady attended the opening of the park, dedicating it as a national monument. "May there never be a wall between these two great nations," declared Pat Nixon. "Only friendship."

No less than Northumberland, America's borderlands were an unknown country to me. In Edinburg, Texas, about twenty miles from the border, I was invited to tour the campus of the University of Texas Rio Grande Valley (UTRGV), a school where 90 percent of the enrollees in 2017 were Latino, the majority of them Mexican American. Located on landscaped grounds with uniform brick buildings, a few graced by elliptical arches with a faintly Spanish air, the school draws primarily from surrounding Hidalgo County, one of the poorest in the nation. Yet the university has been growing rapidly, its programs expanding. In one of its newer facilities, a student center completed in 2005 by San Antonio–based architects Muñoz & Company, the designers had placed an elevator shaft in which a series of *dichos*—traditional Mexican proverbs—were etched into the glass, both in English and in Spanish. As the elevator ascends, the two languages become increasingly intermingled, reenacting the linguistic cross-pollination common to the mestizo sphere of South Texas.

The mixed cultural milieu of the borderlands, though always marginal, managed to exert an outsized influence on American life over the course

*Education Building at University of Texas Rio
Grande Valley, Edinburg*

of the twentieth century. Perhaps nowhere was this felt more keenly than in architecture: In the realm of high design, Frank Lloyd Wright, who set up his winter studio in the Arizona desert, melded the motifs of Mayan and Aztec temples into a unique synthesis, while in less rarified precincts the Spanish Mission style was adopted as the common housing vernacular in the exploding suburbs of the West. A byword for romance, the border became a popular tourist destination and a lure for film audiences—witness *Border Caballero* (1936), *Below the Border* (1942), *Border River* (1954)—while its music, art, and foodways wormed their way into the mainstream. But even as they did, Mexican Americans were often relegated to the sidelines. This was especially so in Hollywood, where they were all too frequently depicted as grimacing banditos, shiftless farmhands, or *damas* in distress.

For all the progress in the political arena, some attitudes had remained unchanged since the days of Santa Anna. Whatever the strictures of the quota system, most Americans did not regard Latinos of any extraction as white, and even before the quotas were replaced there were calls for limiting Latin American immigration. In the borderlands, the ethnic modus vivendi was more idiosyncratic—in Texas in the 1920s, white interviewees described Mexicans as "not so bad as the Negroes," able to eat in restaurants where "the n___ would not"; in California, fair-complexioned Mexican children were simply referred to as "Spanish"—but even Latinos in traditionally mestizo territory endured episodes of blatant discrimination. In Los Angeles during World War II, the Zoot Suit Riots saw Mexican Americans targeted by white mobs for perceived disloyalty, no matter their actual citizenship or record of military service. Those who gave the full measure of devotion were not spared indignity either: In 1945, Felix Longoria, a native of Three Rivers, Texas, was killed in a Japanese ambush in the Philippines; he was then denied burial in his hometown after the local funeral director refused to accept the corpse of a Mexican American on the premises. Eventually, the then newly elected Senator Lyndon Johnson intervened on the family's behalf.

In the wake of the successful civil rights movement, Mexican Americans began to take matters into their own hands. "The Democratic party . . . no longer can take Mexican Americans for granted," said Henry Muñoz II: The Laredo-born activist—whose son's firm was responsible for the UTRGV student center—was a major player alongside Cesar Chavez, Gloria Anzaldúa, and Oscar Zeta Acosta in the Chicano movement, a constellation of organizers and artists who sought to transform Mexican Americans into a fighting political force while molding a more authentic binational identity. Throughout the 1960s and '70s, movement leaders spoke out against media stereotypes and unfair labor practices affecting the mestizo community concentrated in the border states. "Nothing can stop the Chicanos," said Muñoz, and their power seemed bound to swell in tandem with their numbers. Renewed economic instability in Mexico in the 1970s prompted a sudden surge in immigration, both legal and otherwise, making Chicanos an ever more visible presence on the American scene.

Meeting with successes and setbacks, the struggle for immigrant rights became increasingly formalized, with umbrella organizations like the National Council of La Raza (today UnidosUS) advancing the movement's priorities at both at the state and federal levels. Steep cuts in government support in the 1980s left such groups on weakened footing; yet it seemed, in its waning years, that the twentieth century would close out on a happy note for Mexican Americans, albeit courtesy of the least likely of borderlands politicians—a famous fan of cowboy movies and a sometime actor in them himself.

While still governor of California, Ronald Reagan had followed in the footsteps of his old friend and mentor Barry Goldwater, forging connections with Mexican American business leaders to exploit a perceived fissure in the Democratic electorate between blacks and Latinos. In his successful bid for the presidency in 1980, Reagan kept to the same approach, making an emphatic pitch for a measured and reasoned solution to the problems of the border and undocumented immigrants. Speaking to a crowd at his 1980 primary debate with then opponent and future vice president, George H. W. Bush, Reagan looked beyond the issues of the day to the broader historical and geopolitical ones between the United States and Mexico, two countries that he claimed needed "a better understanding and a better relationship than we've ever had." He went on:

> I think we haven't been sensitive enough to our size and our power. They have a problem of forty to fifty percent unemployment . . . Rather than talking about putting up a fence, why don't we work out some recognition of our mutual problems, make it possible for them to come here legally with a work permit, and then while they're working and earning here, they pay taxes here.

As president, Reagan would live up to his rhetoric. In 1986, he signed the Immigration Reform and Control Act, accompanied by a statement that the measure would "preserve the value of one of the most sacred possessions of our people: American citizenship." The bipartisan legislation had been sponsored by Democratic Representative Romano L. Mazzoli, chairman of the House Subcommittee on Immigration, and his opposite number in the Republican-held Senate, Senator Alan K. Simpson, and it granted full citizenship to all who had entered the country illegally before January 1, 1982, provided they had some grasp of English, no criminal record, and paid any outstanding taxes. A year later, the Reagan administration doubled down on the policy—the Immigration and Naturalization Service declared that children whose parents had been beneficiaries of the amnesty would also be shielded from deportation. When Bush followed Reagan into the Oval Office, he went still further, extending the amnesty to an estimated 1.5 million family members of qualified immigrants.

The changes of the 1980s did not come without challenges, not the least for the borderlands, where shifting economic currents reshaped the landscape yet again. Only a few miles south of UTRGV, near the Hidalgo Port of Entry, I saw incongruously large, seemingly half-built houses, the properties (as I was told) of *narcotrafficos* who began establishing a physical presence on the US side three decades ago during the early years of the booming cross-border drug trade. The growth in drugs and drug smuggling would help feed a rumor in some conservative circles that Reagan— a native Illinoisan, after all, who lacked any real feeling for the culture of the borderlands—had become a border hawk late in life, viewing his 1986 amnesty as perhaps the greatest mistake of his presidency. The story appears to be baseless. "It certainly did not originate with anyone who was close to Reagan," noted one conservative analyst: Some versions of the legend have it that Reagan voiced his second thoughts to his former attorney general, Ed Meese; yet Meese, the analyst noted, has expressly denied the claim. So far as his thoughts on the matter are documented, Ronald Reagan stood by his immigration policy till the end. Its legacy for the borderlands is clear enough: For every flimsy, faux-lavish villa around Hidalgo, one could point to dozens more young men and women in the brightly lit student center at Edinburg on a weekday afternoon, many of them the children and grandchildren of the Americans that Reagan helped to make.

III

UNSTABLE WALLS

CHINA

In Feng Menglong's seventeenth-century folk compendium *Stories to Awaken the World*, one episode—entitled *Zhang Xiaoji Takes in His Brother-in-law at Chenliu*—relates how the wayward son Guo Qian was found at last by his long-lost sister after a separation of many years. Describing their tearful reunion, the author erupts into verse, declaring that his hero's many trials have made this moment all the more precious: for, as he writes,

> *If it were not for a bone-chilling spell,*
> *The plum blossoms would not be so sweet-smelling.*

The phrase, which has entered the extensive canon of traditional Chinese proverbs, may be considered equivalent to the English "it's always darkest before the dawn," a cheering reminder that hardship endured will find its just reward in the end.

Unfortunately for visitors to the north of China in December, the plum blossom does not come into flower in the country until late winter. Its fragrance seems a very long way off when one is standing atop a freezing stone parapet in Huanghuacheng, about sixty miles north of Beijing, looking down a ragged cliff where one had expected to find a staircase. At the bottom of the declivity is a frozen lake, and beside that a forest of barren chestnut trees. No choice is left but to turn around and scale once more the ten-story slope leading to the drop. As the wind kicks up and the sun is scarfed up in cloud, it becomes harder and harder to maintain anything like the philosophical optimism of Feng Menglong.

Winter is not, relatively speaking, a popular time of year to see the Great Wall of China. For those who dare, it does have its pleasures, though some of these are inseparable from its perils. Often likened by the Chinese to the tail of a giant dragon, the wall in its endless convolutions frequently vanishes down one mountainside, only to materialize on another some distance away; some portions are open to the public, some are not, and in the winter, with no madding crowd of tourists to follow it is all too easy to go chasing after the wrong length of tail. At Huanghuacheng, where the wall segments are divided by the fingers of a large reservoir, the danger is double, and there are all sorts of ways to end up atop a precarious pile of stones, or in odder places still. That was how it happened—unaccompanied, underdressed, using socks for gloves—that I came to the teetering precipice, and moments later, to the Great Slide of China.

Working my way down after the near-plummet, I found a path that turned into a long meander into a back canyon, leading to a gentle slope where a string of multicolored plastic pennants announced the presence of a seasonal pleasure park. Huanghuacheng's reservoir and its relative proximity to the capital make it a popular spot in the height of summer, perfect for boating parties, lakefront picnics, and for this: a tinny-looking conduit winding down the hill, making snaking switchbacks that perfectly mimic the Great Wall as it threads its way from ridge to ridge. Faded banners featured children, crazed with glee, packed into tiny toboggans. Even accounting for several months' apparent disuse, the slide did not inspire confidence: It was full of leaves, with slight gaps showing in the joins of the halfpipe. There was a sort of stationhouse at the top, also deserted, and only by way of a small service trail behind the building was it possible to return at last to the wall (the *right* wall, this time).

If Feng Menglong only knew. The Great Wall that stands at Huanghuacheng and in much of the surrounding region was built in his lifetime and in the lifetime of his immediate ancestors. The Great Ming, the dynasty that had ruled China for three hundred years, reached its apogee in the sixteenth century; by the middle of the next, only twenty years after the publication of *Stories to Awaken the World*, it would collapse in spectacular fashion, its last emperor hanging himself with a silk sash. The Chinese would not be masters of their own country again for another three hundred years—a very long winter indeed—and, while it lasted, most of the greatness of the Ming walls would slowly tumble in bits and pieces into the precipitous valleys surrounding them. Only in the last thirty years would they be picked up again and partially reconstituted as the world's most uncanny photo opportunity, a family-friendly destination full of thrills, spills, and, occasionally, bone-chills.

The cold isn't always to blame. Trudging slowly back up from the edge, I found it best to go in quick spurts with brief pauses. During one break I looked down to find, baked into the brick of the narrow steps, the tiny paw prints of a medieval cat.

The Great Wall at Huanghuacheng

Franz Kafka, in his short story "The Great Wall of China," wrote of "the many legends which have arisen about the structure [and] which, for individual people at least, are impossible to prove with their own eyes and by their own standards because the structure is so immense." Though the story was intended as fantasy, Kafka's statement holds up: The Great Wall of China's tortured path through the landscape augurs something of the frustrations it poses to any straightforward assessment of its history. Wavering in and out of view, revealing different parts of itself in different places, the wall seems to demand something more than a chronological account. Its legends, in any case, have always been more interesting.

Consider what happened one Saturday evening in 1899, when four newspapermen were standing around Union Station in Denver, Colorado. Each represented a different local paper, and they all shared a serious problem: There was no news. Frustrated, and despairing of finding anything sensational in time for the morning edition, one of the four landed on a novel idea. He told his colleagues that he would make something up, and he encouraged his opposite numbers to join him in the subterfuge.

The others were game, and so the group retired to the bar of the nearby Oxford Hotel to gin up their story, tossing around a number of Denver-related notions. They realized quickly that anything too close to home might easily be disproven: The key to plausibility was exoticism. What they needed was something compelling but distant, recognizable to many but unknown to most, with a catchy narrative hook that would attract attention but not necessarily scrutiny. And then it came to them.

The tale they concocted seems incredible now, but it was somewhat less outlandish in the world as it was then. In older cities all over the globe, defensive fortifications were being dismantled. The devastating power of modern artillery rendered masonry walls obsolete, while the advent of the automobile made them low-hanging fruit for city planners looking to create new boulevards and peripheral roadways. In Vienna, beginning in the 1860s, the city's circumferential fort and its surrounding glacis had been demolished to make way for what would become the Austrian capital's premier bourgeois address, the Ringstrasse. The phenomenon was not confined to Europe: In China itself, Shanghai and Guangzhou would demolish their walls in the early years of the twentieth century and erect new loop highways in their stead, the latter under the supervision of American advisers. If you could do it to city walls, why not a Great Wall?

In the journalists' telling, the Qing emperor was soliciting bids from US contractors to remove thousands of miles of the famous wall and replace it with a roadway running through the Chinese uplands. The articles furnished detailed accounts—all entirely fabricated—of a contingent of engineers traveling from Chicago via Denver to Beijing, ready to submit their proposals to the imperial government. Major American financiers, including the Armour meatpacking clan and department store magnate Marshall Field, were rumored to have stakes in the endeavor, and a bonanza seemed to be in the offing: "Some of the wealthiest and best-known capitalists of Chicago are interested in this enterprise," said one well-placed "source." When all was done and the stories filed, the group felt proud of their little fiction and certain they would escape detection. After all, it would only be in the Denver papers for a day.

Imagine their surprise when, later that week, a feature article appeared in the *New York Times* under the headline "Will China's Wall Come Down?" The Denverites' invention had sprouted legs, and in its journey east it had somehow acquired additional embellishment, now featuring what appeared to be corroborating statements from a Chinese official said to be connected with the project. After rattling around the national press for a short while, the furor at last died down—but not before it gave rise to another, still more bizarre falsehood: Four decades later, a popular misconception would take root in the United States holding that the sham report of the Great Wall's imminent doom had reached China and so outraged the populace that it lit the fuse of the anti-Western Boxer Rebellion, resulting in the murders of hundreds of Europeans and countless Chinese. Though abetted by various pseudoscholarly publications, this rumor had no basis in fact. It was fake news about fake news.

Those are just two of the untruths to which the Great Wall, in all its superb unrealness, has been peculiarly susceptible. Corpses of slaves impressed into the wall's construction crews have long been said to be buried beneath the stone pavers; no bodies have ever been exhumed. It has often been thought that the wall is visible from the moon; the claim not only is specious but also predates the first moon mission by four decades. (Among the more notable qualities of the celebrated "Blue Marble" photograph of the earth, taken by American astronauts in 1972, is how wall-less the world appears.) The wall may or may not have been built in accordance with the geomantic principles of feng shui—most premodern Chinese buildings were—but there is little in the historical record to confirm the claim with regard to the Great Wall in particular. The only reference to that effect is the verbal suicide note, dated 210 BC, of General Meng Tian, right-hand man to China's first emperor and the architect of arguably the earliest version of the wall, who pinned his misfortune following the death of his patron on the fatal sin of having "cut through the veins of the earth" in building the fortifications.

Seen from a place like Mutianyu, another stretch of wall not far from Beijing, the wave of brick and rock that surges up and down the Yanshang highlands does emit a resonance that feels somehow cosmic. On my visit there I was less alone (there was nothing so desolate as the Great Slide) yet an occult atmosphere still hung over the place, as if the wall adhered to a more than martial logic. Perhaps Meng Tian was right—but then the wall I walked at Mutianyu is not Meng Tian's wall. Very little of the wall as it exists today is his, for yet another of the wall's enduring mythologies is that it is an ancient structure, as old as Chinese civilization itself. Some crude earthen barriers can still be found that date to the earliest efforts by various lowland kingdoms to keep raiders from the north out of the fertile plains of central China. But Mutianyu, like Huanghuacheng and most of the wall as it exists in the Western imagination, is the Ming wall, the one built, and the one ultimately forsaken, in the sanguine age of *Stories to Awaken the World*.

The Ming had not always been so preoccupied with their inland frontier. In earlier days, the Yongle emperor, Zhu Di, third in the dynastic succession, oversaw a daring program to expand the empire's commercial and political reach by looking outward, toward the sea. The voyages of the first decades of the fifteenth century preceded Columbus's by nine decades, and the fleet that undertook them was of an altogether higher caliber. Four decks, with a tonnage comparable to a small twenty-first-century bulk freighter, the giant *baoshan* treasure ships traveled in a grand convoy: the eight-masted *machuan*, or horse ships; the *liangchuan*, with its seven masts, bearing provisions for soldiers and animals; the agile *zhanchuan*, light cruisers that were good in a fight. Three hundred seventeen ships in all; the faces of grimacing dragons adorned their prows, giving them the aspect of a fantastical floating bestiary.

Seven of the storied "treasure voyages" were launched by the Ming beginning in 1405. The accounts of the expeditions are outrageous picaresques, the men battling pirates off the coast of Java, abducting royals in Ceylon, fighting off armies many times their size on beaches and in far-off capitals. Their admiral, Zheng He, is still a figure of veneration in some of the older settlements of the Chinese diaspora, and he guided the flotilla by centuries-old star charts and by magnetic compasses, originally developed for feng shui, that brought his ships safely through the Indian Ocean as far as the Horn of Africa: to "barbarian regions," as Zheng He would report, "far away hidden in a blue transparency." And yet after all this—after bringing home tribute from "the countries beyond the horizon, and from the ends of the earth"—the Ming would order the destruction of most of Zheng He's records, condemning him to a posthumous *damnatio memoriae*. His only surviving testimony is the inscription on a single stele. In 1525, the authorities burned all oceangoing vessels.

All at once, the empire recoiled from the world, consumed instead by fear over its landbound frontiers. Since Meng Tian's time and before, a succession of Central Asian nations, many of uncertain provenance, had risen from the northern steppes to harass China. Their most recent incarnation was as the Mongols: Under their leader Kublai Khan, they had pierced the Chinese defenses in the early thirteenth century and overrun the country to establish their own dynasty, the Yuan. The descendants of the Khan had ruled for a hundred years before they were expelled by the august founders of the Ming; driven back across the mountains, the Mongols then fell to division and infighting, while their successors in China waxed in strength and magnificence for two centuries. But now the ancient enemy was stirring once more, and to the Ming their increasing raids could look only like a revanchist putsch, the barbarians straining to regain their lost imperium. In this the Ming were mistaken—this was not the Mongols' object. They were actuated by more quotidian needs: They wanted to buy things, and their Chinese neighbors refused to sell.

"These dogs and sheep are untrustworthy and constantly changing," one Chinese official wrote. The consensus in the south was that the horse-trading rabble beyond the mountains was not worth doing business with.

Few nations were, in the Ming view—the same attitude that helped bring about the abrupt foreclosure of the treasure voyages. The dynamic was self-reinforcing, defensiveness begetting defensiveness: First the Ming cut themselves off from the sea, then from the Mongols; and as the Mongols found themselves turned away from the marketplace, they took sterner measures, provoking still sterner defenses. "In the White Ox Year" (1541), as told in the Buddhist chronicle of the *Jewel Translucent Sutra*, the Mongol leader Altan Khan "commanded [all to join them] and took the Great Realm campaigning towards China." In response, the Ming began to refortify the old string of border garrisons and the line of earthworks that connected them.

In 1550, after a series of daring incursions into the interior, the "never despondent and determined" Altan Khan managed his most stunning military coup yet, charging through the passes where the empire had yet to reinforce the aging ramparts, penetrating as far as Beijing, and putting a good scare into the Great Ming. To the Chinese, Khan was a figure of mysterious terror, surrounded by odd counselors: One was said to hold an elixir that allowed a man to thrive without eating grain (a key asset, grain being the commodity the Mongols were most keen to acquire from the Chinese); another claimed he could make fortifications disappear with a magic spell. Hedging against sorcery, the Ming decided to come to the bargaining table and gave Altan his grain. At the same time, they quietly ramped up a massive building campaign to complete their *bianqiang*, the "border wall," replacing the old rammed-earth construction with brick and stone running along every mountainous saddleback and foursquare towers spiking every peak.

The Ming's construction was remarkably sound, able to bear a high-powered beating. For the grand upgrade of the sixteenth century, the emperors had insisted on masonry facing, not all of which could be conveniently quarried along the wall's route but instead had to be hauled over land (by goat, according to lore) and then dragged uphill. Likewise the bricks that gave the wall its smooth, regular walkway; though kilns could sometimes be placed near construction sites, many operated remotely, and then shipped their wares uphill in wheelbarrows, a Chinese invention. The bricks, most of them approximately fourteen by seven by three inches, sit atop a solid bulwark of rammed earth, tamped down by laborers; on either side of the embankment, the ashlar flanks were laid into furrows cut deep into the ground, and at their top the solid masonry crests were set. Then there were the accoutrements: Though the Mongols didn't possess gunpowder, the Ming did, and their artillery pieces, immensely heavy, were anchored in stony armatures and fixed northward to point through the evenly spaced gaps in the crenels, toward the mountains and the nothing beyond. And then there were the swords, and the armor, and the grain, and all the equipage required to keep a large body of soldiers in fighting trim, for months or even years at a time, all alone in a cold country.

For the twenty-first-century visitor lacking an official tour guide (and illiterate in Mandarin) the difficulty of navigating the twists and turns of the wall is further vexed by its being, not just in appearance but in fact, more than one wall. The Ming built according to necessity, almost haphazardly: Their walls double up in places, both with one another and with the more modest ones of their predecessors, making any estimate of the structure's total length, or of the amount of material consumed in its construction, speculative to the point of high fantasy. Three thousand kilometers? Twenty thousand? The numbers differ from source to source. Other figures are impossible to even guess at. How many workers did it take to tip the stonework, to shoulder the hods? How many died? Around Mutianyu and elsewhere there are inscriptions commemorating the effort, some of them ancient stele bearing the names of great architect-generals, some of more recent vintage. None of them convey, or could be expected to convey, the totality of the truth, the palpable truth not just of how much but of what and why: of why a nation would burn its boats, or what happened to the cat in the kiln.

Scholars have never ceased disputing whether the Great Wall of China was "good" or "bad," whether it lived up to its functional promise and exorbitant cost, whether it saved China or sank it. But these may be the wrong questions. Just as the structure is too physically immense to permit of any ready comprehension, its extraordinarily long life and afterlife make it impossible to pass judgment on its efficacy. Today the wall might be deemed good, inasmuch as it fills China's touristic coffers. At a different time, in a different place, the verdict appears a great deal bleaker.

Eighty years ago, it seemed that the wall had been weighed in the balances one last time, and found wanting. Since just after the turn of the twentieth century, Japan had maintained a body of troops, the Kwantung Army, on the Asian mainland just beyond the wall's eastern terminus at Shanhai Pass—"the head of the dragon," as the Ming called it, where the final defensive tower of their barrier stood buffeted by the waves of the Bohai Sea. By the 1930s, with China's first post-dynastic republic divvied into armed camps ruled by feuding warlords, the increasingly militarist Japanese Empire had grown impatient with its politically fractious mainland neighbor. Rather than wait for Europe to come and play colonizer, the occupying generals resolved to do the job themselves and went looking for a suitable pretext to launch an invasion. One night, the Kwantung garrison commander near Shanhaiguan found one: He blew up a few grenades, fired some rifles into the air, and then loudly proclaimed that his unit had been attacked by local "terrorists." A strike against the nearby Chinese regiment's position around the Great Wall commenced the following morning, January 2, 1933.

Wobbly though it was after three centuries of neglect, the wall still remained a formidable snag for any military attempting to move by land into China, owing mostly to the steep terrain upon which it sat; more vulnerable were the saddle-like passes, and it was there that the rumble of the Japanese columns was now heard. The Shanhai Pass was first to fall, the defenders in the narrow coastal plain surrendering after twenty-four hours of bitter fighting. In the days and weeks that followed, the Kwantung launched an offensive targeting key points all along the wall, tightening the noose around the strategic pass at Xifengkou. Stampeding out of the battlements, swinging high the same single-bladed *dadao* swords their forebears had wielded against Altan Khan, Chinese troops under Lieutenant General Song Zheyuan counterattacked at close quarters near the foot of the wall, denying the Japanese the advantage of their superior firepower. For weeks in March and April, the invaders were held at bay. At last, bit by bit, Zheyuan's men were dislodged from their blockhouses in the valleys, ceding the age-old forts to Japan and melting back toward Beijing. The Great Wall of China, in its last starring role as a military installation, played the loser.

The wall's return as a winner—in the limited sense of becoming a national symbol—was partially explained in a plaque I saw at Mutianyu, the meaning of which I only grasped afterward. Piecing together the scattered rubble has been a major undertaking for the People's Republic of China (PRC) since its reengagement with the West following President Richard Nixon's 1972 visit. (Nixon also came to the wall in winter. He claimed, implausibly, that he "really didn't need the coat.") To assist in the restoration, the Chinese government has solicited donations from international sponsors, and Mutianyu, as the marker on one of its new faux-Ming terraces explains, was brought back to life through the good offices of Düsseldorf-based chemical maker Henkel. The firm's corporate logo is etched into the top of the speckled stone, and below it is an inscription, declaring that while the wall was once "intended to ward off enemy attacks," today it has risen again to "bring together the people of the world."

A lovely thought; as happy endings go, fairly redolent of plum blossoms; yet it speaks to a condition that is alarmingly pervasive and not a little pernicious. With China's emergence as a global industrial dynamo, every aspect of national life has been borne along on a tide of change that has cast even old familiar objects and relations into an unaccustomed new order, tossed indifferently into a crowded marketplace, there to be bought and sold. The wall I walked in Mutianyu was not only not an ancient wall—it was not even the Ming's—it was Henkel's, and their marker is a shrine (as sociologist Armand Mattelart has written) to the company's "appropriation of this morsel of cultural heritage"—the Great Wall of China, brought to you by Germany's favorite laundry detergent.

Between the inequities of the Ming in building the wall and the travesties of capital in rebuilding it, there is not much use in comparing and contrasting or declaring which evil is the greater or lesser. Behind the constant effort to rate the Great Wall of China's success there lies, in many instances, the desire of contemporary political actors to appropriate it to this or that cause: to definitively prove or disprove that the Chinese wall, and by extension all other walls, "works" or does not "work." Again, this kind of assessment is all too reductive—though it might be enlightening to consider the thoughts of the Chinese on the subject.

Formally, the PRC's current attitude toward its most valuable piece of real estate approaches that of the first US president to visit it. "As we look at this Wall," declared Nixon, "we do not want walls of any kind between peoples." The sachems of the People's Republic are only too happy to have this relic of the imperial past, but like Nixon they do not endorse the politics that begat it. Quite the opposite: For them, the wall is most useful as bait to lure in the horse-trading "dog and sheep." At the same time, the government's official position does not rise to the level of out-and-out denunciation of the Ming or their policies. Although ancestors are still much revered in today's China, it is not for the sake of the long-dead emperors that strident critiques of the wall are frowned upon. It is because such talk is a form of sedition against the present leadership. For a brief while, it was a popular one.

River Elegy premiered on China Central Television in 1988, a multi-part documentary that chronicled Chinese history from a perspective that was bracing, novel, and, as it transpired, extremely dangerous. Statements critical of the cornerstones of traditional Chinese culture, the wall included, had been aired in the country before: As early as the 1920s, pioneering Chinese liberal Lu Xun had deemed the structure an unmitigated disaster, writing that "in reality . . . it has never served any purpose other than to make countless workers labor to death in vain." Under Mao and his successors, such pointed remarks could only be sanctioned when in the service of the party agenda, and the writers and producers of the six-episode series slipped their political leash and then some. The narrator of the program embarked on a windy jeremiad that pointed the finger at much more than the pretensions and paranoias of an empire long defunct:

> And yet, if the Great Wall could speak, it would very frankly tell us, its Chinese grandchildren, that it is a great and tragic gravestone forged by historical destiny. It can by no means represent strength, initiative, glory . . . Because of its great size and long history, it has deeply imprinted its arrogance and

self-delusion in the souls of our people. Alas, O Great Wall,
why do we still want to praise you?

Audiences attuned to the codes of censored media understood that this was
the language of metaphor: The chauvinism of the wall's builders stood for
the chauvinism of the modern regime and its resistance to democracy, to
freedom of conscience, and to all those exotic notions labeled by the Central Committee as indelibly Western and corrupting. The government also
recognized the message—and for their trouble the makers of *River Elegy*
faced arrest, imprisonment, and exile. The persecution intensified in the
wake of the pro-democratic Tiananmen Protests of 1989, the last (to date)
paroxysm of reformist fervor to seize China that unfolded and then folded
only a year after the program aired.

The authorities had had their revenge. So, in a way, had the Great Wall,
though it is difficult to feel the victory as in any sense positive: the triumph of an image over an idea. Next to the slide one almost discerns the
outline of a tank, and perhaps the couple kissing on the parapet are in the
employ of the state . . . And perhaps there are other values, besides those
of the market or the military, that ought to bear on whether the wall has
"worked" or not—human values, however we may choose to define them.
Taking the qualitative measure of any building is practically impossible
("good architecture," as design critic Andrew Leach has written, "can be
comfortable or uncomfortable, functional or otherwise, beautiful or ugly")
unless undertaken with the right set of principles. Absent that, the wall
will always hover in the distance, just out of reach.

CRISIS

What had seemed in the late 1970s and early '80s a purely cyclical spike in unauthorized crossings of the US-Mexico border turned out to be closer to a secular trend. From 900,000 in 1980, the numbers of apprehensions at the border surged to 1.7 million a year by the middle of the decade, dropping briefly only to rise again during the early and mid '90s. The escalation stemmed from Mexico's ongoing economic stagnation—in sharp contrast to the burgeoning job market in the States—and by 1994 the number of Mexican-born individuals living in the United States was grazing the five-million mark, with fully a million of them in California, their destination of choice. That year, the citizens of the state approved Proposition 187, a measure denying a comprehensive array of public services to undocumented immigrants. Supporters of the ballot initiative included Republican governor Pete Wilson, whose reelection campaign sponsored a television advertisement that consisted of security camera footage, taken at night, featuring shadowy figures dashing across the border. A gravel-voiced announcer intoned the phrase: "*They keep coming.*"

The law was ultimately blocked by federal courts, but not before it helped give rise to a new dynamic in California politics and in national politics at large. Oddsmakers had counted on Wilson to fall short in his bid to return to the statehouse; aligning himself with Prop 187 helped him to pull off an electoral upset. Looking back decades later, Wilson expressed no regrets about his decision to back the law, though he was forced to concede that the measure (and by extension, he) did not prevail on the merits alone. "Do I think there are racists in the world?" he asked rhetorically. "Of course I do. Do I think there were some in California at that time who were probably pleased with 187? Yeah, I do." Turning a blind eye to the dicey ethics, politicians across the country could now point to California as proof that, in a tough fight, tough talk on immigration could pay off.

In the same year, the US Immigration and Naturalization Service (INS) announced the launch of Operation Gatekeeper. Under pressure to neutralize the issue as a prospective Republican talking point, President Bill Clinton ordered a twofold increase in funds for enforcement to facilitate a more comprehensive approach to the prevention of border infiltration. In the INS's westernmost enforcement sector, comprising most of the territory between Tijuana and southern San Diego County, two hundred additional enforcement officers were put on duty, while new lighting and other detection equipment were installed to discourage unauthorized entry. Most importantly, INS ramped up the installation of metal fencing, already pioneered in San Diego, where it ran fourteen miles from the Pacific Ocean to the dusty sable hills of the Peninsular Ranges.

The material of which these first fences were composed had a most unusual provenance. Not long after assuming his post as commander of the joint-service Military Assistance Command, Vietnam, in 1964, General William Westmoreland began preparations for the second part of his projected three-stage program for victory against the Communist forces of North Vietnam. "The front line was nowhere and everywhere," the general would later write, and his plan called for aggressive, targeted action by a highly mobile American military that could strike at will anywhere below the seventeenth parallel. Airpower was to be a major component of this approach, particularly the stout UH-1, "Huey," helicopters that could insert troops into combat and then extract them swiftly and return them to the rear. In order to establish forward bases for airborne operations, the military required landing surfaces that could be transported and thrown down in a hurry wherever they were needed. Steel sheets known as Marston matting—narrow strips joined by interlocking clasps—had been in use for this purpose since the Second World War, but the heavier loads of 1960s aircraft required a more durable material, without the typical perforations through which vegetation would quickly spring in the teeming Vietnamese jungle. The American military began to favor solid, corrugated mats, in particular a model known as the M8A1.

"In the face of American airpower, helicopter mobility, and fire support," Westmoreland declared, there was "no way" the enemy could long endure. Events were to prove otherwise. By the early 1970s, the United States was obliged to withdraw from Southeast Asia, and the military now had to reckon with the vast support infrastructure (ice cream factories, miniature golf courses) it had put in place. Much of it would simply be abandoned, as would untold numbers of M8A1s. As they had following earlier wars, the local population commandeered what was abandoned and repurposed it to their own uses, fashioning the slender steel planks of the M8A1s into everything from garden walls to highway guardrails. Many of the landing mats, however, made it back home, where millions were put into circulation, alongside unused fatigues and flashlights, as army surplus. Millions more simply moldered in government storage for decades—until the 1990s, when some forty-three thousand of them were given, gratis, to INS.

M8A1 mats are each a quarter-inch thick, twelve feet long, and just under two feet wide. For their redeployment in the border fence, the rail-like strips were welded together into panels about eight feet in height, many of them dabbed with painted-on serial numbers for ease of identification and replacement. The latter issue would seem especially pressing: Though the 147-pound planks are fairly durable, the links between them are less so, and the long file of sheets running along the Tijuana border had less resemblance to a solid screen than to a metallic crazy quilt, the panels meeting at odd angles as the fence jogged along the coastal hills. As a visual advertisement for control, the landing mats did not present a terribly persuasive image, and on the Mexican side a miniature ridge of dirt—perhaps made by human hands, perhaps simply a windrow formed by vehicles—built up on the road running parallel to the fence, substantially reducing its effective height. It was easy enough to stand atop the mound, grab ahold of the lip, and vault straight over.

Nonetheless, three years after the launch of Operation Gatekeeper, INS could boast of substantial gains in the San Diego–Tijuana area. What had been by far the department's busiest zone, accounting for nearly half of all arrests on the border, saw a 40 percent decrease in illegal traffic, bringing the headline number to a seventeen-year low. The fence seemed to be a major component of that success, with the western sector's now three thousand officers beginning to shift their attention away from the cordoned-off area and toward the town of El Centro, farther east, where arrests soared from 36,000 to an astonishing 146,000 over two years. Parallel initiatives elsewhere on the border (Operation Hold the Line in Texas, Operation Safeguard in Arizona) as well as new legislation (in particular the Illegal Immigration Reform and Immigrant Responsibility Act of 1996) would erect similar barriers, achieving comparable results. By 1997, with less than seventy miles of fencing in place, the Department of Justice was already declaring that the battle for the border would shortly be won. As Alan Bersin, then the Southwest Border Representative for Attorney General Janet Reno, announced to CNN, "We have a border that is marked. A border that is lit. A border that is under control for the first time in American history."

Already, however, Bersin might have had reason to temper that assessment. A year prior, the president of the National Border Patrol Council—the union representing INS enforcement officers—testified to the California State Assembly that local border officials were deliberately fudging their figures in order "to create the illusion that Operation Gatekeeper is effective." Anonymous testimony from one agent in the coastal division suggested that violations were continuing unabated, while senior staff was essentially giving up: Zeroes were scratched off nighttime sighting logs, "150 aliens" being recorded as "15 aliens." Some supervisors were encouraging agents to send aliens back, without reporting or processing, wherever they could be gotten through or around the new metallic barrier. The fence seemed almost less of an impediment to Mexicans fleeing north than to harried INS officials trying to ship them south again.

There was something else as well. Only eight weeks after the launch of Operation Gatekeeper, in December 1994, the Mexican central bank, in an effort to stem a burgeoning capital crisis, devalued the peso. The near collapse of the national economy that followed was worse, as measured by percent decline in GDP, than anything the country had known—worse even than the recession that would follow the global economic crash in 2009—and it brought with it poverty and hunger that touched every city street and rural road in Mexico. All those blurry specters seen in all those nightscopes and in the flickering surveillance tapes were running away from a menace of such scale as to render a quarter-inch of military surplus a paltry deterrent at best. For a second time, the steel ribbons were being enlisted in the service of a losing fight.

"Illegal aliens should not receive public benefits other than emergency aid, and those who become parents while illegally in the United States should not be qualified to claim benefits for their offspring." With this sentence, written in 1996, the language of the anti-immigration movement entered the Republican party platform for the first time. The Clinton administration's aggressive action on the border notwithstanding, the president had come out against Proposition 187. The opposition saw an opening, and an express endorsement of the California initiative was also included in Bob Dole's official immigration plank.

Slowly, without the direction of any single mastermind or cabal, a shift was underway. The assiduous efforts to court the Latino vote of Republican candidates from Eisenhower clear through Reagan would now give way to a new dynamic, with the GOP becoming more and more identified as the anti-immigrant party. The prototype and analog of this transformation was the infamous Southern Strategy, Richard Nixon's gambit to attract traditionally Democratic working-class whites through coded appeals to racial prejudice. Just as the party in the late 1960s had staged a quiet retreat on civil rights under the cover of a small-government mantra, Republicans would now claim (if only intermittently) that they merely favored "legal" as against "illegal" immigration, or else suggest (if only in the abstract) that some legislative means might be found, at some unspecified future date, to square the undocumented with the law. Neither was convincing, nor were they meant to be. They were merely camouflage for an incipient realignment.

Still, as late as 2014, a majority of Latinos reported that they had voted for a Republican at least once in their lives. Fully 40 percent of the Latino vote went to George W. Bush in his 2004 reelection, a decisive factor in his narrow popular vote victory over John Kerry. In his politics as in his persona, Bush represented the last, best hope of the Republican effort to mask their increasingly anti-immigrant policies behind a veneer of accommodation. Bush himself spoke Spanish, albeit haltingly (most memorably in a series of Spanish-language advertisements during his second presidential campaign) and his family included his brother Jeb's Mexican-American wife and their mixed-race children (those whom the elder President Bush once infelicitously referred to as "the little brown ones"). In view of his deeply felt Christianity, W.'s frequent expressions of compassion for immigrants regardless of legal status were likely in earnest. These sentiments were made all the more credible by the fact that the president, with his oft-noted lack of curiosity, may never have grasped how his compassion was being used as a smokescreen by some of his partisan fellow travelers.

It was George W. Bush's signature that was appended to the Secure Fence Act of 2006, the legislation that sounded the opening in a new, more concerted stage of barrier construction. The vote on the bill took place in a context markedly different from more recent debates on immigration policy: While Bush's position was more sympathetic to immigrants, Democrats appeared, ostensibly, more sympathetic to wall-building. In 2017, White House budget director Mick Mulvaney would note, with some accuracy, that his pro-wall administration didn't understand "why the Democrats are so wholeheartedly against it. They voted for it in 2006. Then-Sen. Obama voted for it." Indeed, the Secure Fence Act, calling for vastly expanded border infrastructure, passed the Senate by an overwhelming majority, 80 to 19. It did so because a competing draft in the House, known as the Sensenbrenner Act, was so obnoxious to pro-immigrant forces that Democrats were hard-pressed not to vote for the more moderate alternative. Named for its sponsor, Representative Jim Sensenbrenner of Wisconsin, the House measure would have not only changed present law to upgrade illegal entry from a misdemeanor to a felony, but also imposed upon anyone who housed or assisted an illegal immigrant "the same imprisonment term as applies to the alien so aided." Between mass criminalization and more fences, Democrats chose the fences.

The fence as described in the 2006 law bears only a passing resemblance to the fence as realized. "There should be 700 miles of double-layer fencing built along our southern border," complained Senator Ted Cruz in 2015; by then, a scant thirty-six miles of secondary fencing was in place, following pleas for a more nuanced approach from the Department of Homeland Security (DHS) and Customs and Border Protection (CBP), the subagency now overseeing the project. Congressional testimony from CBP representatives later claimed that only 653 miles could be identified as "appropriate for fencing and barriers," and consequently Texas senator Kay Bailey Hutchinson—Cruz's predecessor—advanced a 2008 amendment that restored to the DHS the prerogative to build whatever type of fence it wanted, where it wanted, in whatever length it thought best. Conservatives of Ted Cruz's stamp would howl. But most, including President Bush, seemed happy enough to have the matter remanded to the bureaucracy, safely removed from the political playing field.

Varying from place to place as CBP saw fit, the fences that were built as part of the 2006 initiative were odd individually and odder in the aggregate. Near Naco, Arizona, CBP opted for a meshy matrix; near Tucson, they chose a line of spiky metal asterisks, like the anti-tank "Czech hedgehogs" of the last century. In the Imperial Desert of California, the agency erected a "floating fence," sitting lightly on the desert floor with raked buttresses that allowed it to shift in the wind and with the shifting sands. The "sand dragon," as some called it, cuts across an area that used to be regularly traversed by ATV drivers, who in years past would speed over to the Mexican town of Algodones for tacos.

One popular model appears at the border's eastern end, around Brownsville, Texas, where I saw it in December of 2017. A ribbed enclosure of iron about eighteen feet high, its individual vertical posts are angled such that the visitor sees through them only in oblique views: Walking or driving alongside it, Mexico flickers past like a picture in a zoetrope. In the middle of downtown Brownsville, the fence stands about twenty yards back from the Rio Grande, and the river's de facto confinement has left it entirely untouched, the pristine water flashing in the sun and the rushes swaying serenely on the banks as if Moses's basket were about to bob past. The black iron bars, rooted in thick concrete footings at least two feet wide at the base, are remarkably lacking in any sense of tactility or material presence—

making it only too tempting to touch them, if only to figure out what they're made of. Through the unkempt alluvial plain near the Gulf of Mexico, this type of fence runs alongside rural highways, through open fields, materializes at the ends of cluttered alleys and in the backs of empty parking lots.

The spectacle of the fence standing in front of the river—of one barrier standing in front of another—makes for a confounding double vision, one that's repeated elsewhere on the border, especially in places like Otay Mesa, California, where the Secure Fence Act resulted in a newer, higher fence being constructed directly alongside the original landing mats. Seeing them together prompts the question: If two, why not three? Why not more? One person sensible to that riddle was Barack Obama, who often found himself confronted by political opponents who doubted CBP's commitment to barrier-building under his administration. Standing in front of a newly completed section of fence in Texas in 2011, the president put the question to congressional Republicans demanding a secure border before considering comprehensive immigration reform: How much security would be enough? "All the stuff they asked for we've done," said Obama. "But even though we've answered those concerns, I suspect there will be some who will try to move the goal posts . . . Now they'll say we need to quadruple border patrol. Or now they'll say, we want a higher fence. Maybe they'll need a moat. Maybe they want alligators in the moat. They'll never be satisfied."

Obstinacy from border hawks continued despite, as the president recognized, the meaningful strides made by his White House on the immigration front. Between 2009 and 2014, the total number of Mexican nationals living in the United States decreased by 140,000, its first net decline since the 1930s. Apprehensions at the border continued a downward plummet that had begun after the turn of the millennium—suggesting, perhaps, that the 2006 law, and the qualified commitment to it of both the Bush and Obama administrations, had had a salutary effect after all. As ever, this was a matter of perspective: The fences extracted a terrible humanitarian toll, channeling migrants away from conventional crossing points into the most unforgiving border terrain; the abandoned shoes and backpacks of the dead and dying now littered the desert floor for miles, while those who made the trek only to run into the fences were regularly sliced by concertina wire or concussed in a fall. Even with all this, the fences might not have been the real reason more Mexicans appeared to be staying home. Just as economic malaise in Mexico had driven much of the 1990s surge in illegal immigration, declining economic conditions in the US in the late 2000s were undoubtedly an essential factor in the trend's reversing itself so abruptly. Without the promise of a job on the other side, it was hardly worth it to cross the border at Otay Mesa, in the Imperial Desert, at Tucson, or anyplace else. Higher than any fence, deeper than any moat, the Great Recession could not be lofted over by drone, could not be breached or scaled. It was the greatest wall of all.

The bulk of the fencing that currently exists between the United States and Mexico represents the living bequest of America's two previous presidents to the southern border. Neither Barack Obama nor George W. Bush imagined that this would be so: Both advanced progressive immigration policies in the mold of Ronald Reagan's; both imagined that the erection of fencing—and in Bush's case the 2003 reorganization initiative that created Immigration and Customs Enforcement (ICE)—would merely be down payments on a comprehensive solution. Instead, the fences now stand as their lasting monument in the borderlands. The structures have taken an already haunted landscape and rendered it even more so, intensifying an endemic air of angst.

Such is the atmosphere around Boca Chica Park, a public shoreline twenty miles from Brownsville at the easternmost end of the border. On my visit, I managed to walk the length of it to the point where the Rio Grande enters the Gulf of Mexico. Though warm and sunny, it seemed to me a beach with all of a beach's festive atmosphere vacuumed out of it. The nearest fence is almost fifteen miles away, but its construction has tended to make Boca Chica more attractive for trans-border traffic—at low tide, one can simply walk across the river—obliging CBP to step up patrols and install sensors and other monitoring devices. Reaching the mouth of the river, no more than twenty yards wide where it empties into the sea, I could stand on one side and shout across to Mexican fishermen on the opposite shore. But no one was in the mood for friendly greetings at Boca Chica.

What few visitors I saw walking or driving on the American side of the beach appeared to regard me, and one another, with barely veiled suspicion. I asked an older couple, seated high up in an RV, if I could charge my phone in their cigarette lighter. After a colloquy of a minute and more, they resolved that no, I couldn't.

Where the river meets the sea: Boca Chica State Beach,
outside Brownsville

For the year-round residents of the area, the fencing has landed like an alien intruder in their midst. Only a few miles inland from Boca Chica is the farm of the Benavidez family. Residents of South Texas since the early nineteenth century, generations of Benavidezes have wrought a modest crop of cotton and squash from the hard, cracked soil; in 2008, they were approached by the federal government and informed that a narrow strip on the southern end of their seven-acre tract was to be requisitioned by the government and that the land beyond it would be cordoned off from the rest of their property by an eighteen-foot-high fence. The family was unsympathetic to the proposal. "It's going to be ugly," claimed seventy-seven-year-old Ida Benavidez, "and it's not going to work." Looking to halt the project, the family joined forces with other locals—B and B owners, citrus growers, bird enthusiasts—whose land was also under threat.

There was little that could be done, and in time the fences sprouted up all over the lower Rio Grande. The government, as the US solicitor general claimed, simply had no choice: The wall had been mandated by Congress, and there was nowhere else for them to build it, as international law proscribed its being constructed any closer to the river. Following the Mexican–American War, the two countries signed a series of agreements specifying that neither was to build on the river or alter its course without prior consent of the other. There have been multiple infractions of this by private actors, but the US government has stuck to the letter of the law. For that reason, the acquisitions required by the Secure Fence Act had to be some distance away from the riverbank itself. By the end of the Obama years, an untold expanse of American territory had been effectively cut off from the United States, trapped behind fences and accessible only to owners via keypad-operated gates. Another Brownsville-area resident whose land was being appropriated could trace her family's ownership claim back to a land grant of the Spanish crown. "All this history," she told a reporter. "It just doesn't seem right."

Physical disruptions to the borderlands were accompanied by a change in the region's social and economic profile, also driven by the new policy. The ramping up of border security in the mid-2000s brought on an increase in border patrol agents, whose numbers between 2006 and 2008 were set to leap from under 12,000 to 18,000. Since most of these agents were of Latino extraction, CBP quickly became an even larger presence in the Spanish-speaking community along the border—a delicate situation given that, unsurprisingly, many families in the area include both American-born and Mexican-born members. The resultant problems were compounded by lax vetting procedures during the hiring spree, with sometimes alarming results. In 2001, Oscar Antonio Ortiz, a navy veteran and former construction worker in Utah, applied for and secured a job at CBP; after three years of service at the border, it was revealed that he had been smuggling Mexicans into the country while in uniform, bringing more than a hundred immigrants into the country—work for which he was uniquely qualified, since Ortiz himself, unbeknownst to his employers, was also an undocumented alien, born and raised in Tijuana. His supervisors, according to reports, had noticed nothing, remarking on his "radiant, confident, poised and courteous demeanor," as well as his excellent language skills and personal grooming habits.

The incident was by no means isolated, with a number of other officers accused and convicted over the years since for everything from bribe-taking to running illegal drugs to harboring illegal aliens in their own homes. Doubtless the incidence of such illegal activity was influenced in part by what was happening immediately across the border at the very same time: an intensification of cartel violence among Mexican groups for control of the lucrative illegal drug trade. In Matamoros, just a few miles from the Benavidez's farm, murders and kidnappings skyrocketed in the early 2010s, eventually earning the region a "do not travel" rating from the US Department of State; when the wind blew in the right direction, bursts of gunfire could be heard in downtown Brownsville. Even as the cross-border flow of immigrants dipped precipitously after 2008, the ongoing mayhem in Mexico made it seem even more of a threat to anxious Americans.

Alongside this narrative was a different one, less remarked upon, that added another sour note to the already-discordant border debate. Even as the Great Recession abated, job growth remained sluggish in many American working-class communities. Meanwhile, despite ongoing cartel activity, northern Mexico experienced a minor economic miracle. Between 2009 and 2014, exports to the United States of machinery, plastics, and appliances doubled across the board. The country became, as one McKinsey study put it, "a prime destination for investors and multinationals around the world," with accelerating job growth concentrated in the giant maquiladoras that catered to the American market. A sneaking sense that America's once-thriving industrial cities had somehow been sold out to Mexico—that "at least 750,000 American jobs were lost as a result of NAFTA," as ardent anti-free trade newsman Lou Dobbs (dubiously) claimed—began to take hold, and in this narrative the Obama and Bush administrations, who supported the trade deal, were deemed every bit as culpable as the Clinton administration that had crafted it. The promise of NAFTA, critics complained, had been general economic uplift that would benefit middle-class Americans while obviating the causes of both Mexican immigration and Mexican crime. Where were the results?

What many Americans did not see was the dramatic shift going on in places like Brownsville. By 2014, communities along the border had pulled out of the recession thanks in part to the brisk cross-border trade—studies suggested that for every 10 percent increase in Mexican factory-worker wages, employment in towns on the Texas side grew by up to 2 percent. Cultural ties had always bound the two sides together; now they shared vital economic interests as well. Just north of Boca Chica Park, the Port of Brownsville, connecting the factories of northern Mexico to the Intercoastal Waterway via adjoining rail networks, saw such rapid increases in traffic that the federal government signed off on a multimillion-dollar plan to significantly improve the facility. That same year, billionaire investor Elon Musk chose Brownsville to host his own private Cape Canaveral for his aerospace venture SpaceX. "Brownsville's destiny has changed," declared one local civic leader. All this was happening even as the mileage of border fencing in the area grew.

Coming as an uninvited guest to the borderlands, the fencing now encroached upon communities that for all their ostensible struggles were actually poised to thrive. The structures created displacements and deepened tensions that might have been better off, and certainly little worse, had nothing been built at all. In San Diego in 2009, the construction of secondary fences forced the closure of Friendship Park—the binational public meeting place created during the Nixon administration—sparking protests that led CBP to reverse course three years later. Even then, the park was never the same, with a new permanent fence (replacing more modest ones dating to the 1990s) that extended several hundred feet into the surf below, marring the peaceful scene forever. But then the measure of the fence's success was never supposed to be taken at the site where the fences were built or among the people who lived there. The structures were intended for a different constituency, one that truly found its voice only after they were built.

* * *

It was turning to late afternoon at Boca Chica when I finally started to retrace my path and make my way back from the river to the main road. From where I stood atop a berm, looking past where the dunes gave way to the brush, I could see an expanse of flatland that, as a sign by the road informed me earlier, marked the site of Palmito Ranch. In 1865, over a month after the fall of Richmond, a Union force under a hotheaded commander faced off there against a Confederate detachment with whom they were supposed to have had a nominal truce. The mostly African American soldiers from the North confronted a Southern force whose Mexican allies had supplied them with French cannon. It was the last battle of the Civil War, and the Union lost.

Closer at hand, rising between the beach and Palmito Ranch, stood the menacing-looking SpaceX compound, a bristling framework of piping surrounded by chain link. The launch site remains dormant for now, though this has less to do with the problems of the border than the company's own technical failures. In June 2015, mere months after they'd acquired the site, their Falcon 9 rocket sputtered halfway to near-earth orbit. The resulting spectacular explosion has since become a popular YouTube phenomenon—but it was almost buried in the headlines when it occurred, coming as it did in the middle of a very eventful news cycle. Just twelve days before the Falcon explosion, an announcement had been made that instantly sucked away any media oxygen that might have been spared for SpaceX or anything else.

While the American economy had largely recovered from the depths of the Great Recession, roiling discontent was still the order of the day and, with an election year approaching, the likely candidates—Hillary Clinton among the Democrats, former Florida governor Jeb Bush, Wisconsin governor Scott Walker, Ohio governor John Kasich, and Florida senator Marco Rubio among the many Republicans—seemed all too staid and familiar. At last, an eccentric Manhattan real estate developer threw his hat into the ring. For some, he seemed to jibe with the moment, affording a relief from political routine. For the rest, his outsider candidacy appeared likely to go the way of the ill-fated rocket.

The whole phenomenon bore more than a passing resemblance to the failed efforts in 1992 and 1996 of Ross Perot, another self-professed self-made billionaire running what appeared to be a spirited vanity campaign. Perot, notably, had been an early opponent of NAFTA, insisting that the trade pact would alter the American economy to the disadvantage of native-born workers: "While no one was watching," he claimed in 1993, "NAFTA negotiators radically revised the nation's immigration laws." When he burst on the national scene, Perot's economic nationalism inspired no small amount of enthusiasm among disenchanted white middle-class voters, but his policy prescriptions were always vague, and his personality, though colorful, turned out to be a liability, leading to gaffes aplenty. He still garnered 19.7 million votes in 1992 (Clinton won with nearly 45 million, out of a total 104.4 million votes cast) and 8 million in 1996, but failed to secure a single electoral college vote in either election and is now mostly remembered as a late-night laughingstock.

Every indicator suggested this new entrant in 2016 would end in much the same place—indeed he effectively began there. For his announcement, Donald J. Trump greeted the media in the lobby of his eponymous Manhattan high-rise, looking somehow both lost and impatient as he slowly descended an escalator. Like Perot, he proceeded to deliver an address that featured none of the accepted signifiers by which politicians typically project their seriousness and readiness to lead. He repeated words, went off script, waved his arms around with childish insouciance. His program, insofar as he outlined one, was even less clearly articulated than Perot's—on defense, "Nobody would be tougher on ISIS"; on health care, "We have to repeal Obamacare, and it can be—and—and it can be replaced with something much better"—and to top it all off, he managed to take Perot's soft-sell opposition to international trade and turn it into an outlandish boast. "I will be the greatest jobs president that God ever created," he said. "I'll bring back our jobs from China and Mexico."

And then he went a step further. The problem, the newly announced candidate suggested, was not merely that the Mexico was beating the United States economically. It was that the Mexican people were engaged en masse in a plot against the United States. Those who entered the country illegally were "murderers and rapists," proof that Mexico was "not sending their best." The now-infamous libel appeared to be the most fatal misstep in an announcement already rife with them; a candidate couldn't possibly sell himself to the broader public by appearing so ignorant, so angry, so bully-ing. He spoke with an accent barely softened from the days of his Queens childhood, had been born into fabulous wealth, and had lived his entire life in cosmopolitan circles far removed from the small towns and quiet sub-urbs where anti-immigrant sentiment was presumed to lurk. His sudden fulminating about murderers and rapists rang laughably false.

Equally absurd was his analysis of the cause of the problem. "We have no protection," he insisted, "and we have no competence." Despite claim-ing to have had conversations with border officers (who might have taken umbrage at the competence swipe), the candidate did not, at any point during the nearly hourlong announcement, once use the word "fence," nor acknowledge that any impedimentary infrastructure already existed. This was perhaps not surprising, since in all likelihood he had little or no knowledge of the 600-plus miles of fencing already in place, much less seen it firsthand. There is no conceivable reason why this Manhattan real estate developer should have spent any meaningful amount of time on the border, given that he had no real business interests in its proximity and had evinced only passing interest in border policy prior to announcing his candidacy. In a rhetorical flourish facilitated by sheer ignorance, an effort lasting twenty-five years and costing billions of dollars all disappeared in a flash—the Vietnam-era matting; the razor-wire topped Bush-era fences; the heavy bollard-like slats that surrounded Brownsville and ran out onto the dry expanses around Palmito Ranch.

Gone too were all the practical challenges that had attended the con-struction of those troublesome barriers, the struggles of the rancher fami-lies, the shifts of immigrant movements from one sector to the next, the budgetary and bureaucratic battles that had ensued. The borderland's entire history, in fact, was dispelled at once, the region reduced to a single problem that wanted only the will to set it right. And what was this instantaneous cure-all, this common-sense solution obvious to anyone bold enough to speak it and to do it? "I would build a great wall," declared the freshly minted candidate, "and nobody builds walls better than me, believe me, and I'll build them very inexpensively. I will build a great, great wall on our southern border."

With that, the audience of assembled journalists and hangers-on, along with the millions who would watch the speech online and on television in the months to come, were all at once transported. The marble-and-gold interior of the Fifth Avenue tower receded, and in its place there manifested a vision: that of an endless monument, snaking over mountains, impervious, impossibly high, capable of withstanding anything that nature or man could possibly hurl at it. The image was familiar to all, and everyone knew that it would last forever, outlasting dynasties, the projected essence of a whole people. It was a scene far more arresting, far "greater," than the dusty flatscape of South Texas with its rusted metal barriers. Not just any wall, but a great wall. *The* Great Wall.

The candidate could not have conjured it any more effectively, even if he had not made reference to "China" twenty-seven times during the same monologue, even if the second "great" suggested that perhaps it was no more than an emphatic turn of phrase. In fact the repetition of the word was only to imply that America, and the man who promised to lead it, would requisition that already-great entity and imbue it with a quality that would transcend any pedestrian concerns as to whether the Chinese one ever "worked," whether it was "good" or "bad." It was, in one way, a brilliant aperçu: *Of course* the Great Wall was great. That was its *name*.

IV

THE ART OF THE WALL-ABLE

THIERS

One might have thought that the world had already learned its lesson when, in 1830, the Orléanist king Louis-Philippe was elevated to the French throne and immediately began to agitate for a new urban defense system for Paris. By then, advances in gunnery and tactics had rendered fortified cities more or less irrelevant, as the French themselves had ably demonstrated: In the first decade of the century, Napoleon had revolutionized warfare by mobilizing huge numbers of troops and advancing them rapidly, devastating opposing armies in the field with combined assaults while engaging in as few sieges as possible. As if to drive the point home, his capital, despite its own ring of stone, had been swiftly captured by the allied monarchies of the continent following Napoleon's disastrous adventure in Russia. Paris needed many things. A wall was not one of them.

The city had grown only slowly in the years following the royal restoration, creeping up toward a population of 800,000 from a trough of 700,000 after the war-torn Napoleonic era. But the increase was enough to put pressure on what was already an unsettled civic milieu. "The modern Babylon," one character called it in *Confession of a Child of the Century*, Alfred de Musset's 1836 novel portraying an urban society beset by malaise and atomization. (The image struck a chord—the youth of 1830s Paris would fight over Musset's discarded cigarettes.) In the book as in life, landless aristocrats, underemployed artisans, and socially ambitious merchants all stewed together in a social bouillabaisse, seasoned by growing numbers of former agricultural workers from the provinces. Physically, the city they inhabited was still unmistakably medieval, full of winding streets with no recognizable grid or pattern; most houses lacked any internal plumbing, and foul odors wafted off the polluted waters of the Seine, with worse ones emanating from insalubrious industries (among them a large horse-rendering plant in the northeast of the city legendary for its "harmful miasmas"). Napoleon had promised to transform Paris into "the true capital of Europe," "something fabulous and colossal," but his improvements had mostly been cosmetic. The short-lived Bourbon monarchy that followed actually did better, organizing the police and giving them proper uniforms, as well as erecting the first public gaslamp at the Place du Carrousel, a pompous affair perched atop a Doric column. In a contemporary engraving, a mix of Parisian types stand around it, all of them gawking at the new contraption as they might at one of the public beheadings that took place in the same spot a generation earlier.

The advent of improved lighting had not totally displaced revolutionary fervor. The Bourbons had been cast down, and Louis-Philippe brought up, after a fierce political convulsion seized the populace: In July of 1830, in the city's first mass movement since the 1790s, the lower and middle classes arose in united opposition to the repressive policies of King Charles X, storming his palaces and sending his Swiss guards into panicked flight. Thousands of barricades appeared in the streets, and inside of three days— les Trois Glorieuses—Charles was deposed and his Orléanist cousin put in his place, inaugurating what came to be known as the Monarchy of July. Louis-Philippe steered a course to the crown by navigating between the competing camps of anti-monarchists and Bourbon legitimists, eventually appearing to all factions as the least-objectionable option. Surrounding himself with merchants and former Bonapartists, he promised to be a tame monarch, one with a healthy regard for the will of the people; the aging Marquis de Lafayette, the hero of two revolutions and a champion of constitutional monarchy, appeared with the new-crowned king on the balcony of the Palais Royal: "Citizens," he shouted, "We have now the best description of republic!" His enthusiasm would not last long, as Louis-Philippe shortly revealed himself to be a temperamental conservative, anxious to keep his unruly subjects in their place.

The city that was now his capital had already been crisscrossed with walls time and again throughout its history. From the days when it was still known as Lutèce—the primary settlement of the Gallic Parisii tribe—the future Paris likely had some form of perimeter defense, though this was swiftly overwhelmed by Julius Caesar when he arrived with his armies in the first century BCE. The pre-Roman wall had left no permanent trace, nor had the ones on the Left Bank that the Romans built in its place. As the Roman order went into decline, the Frankish kingdoms that came after were beset by Viking raids and proceeded to erect walls around the Left Bank to keep out the raiders who sailed into the heart of the city on the Seine. In 885, the Norse returned and attempted to ransack the city again; a monk in the abbey of Saint-Germain-des-Prés described the scene: "On the walls, the towers, and all the bridges, battle was joined . . . Loud were the horns, urging inhabitants to leave their tables." For the first time, the walls held against the invaders, and the Vikings were forced into retreat.

Portions of those defenses have since been discovered, but they were unknown in the age of Louis Philippe. More easily seen in the nineteenth century were the walls built in successive rings around the city beginning in the high middle ages, when King Philip II, Philip Augustus, surrounded the whole of the capital with a mighty fortification, a vast undertaking begun in 1190 and only finished twenty-five years later. Paris was still a small city, and the enclosed portion corresponded to what by the 1830s were only the innermost districts, running on the Right Bank from the Louvre castle (first built by Philip II as the wall's westernmost bulwark) to the latter-day Quai des Célestins in the east, with a comparable loop on the Left Bank. A century later, Charles V would create another, larger wall, strictly on the Right Bank, leaving the other half as it was; another two hundred fifty years and another king, Louis XIII, expanded the northern perimeter yet again, partially demolishing Charles V's work. While these latter improvements ensured that the city's northern half was always protected, the Left Bank was left to sprawl beyond the 1190 wall into the surrounding farmland without any check to its growth; as there were no princely palaces on that side, its invasion was less a matter of royal concern. But with the ascent in 1643 of Louis XIV, the concern evaporated altogether, as France entered an era of swelling power and confidence. Le Roi Soleil deemed all of the city's walls outdated, and instigated a process of comprehensive demolition that saw the defenses transformed into the first of the *grands boulevards*. Some of these—Beaumarchais, Italiens, Madeleine—remain among Paris's best-loved thoroughfares.

Yet the city's wall-building days were not over. In the waning years of the ancien regime, one last ring was built around the outskirts—though it was not for holding off foreign armies. The *ferme générale*, the revenue service of the king, was responsible for taxing all goods coming into and going out of Paris, a very lucrative enterprise for the private licensees who were granted the royal concession. In the 1780s, this rather mercenary operation constructed a network of customhouses connected by a continuous barrier to regulate the flow of trade. The *ferme* was by no means a well-regarded institution among the locals, and its wall became the object of popular satire: As one folk rhyme put it, "To augment its salary / And limit our vision / The *ferme* has deemed it necessary / To put us all in prison." At the very least, the city's incarceration was an architecturally distinguished one, the blockhouses having been designed by Enlightenment-era master Claude Nicolas Ledoux. While highly regarded by later generations of architects, Ledoux's classically inspired buildings only prompted more scorn from Parisians, including this invective from a well-known epigramist:

> In vain, with words of mocking gall,
> One boos the gross extravagance
> Of that grotesque, colossal wall
> In which they've hidden us in Paris.
> But as for me, I think it's fine—
> The plan is perfect for the city.
> There's an adage, Le Doux, a favorite of mine:
> "If you're stuck in prison, make it pretty."

This somewhat decorative wall was the one in place when the enemies of Napoleon surrounded the city in 1814, and it was the one most visible when Louis-Philippe ascended the throne. No doubt it would have been easy enough to improve on its military effectiveness—it was never built to stop anything more imposing than a wagon of dry goods—but Louis-Philippe had other things on his mind besides external threats. He had, after all, risen to power courtesy of an insurrection, the very one that had inspired Eugène Delacroix's *Liberty Leading the People*. The painting, featuring the Phrygian-capped Marianne bearing the republican flag alongside gun-toting *citoyens* old and young, was enough to make any leader worry: What if the people were to rise again? Louis-Philippe—"careful of his health, of his fortune, of his person, of his affairs," as Victor Hugo said of him—feared exactly that. So did his supporters, and in short order they set about building Paris's last city wall, largely under the pretext of protecting the Parisians but more importantly to protect themselves.

An even more colorful, more incisive observer of Paris's street life than Musset, Victor Hugo chronicled the city's architectural past (or his imagining of it) in his *Notre-Dame de Paris*, conjuring a medieval world where buildings served as the only common language available to the city's then-illiterate masses. Architecture was "the book of stone," Hugo wrote, "the great handwriting of the human race," a position of privilege from which it was toppled by the advent of the printing press in the fifteenth century. In his own time, Hugo would live to see the city's architecture slip a notch lower, muscled aside altogether to make way for a new manifestation of power. As Hugo watched the old houses and gardens turn to rubble in order to make way for Louis-Philippe's wall, he was bemused. "Fascinating," he wrote. "Paris demolishing itself in order to defend itself."

It had already taken nearly a decade to begin the demolition, and it would be many years more before the construction that followed was complete. In 1833, acting on the king's instruction, Marshal Jean-de-Dieu Soult, a venerable figure of the bygone Napoleonic empire, presented a formal plan to France's Chamber of Deputies for a new citywide fortification. The system he outlined included seventeen strongholds around Paris, each in the shape of a pentagon housing eighty artillery pieces along with ammunition, supplies, and a thousand men. Rather than demolish the old *fermes* wall, the marshal recommended keeping it and increasing its height while bedecking it with new watchtowers and forts and another three hundred cannon for good measure. Detailed as the scheme was, it suffered from at least two major flaws: Its presumed cost ran to thirty-five million francs, an exorbitant sum at the time; worse, the estimate was furnished by Soult, the so-called Plunder Master General, who had earned notoriety as a war profiteer after selling off purloined artworks during his years with Napoleon. France's Chamber of Deputies demurred.

In 1835, the body came around to another option, one that entailed razing the Ledoux barricades and building a single, smaller ring of bastions, fit more snugly around the city. The idea was far more economical, and it had the support of the king—its greatest liability, as it turned out, since it set off a reaction that would repeat again and again in the years to come. The program, with its vast complement of men at arms, looked even more prison-like than the *fermes*, and immediately the cry rose up from the press organs of every republican and anti-Orléanist faction in the city. "It is a plan to put down liberty," as one observer put it, "not to defend Paris!" So vociferous was the opposition that for five years the proposal was sidelined. When it at last returned in 1840, its detractors were still numerous and vocal; they would remain so even after the wall became a political inevitability, indeed even after it was built.

The figure who carried the project forward in the teeth of so much opposition was neither Soult, nor the king. Adolphe Thiers had already been in and out of public life, and in and out of government, for more than a decade when the wall proposal resurfaced. He had been instrumental in bringing Louis-Philippe to the throne and served as prime minister once before during his reign; his tenure had not been a happy one, and his return to the post only a year later promised to be no better. But then Thiers was nothing if not adaptable. Liberal, conservative, pro-establishment, anti-establishment—he had taken on or would take on almost every available position on the political spectrum. In his earliest iteration, as an historian of the French Revolution, he had written that "in politics, we must repair the evils and never avenge them," and though his subsequent career didn't always live up to that magnanimous creed he did show a remarkable ability to overlook slights and turn enemies into friends. It was only by way of Thiers's deft maneuvering, weaving between the king's insecurities and the people's, that the wall was built at all.

This wily "old umbrella," as Thiers called himself, had been able to survive "many showers," and though no admirer of royals (it was he who coined the popular description of constitutional monarchy, "the king reigns, but does not govern") he won Louis-Philippe's favor by securing 140 million francs for the construction of the king's long-sought wall. To appease his liberal friends, he was able to move the fortifications housing year-round troops farther from the capital; to appeal to the various elements of the right, he sold the project as a patriotic necessity, a bulwark against rising British aggression. The flare-up in tensions with France's old foe turned out to be temporary, ending even before 1840 was out—as did Thiers's second premiership, which concluded as acrimoniously as the first. But by then the wall had assumed a life of its own. The structure known to history as *l'enceinte de Thiers* would stand as arguably his greatest physical endowment to the city where he spent most of his life.

Designed by General Guillaume Dode de la Brunerie, the wall was far more elaborate than Soult's original proposal, a hybrid design combining different techniques in urban defense. The continuous sloping perimeter was punctuated by ninety-four bastions, some poking outward in the form of a half-hexagon, others a half-octagon, and still others in an irregular triangular shape. Beyond the primary wall, Dode also called for the construction of an additional fifteen detached forts, creating forward positions that would be fully staffed with soldiers even in peacetime. Over the three-year construction timeline, a thousand soldier-engineers were enlisted in the effort, overseeing a workforce that eventually grew to 21,600; this number included private contractors as well as infantrymen-turned-builders, casting down their rifles to pick up implements as simple as shovels and wheelbarrows. Digging out the foundations, the crews transferred the excavated earth to the outer ring around the wall to pile up the sloping glacis. Accommodating the workforce was a stupendous logistical challenge, with portions of many outlying villages turned into temporary camps, where living conditions were frequently poor—twice the builders attempted to strike, and twice they had to be put down by their own brothers-in-arms. In spite of it all, and in a rare accomplishment in the history of France's *grands projets*, the wall was completed under-budget and mostly on time, with only minor improvements continuing into 1848.

When it was done, it was the last word in urban defense—in more ways than one. Seen in section, the "wall" was actually a dense layer cake of fortifications, almost five hundred yards thick: Besides the wall, the bastions, and glacis, there was a *rue de rampart* running behind the wall for circulation, a ditch in front of it to trap invaders, and a ridge directly in front of the glacis on which additional defenders could be placed. Louis-Philippe may have been anxious to keep Parisians mindful of his military might; the military, however, wanted something that could at least slow if not stop a modern army, and the wall's multiple emplacements for cannon batteries gave it a reasonable chance of doing just that. Where Paris's ancient walls had been defensive structures in themselves, capable of blocking projectiles, these walls were a strategic armature, a tool that might, in combination with the detached forts, give the French army time to outmaneuver an enemy. This approach was a foretaste of things to come: In years after, forts outside cities would become more common than walls surrounding them. Paris's was arguably the last of its kind in the West.

More important was its effect upon Paris. The wall was built well beyond the formal city limits at the time, swallowing up outlying suburbs and more than doubling the city's area. Passing through what had been bucolic villages, farms and fields, the wall arrogated to the municipality a vast new quantity of territory into which it could expand, turning the city from a single, tightly interwoven fabric of neighborhoods into a heterogenous collection of different communities and topographies. The completion of *l'enceinte* marked Paris's official inauguration as a new entity, the premier urban form of the nineteenth century—the metropolis.

None of this had been in Thiers's mind of course; it wouldn't even become evident until a whole new political regime had been put in place. In 1848, even as the trees were still being planted along the wall's inner pathway, Louis-Philippe's anxieties became real when Paris rose again. The defense network he had hoped would help forestall a popular uprising proved useless when the police and key segments of the military, as tired as other Parisians of the king's excesses, went over to the insurgents. In a few days, the Monarchy of July was over, and a new republic was installed. Thiers would not be at the helm this time, though the man who would, Napoleon's nephew Charles-Louis Napoleon Bonaparte, was considered a lame poseur—on his election, Thiers dismissed him as "a dimwit whom we will lead." He was wrong.

Four years later the police commissioner arrived at Thiers's residence to arrest him in person. As he languished in a prison cell, Louis Napoleon's army executed a perfectly orchestrated coup, thanks in part to the detached forts outside the main perimeter which the new regime now filled with republican prisoners. Having dispatched of the opposition, the president went on to assume dictatorial power, proclaiming himself Napoleon III, the numeral an acknowledgment of the first Napoleon's half-forgotten son who died young in Vienna. Karl Marx would call the new order laughable, a "parody of restoration of empire." To most observers it appeared serious enough, at least at first.

It was during the Second Empire that Thiers reached his career high as a man of principle, and his career low as a man of action. Following his brief incarceration, he went into exile; he remained abroad for a year, until the new-crowned emperor, his regime firmly in place, allowed Thiers to return to Paris. The assembly was now hardly more than a rump body, and Thiers saw little hope for democracy, remaining on the sidelines for the better of a decade while resuming his work as an historian. He returned to politics in 1861—only to flail in opposition as the "dimwit" continued to outmaneuver him. Thiers and his allies had grossly underestimated their former protégé: Napoleon III had restored universal male suffrage, ensuring broad popular support for his rule, and had then set about dramatically remaking Paris on a bolder model than even his illustrious uncle could have imagined. Under the direction of his new prefect of the Seine, Georges-Eugène Haussmann, the city expanded to the very edges of Thiers's wall, with more wide boulevards, more fabulous architectural monuments, and much-improved housing and infrastructure for its growing masses. Against all this grandeur, Thiers could only fume.

Even his namesake wall received an update, becoming an integral part of the emperor's new Paris. France had no national rail network until the 1840s; one of the first short routes to go into service around Paris was built in 1836 at Thiers's direction, though the prime minister regarded the locomotive only as a "plaything . . . that will never carry voyagers." Napoleon III took a different view, encouraging the expansion of the nation's private railroads, and soon his military followed suit, undertaking to build a railroad of its own. Known as le Chemin de fer de Petite Ceinture—popularly the *petite ceinture*, the little beltway—the new railroad would add yet another layer to the city's *enceinte*, tracing an irregular oval along the inner flank of the wall's walkway. Built in cooperation with Paris's rail companies, the government-backed project solved two pressing problems at once, ensuring faster transportation of heavy armaments while also ending a vexing bottleneck caused by the competing privately held lines, which had refused to create any links between their respective terminuses. Once complete, in 1869, the *petite ceinture* solved both problems at once: In peacetime, it would act as a convenient freight and passenger route; in the event of war, it could be rapidly commandeered by the army to move men and materiel between the various wall bastions.

The latter eventuality seemed remote. Though basking in the reflected glory of his forebear, Napoleon III was no soldier, and the few military exploits of the Second Empire (in Italy, the Balkans, and in Mexico) had been limited in scope and duration. Only the emperor's naïve conceit, combined with a sudden surge in French jingoism, allowed him to be manipulated into a conflict for which he and his country were woefully underprepared. By the late 1860s, Prussia, under its cunning chancellor Otto von Bismarck, had become a rising power on the continent, turning the patchwork political map of Mitteleuropa into an incipient nation-state. To lasso the last of the errant German principalities, Bismarck felt he needed a war with France; he had been spoiling for one for years, and in 1870 he managed to bait the French into declaring it. Thiers was one of the few parliamentarians in France who tried to resist the call to arms. "You are not ready," he declared to a prominent general on the floor of the assembly. The general laughed off the claim, insisting that French soldiers "didn't lack so much as a button on their garters."

When war broke out, the Thiers wall went into action as a defensive structure for the first time, with the *petite ceinture* ferrying provisions and ammunition to the men stationed on *l'enceinte*. Yet within mere weeks—notwithstanding the condition of their soldiers' garters—battles on the Rhine frontier turned disastrously against the French. Napoleon III was captured at Sedan, falling into the hands of the Prussian army. As his empire rapidly collapsed, there seemed nothing to halt the advance of Bismarck's forces as they swiftly surrounded the capital. Parisians girded themselves for invasion. The wall, so long viewed with suspicion by the citizenry, now appeared to be their last hope.

Digging in and building temporary structures along *l'enceinte*, the remnants of the professional army attempted a last-ditch defense, aided by hastily summoned National Guardsmen. They needn't have bothered: Prussian artillery situated well away from *l'enceinte* cleared the ramparts and brought death and destruction to the city proper. In January 1871, after three months of German encirclement, the provisional republican government that had stepped in to fill the vacuum left by the emperor officially proffered its surrender. But capitulation only served to shatter France's tenuous political unity. In Paris, long-suppressed elements of the political left were now able to act with impunity, and they mobilized the people of the city in radical opposition to the prevailing order. Sympathetic National Guardsmen sided with the Parisians, and in February the city declared itself an independent body—the Paris Commune, an egalitarian experiment that promised to build a new society on the rubble of the old. Even as it raised its red standard over the Hôtel de Ville, the reconstituted national government, headquartered at Versailles, vowed to crush it, and to lead the charge they appointed a new prime minister: Adolphe Thiers. The "old umbrella" now faced his greatest test.

Surrounded by the wall Thiers himself had built, the Communards awaited their fate. Having survived one blockade by the Prussians, they now had to endure another from their own countrymen, as the Versaillais—the loyalist forces of Thiers—took up positions around the city. While the Communards were still able to hold positions along *l'enceinte* as well as in the exterior forts, the split between the regular army and the National Guard had left them shorthanded, with forces numbering only about six thousand. The lack of personnel was compounded by a deficit in leadership: As the Commune's high-minded committees debated ideological minutiae and issued unenforceable proclamations, the Versaillais pounded the fort at Issy south of the city. When the fort succumbed, the Commune roused itself at last to mount a defense, dispatching reinforcements who were also, almost immediately, forced to raise the white flag.

The final drama began unfolding at the wall's most southwesterly entrance, the Porte de Saint-Cloud near the neighborhood (formerly the village) of Auteuil. Massing their troops around *l'enceinte*, the generals of the Versaillese sought out a weak point in the Commune's defenses, unaware how weak they already were—in that part of the city "we had only [one] cannon . . . to answer the hundred Versaillese pieces," claimed one former communard. The generals only realized their opportunity when a traitorous guardsman appeared atop Bastion No. 64, waving a handkerchief and shouting down from the wall, "You can enter; there is no one here." Creeping into the city in small platoons, the national army soon controlled most of the wall in the southwest. Thiers, according the development rather more drama than it actually possessed, informed his government that the "gate of St. Cloud has fallen under the fire of our cannon."

Having seized the advantage, the prime minister would offer no quarter to the rebels. As corps after corps entered through the southwest breach, seizing the various bastions as well as other strategic points, the Communards fell back to the streets, erecting barricades across Haussmann's broad boulevards just as their revolutionary predecessors had done in 1830 and 1848. Thiers had sided with Parisians on both occasions; now, turning the cannons from the forts and bastions to face inward, the military under his command began bombarding the city. Shells started exploding not two hundred yards from a concert in the Tuileries being held for orphans and widows of the war. "Citizens," said the conductor, "M. Thiers promised to enter Paris yesterday. M. Thiers has not entered . . . I invite you to come here next Sunday, to the same place, to our second concert." But of course Thiers had entered, and there would be no more concerts for the Commune.

By May 27, separate bodies of republican troops had worked their way along the wall from opposite directions, joining up in the far northeastern quadrant of the city near the cliffs of the Parc des Butte-Chaumont and the Père Lachaise cemetery, the last redoubts of the National Guard. On that day, supported by artilleryfire from the bastions to their rear, the Versaillese stormed the remaining strongholds; in the graveyard, they fought from tombstone to tombstone until they had rounded up every last armed revolutionary and summarily shot them against the cemetery wall. How many were killed in like fashion all over the capital would be a subject of debate for decades to come, though as an American who witnessed the carnage claimed, "their numbers were proved by the quantity of blood which ran in streams through the gutters." The death toll was certainly made the worse by the fact that no one, whether complicit in the Commune or not, could now escape, since the army controlled every gate of *l'enceinte*. Prosper-Olivier Issagaray, a Communard who would later marry Marx's daughter Eleanor, watched as his fellow Parisians, trapped in their own city, fell prey to an "army transformed . . . into a vast platoon of executioners." Thiers, meanwhile, was jubilant, telling the assembly that the "cause of justice, order, humanity and civilization has triumphed." His house in Paris had been razed, but it would later be rebuilt at public expense.

It had been nineteen months almost to the day since the last American presidential election when I came to Paris to pay a visit to *l'enceinte de Thiers*. Technically this was a return: I had studied in Paris as an undergraduate and lived in the Fifteenth Arrondissement; my Métro stop, Porte de Vanves, was named after one of the southernmost gates of the wall, and my apartment was only a few blocks away from the old perimeter. It is a testament to my poor French at the time (which, admittedly, hasn't improved much since) that it never occurred to me, in all the months I was there, why the major thoroughfare down which I regularly walked was called the Boulevard des Maréchaux—the Boulevard of the Marshals. This was the Rue Militaire, the roadway that ran on the inner margin of the wall. Day after day, I passed along the route of what had once been Paris's last city wall, having no idea it had once been there.

In fairness, there was not much besides the street name to identify it. Of Thiers's wall itself almost nothing remains today. Two of the ninety-plus bastions located around the city are still largely intact, one in the northwest and the other far to the east near the Porte de Bercy. The latter is an especially magnificent ruin, though isolated, surrounded by bands of highway on three sides with the Seine just to the south. This was Bastion No. 1: Its massive footings rise in a slight slope about twelve feet above the sidewalk, the masonry still in good if weathered condition, each block exactly like the last and mortared fast together in a remarkable testament to the skill of the builders. The last of Europe's great city walls was certainly well built, and the consistency in its construction is visible in its few remains: in the archway of the Poterne des Peupliers (still standing firm under the *petite ceinture*, converted in this section to a park), and a little farther west at the Porte d'Arcueil, a blockhouse now serving as a cultural center with an ultracontemporary metallic roof.

*The Petite Ceinture (now café seating) near the
Porte de Saint-Ouen, Paris*

The most obtrusive physical leftover is the *petit ceinture*, portions of which open up in the middle of elegant boulevards and parks that have been laid over the majority of the wall. Near the Porte de Saint-Ouen, an 1863 stationhouse still stands, converted into a café and events space; in 2018 the venue debuted an outdoor terrace on the former northside platform, accessible via narrow stairs and giving diners a perfect view of the disused tracks and the walls of the cut, now decked with outrageous multicolored graffiti. In the Parc Montsouris on the opposite side of town, the railway has been rehabilitated as part of the Réseau Express Régional (RER) transit network, one of a number of such conversions that have been floated over the years. Few have been completed or gone beyond the testing stage.

Other kinds of post-wall projects have proven easier to realize. Beginning after World War I, block after block of social housing was built in the space once occupied by the nearer side of the glacis; a little farther out, the city constructed the Boulevard Périphérique, Paris's circumferential highway, beginning in the late 1950s. As one writer described it in the 1920s, the *zone*—as the decommissioned area of the wall had come to be called—was "a circular enclosure in which the imagination can conceive of anything": Surrounding Paris like the rings of Saturn, it bore witness to all the dreams and schemes of the century, as parties and prime ministers tried again and again to bend it to their political purposes.

Which, as the wall's creator knew full well, was exactly how it all began. Any illusion Adolphe Thiers might have had that the wall that bore his name was built primarily for defense had vanished long before Prussian shells began arcing over it to land on the heads of his fellow ministers. Thiers had built *l'enceinte* as a sop to a king he did not support; watched as it became an apparatus of an empire he despised; and then, in the critical moment, commandeered it to corral the very people who had prompted the king to demand it in the first place. The wall long outlived him, surviving clear through the First World War—when, once again, it saw no military service: Although the German army came nearly as close to the capital in 1914 as they had in 1870, the French had long before decided on external forts as a superior model. The Thiers wall played many parts during its lifetime and has kept on playing them even in death. But under it all, its true identity remained fixed: It was an instrument of domestic statecraft.

Architecture, for better or worse, is always an accessory to power—though naturally who wields that power makes all the difference. Right atop Bastion No. 1, once I'd safely circumnavigated the high-traffic arteries surrounding it, I walked into what is now a dirt-filled precinct to find that part of the bastion was occupied by another new building. Small children ran around in the unlandscaped lot minded by their parents who regarded my arrival with only mild confusion. One of them explained to me that the building was "*des abris d'urgence*": emergency overflow housing. As Paris's historic center has grown impossibly expensive, the city's housing crunch has gotten worse, and the crisis has been deepened in recent years due to the influx of new immigrants and refugees entering from North Africa and the Middle East. Expected to be onsite for another seven years, the economical but quite handsome construction of wood and steel had been completed six months prior, providing 308 units to individuals and families who otherwise might be sleeping in the Bois de Vincennes nearby. It was yet another attempt to put the defunct fortification systems to some social good use—or at least to relieve political pressure on an increasingly beleaguered centrist government. It was not, in any case, a public building. Feeling I'd intruded, I smiled and quietly wandered off, back to the busy thoroughfare below.

I walked a long way west until I found a café I'd known years before. I asked for a coffee and the WiFi password, and as I looked into my phone I was immediately confronted by a news report stating that "the border wall has begun construction" in San Diego. It was "fake news," or at least fake-ish: Enhancements to previously fenced portions of the border were often construed as being "the" wall, a confusion the administration did nothing to counter as it bucked up the spirits of their pro-wall base. The error had appeared in the press several times before (and it would again, repeatedly). Still, it jarred: a pointed reminder of who was in the White House and of how he got there.

REACTION

The Embarcadero was swarming with foot traffic—buskers and baby carriages, tourists with bread bowls of chowder—on a fine summer day, the first of July 2015, as Jim Steinle walked with his family along the San Francisco waterfront. As they made their way down the paved catwalk of Pier 14, Kathryn, Steinle's daughter, began complaining that she didn't feel well, sensing (as police would later report) that "something had taken place." All at once she fell to the ground. Her father administered CPR until paramedics arrived. Hours later Kathryn Steinle, thirty-two years old, was dead at San Francisco General Hospital.

What had happened that afternoon was that a .40 caliber bullet had entered through Steinle's upper back and lodged itself in her aorta. The gun had been fired from several yards away, its sharp report drowned out by the noise of the crowds on the pier. It was only a few hours before police apprehended a suspect, José Ines García Zárate, who claimed that he'd found the gun on the ground and that it had accidentally discharged when he attempted to pick it up. The weapon, it was later discovered, had been stolen several days earlier from the vehicle of an agent for the Bureau of Land Management.

Steinle's death occurred in the midst of a most grisly year for shootings in America, including the mass murder of nine black churchgoers in Charleston, North Carolina, by a self-described white supremacist only two weeks prior. Amid so much mayhem, the killing of a single young woman in San Francisco received only muted coverage in the national media—until, that is, it was revealed that the alleged perpetrator was not only an undocumented immigrant, but one with a lengthy criminal record who had been deported from the United States and then reentered illegally on no fewer than five occasions since 1991. Even this revelation did not quite land the Steinle case on the front pages of major metropolitan dailies. It did, however, attract considerable attention from other quarters.

"Another victim of the war on white people," declared one commenter on Breitbart.com. "100% of ILLEGALS are CRIMINALS!" claimed another. "God bless Kathryn Steinle and her family . . . A deadly pox on all politicians. The blood on their hands will never wash off." The conflation of Zarate's criminality with his status as an alien was complete and remarkably literal. "If we can send a spaceship to Pluto," noted "Tom Smith," "we can send a Mexican from San Diego to Tijuana."

To members of the anti-immigrant movement, the solution to this extraterrestrial invasion was startlingly clear. Breitbart's commenters fairly bubbled with suggestions: "Electrified razor wire is a good start!" . . . "Build the wall even if you have to starve every Liberal in USA to do it" . . . "If construction workers start getting killed, send in the national guard to wipe the cartels off the face of the earth." Other proposals were somewhat less colorful, if no less vivid. "This wall must be old fashioned Hoover Dam concrete," opined "The Order." "10 feet thick. 30+ feet high . . . Then, the wall will stand for a thousand years. It will be beautiful."

The insistence on beauty continued to be a running theme among wall advocates ("Spend the money to make it look nice," as yet another Breitbarter put it), and the refrain was taken up with gusto by their new champion in political life, who repeatedly made aesthetic quality a prime objective of the border scheme articulated in his announcement speech, made only three weeks before Steinle was killed. "We are going to build a big, beautiful, powerful wall," the candidate would later assert, while at other times he would refer to the proposed "door" in the wall, presumably for the use of legal immigrants, as likewise being "big" and "beautiful." At the same time, he began to fix on the Steinle case as proof that the wall was necessary, frequently using the same language to describe the slain woman that he deployed in talking about the wall, referring to "beautiful Kate"—just another in a long string of epithets that would include "crooked Hillary" and "Lyin' Ted."

"Beautiful", "great," and most of all "huge": This was the vision of the wall most frequently put forward by Donald Trump. Politicians could build fences; a builder would build a *wall*. Without question, the image of something solid and continuous was the one fastened onto by supporters, as for instance one who arrived at a Florida rally in a Spandex bodysuit painted with the outlines of bricks and a hat bearing the words "Trump Wall." But this was not the only image circulated by the candidate. Over the course of the next year and more, the wall would occasionally be allowed to shrink, becoming something much less physically imposing, ultimately taking on various guises as described in public statements on social media and in interviews. The earliest known date at which the infamous smartphone addict expressed his support for the proposal was in a tweet dated August 5, 2014, as succinct as any statement he's made on the subject since: "SECURE THE BORDER! BUILD A WALL!" After officially throwing his hat into the ring, the presidential hopeful fended off Jeb Bush, insisting his plan was "not a fence, Jeb, it's a WALL, and there's a BIG difference!"—plainly indicating that only a firm, uniform structure would suffice to keep undocumented aliens out.

Then, only days after he had announced his candidacy, he appeared to hedge on the promise, telling CNN, "You don't need a wall for the entire piece because we have wonderful people, Border Patrol people, that can do the job. But you do need walls in certain sections, without question." Shortly thereafter, at a news conference in Iowa, the two-thousand-mile, "great, great" version resurfaced (along with the claim it would be "easy") only to disappear again thereafter. The wall would be solid, or see-through, the same in all places or adapting to local conditions, and while it was officially codified in the Republican platform of 2016 with the claim that it "must cover the entirety of the southern border and must be sufficient to stop both vehicular and pedestrian traffic," it was never clear how the wall appeared in the mind of its highest-profile proponent.

The ambiguity was no doubt an effect of the idea's mixed parentage. Although advocates of increased border fencing had occasionally referred to the project as a "wall," there was no coordinated effort to explain what that meant, much less build it. The Minuteman Civil Defense Corps, who began vigilante patrols at the border in the early 2000s, succeeded in drumming up several hundred thousand dollars for a multilayered structure of their own in Arizona, but they typically referred to it as a "fence"—rightly so, in the view of one of their own numbers, who claimed the structure the group envisioned "wouldn't stop a tricycle." (The Minuteman leader who launched the fundraiser was subsequently convicted of child molestation.) Though figures from the Minuteman movement would line up behind the new anti-immigrant candidate in 2016, the wall notion likely came by other channels, and there are competing assertions as to who, if anyone, first fired the imagination of the New York developer and steered him toward the concept. One member of his political inner circle, Stephen Miller, seems a likely source, given his strident anti-immigrant positions; certainly he can claim precedence, having been known, as a third grader, to spend hours building mock walls out of tape and glue. But the most credible assertion comes from Sam Nunberg, a protégé of sometime campaign adviser Roger Stone, who had first come to the attention of the candidate for his opposition to the Ground Zero Mosque, a Muslim community center that was neither a mosque, nor at Ground Zero. Nunberg, as he told a reporter, was attracted to the idea of a wall for its simplicity and for its being, he claimed, "fun," especially as compared to other, more even-handed solutions. Other candidates could muster no more than a "Maybe we do this, maybe we do that" approach, he said. "No, fuck that! We are building a wall."

Whoever was responsible, the most compelling feature of the proposal from a political perspective seems to have been the invention of the businessman-turned-politician who first articulated it. This was the mechanism by which the massive structure would be built: As he said in his announcement speech, "We will make Mexico pay for it." The claim did not appear as spoken in the (much briefer) prepared version of the announcement originally circulated to media by the candidate's exploratory committee, but seems to have been extemporized on the spot. In the weeks to come, it would take on the appearance of well-considered policy, an attempt to inoculate the proposal against criticisms leveled at its expense. Like the physical aspects of the wall, it would also be subject to countless qualifications and refinements—as for example that Mexico would not literally "pay" for the wall, but rather that tariffs on Mexican goods (which would, of course, be paid by Americans in the end), reductions in the trade deficit, or taxes on remittances sent home by immigrants would all contribute to funding the project. But none of these fiscal fine points were really of interest to any of the idea's fans. The notion that Mexico would pay for the wall was satisfying on its own merits, the wall being a kind of collective punishment all its own, retribution for outrages like the death of Kathryn Steinle.

As for Jim Steinle, whose daughter called out repeatedly for his help as she collapsed to the hot asphalt, he and his wife emerged from their personal horror to find that they had become political mascots. "For Donald Trump, we were just what he needed," Liz Sullivan, Kathryn's mother, told the *San Francisco Chronicle.* "Beautiful girl, San Francisco, illegal immigrant, arrested a million times, a violent crime and yadda, yadda, yadda." Appearing on Capitol Hill mere weeks after Kathryn's death, Mr. Steinle repeatedly fought back tears as he implored lawmakers to pass legislation that would ensure undocumented immigrants with prior convictions were fast-tracked to deportation. Yet both he and Sullivan were adamant that their grief, and their "Kate," did not belong to anyone save themselves. When the candidate pointed to Steinle's death as proof that Mexico was "not sending their best," Jim Steinle bristled. "That's the Donald being the Donald," he told the press, "We're not going to get caught up in that."

The Breitbart commenters were undeterred: For them, the wall would solve all. Some of their recommendations for its construction were remarkable for their specificity, in particular an idea for a structure with "electricity . . . at the upper third, then it activates the lower third once the upper is touched, then they're stuck in the middle. Going up they die, down they die, jump they break both legs." The writer added, "I haven't worked out the details yet."

In popular accounts of Mexico's ongoing crime wave, Ciudad Juárez had often been made to stand for all that was wrong with the country, a hotbed of violence where drug dealers ruled the streets. I visited in the summer of 2018, and I confess I did not find the atmosphere encouraging, even by the standards of the developing world—whole streets of ruined store-fronts, hotels posted with hourly rates, bicycles and junk cluttering even the elegant courtyard of the Centro Municipal de las Artes. Whatever its supposed hazards, however, the city mostly went about its business: Though it no longer attracts the American tourists who, in the early twentieth century, flocked to popular nightspots like the Kentucky Club, it remains a hub for cross-border commerce. It also draws more prominent visitors, as it did in February 2016, when Pope Francis arrived in Juarez during a swing through Mexico.

The streets of Juarez

His Holiness led a mass at the Chamizal, on the Mexican side of the park built to commemorate the Johnson-era agreement that settled the long-simmering land dispute. There, mounting a platform that overlooked the Rio Grande and El Paso, the pope addressed the faithful on both sides, as well as the nations of Central America whose internal crises had been driving additional migrants northward in growing numbers. "We cannot deny the humanitarian crisis which in recent years has meant the migration of thousands of people," he said, in what many read as an explicit swipe at the "Make America Great Again" movement. In response, its leader called the head of the Catholic Church "a very political person" during an interview on Fox Business Network.

Spats like this would do nothing to improve the long odds that the mainstream media placed upon the latest entrant to the presidential sweepstakes. The wall in particular was viewed as a drag on the candidacy: Vox.com included the wall proposal among its "Eleven Bonkers Quotes" from the announcement speech; late-night host Seth Meyers likened the candidate to a character in the fantasy series *Game of Thrones*, manning the show's anti-zombie wall. (The object of Meyer's satire eventually cottoned to the comparison, posting an Instagram shot inspired by the program's ad campaign that featured his face along with the slogan "The Wall Is Coming.") Even conservative commentator Dinesh D'Souza mocked the idea, posting a photo of an ivory-white wall topped by Taj Mahal–like details, with the same garish sign on it that the famous real estate firm put on all of its high rises. (D'Souza would later warm to the cause, eventually receiving a presidential pardon after he was convicted of campaign finance fraud.) The "quixotic bid," as Politico.com termed it, would not become any less so by grace of a far-fetched border gimmick.

Other Republican hopefuls in the race appeared to feel the same way. Former Florida governor Jeb Bush took a strong stand against the proposal, provoking his opponent's ire by using the "f-word": "We don't have to spend hundreds of billions of dollars on fencing," claimed Bush's official campaign statement, "when we can use new technology, improve the Border Patrol's access to streams and rivers on the border, [and] beef up our patrols." Chris Christie of New Jersey was prepared to lend the proposal only partial support, calling for a wall "where appropriate," chiefly in cities; John Kasich would go further, stating he would "finish the wall," though the phrasing suggested he endorsed not a new structure but the completion of the existing fences. (His stated policy on the twelve million undocumented individuals already in the United States was radically different from his peers', calling for legalization for all noncriminal immigrants.) More direct critiques of the "great" and "beautiful" wall came from other forces on the political right, including the Center for Immigration Studies, a Washington,

D.C., think tank advocating reduced immigration. "[It's] more of a slogan than a policy idea," the group's Jessica Vaughan told CBS. "He's right that we need to do a better job of border security, but his idea is presented in a very cartoonish way, without nuance . . . The fence is very effective where it can be patrolled, but in other areas it's a complete waste of money."

Not all conservative elites were so keen to stand on principle. As the election season heated up in late 2015 and 2016, Senators Ted Cruz and Marco Rubio, both sons of Cuban immigrants, began to try to outdo their Manhattanite opponent, and one another as well, in shows of anti-immigration fervor. Both pronounced themselves unwavering proponents of the wall, and Cruz in particular was at pains to point out his support for the Secure Fence Act as well as his instrumental role in defeating the 2013 comprehensive immigration reform bill. In a December 2015 live debate, Cruz lashed out at Rubio for his support of the legislation, saying that he "chose . . . to stand with Obama and Schumer and support a massive amnesty plan." Rubio struck back, pointing out that Cruz had formerly voiced approval of plans to afford a path to citizenship for the undocumented. By February, Rubio thought he had found a way to weaponize the wall against its own master. "If he builds the wall the way he built Trump Towers," said the Florida senator, "he'll be using illegal immigrant labor to do it," a dig at the developer's occasionally murky employment practices. As for Cruz—whose attempts to reclaim the wall idea as his own helped earn him the "Lyin' Ted" sobriquet—the February debate saw him take aim at his accuser. "Falsely accusing someone of lying is itself a lie," he said, "and something Donald does daily." The syllogism was sound, though it might have been aimed a bit high for the audience.

Abstraction was no way to connect with the pro-wall crowd. Before the February debate took place, the large field of aspirants had already endured their first electoral live-fire exercises—the Iowa caucuses and New Hampshire and South Carolina primaries had proven that Republican politicians should be as loud and proud as possible. Iowa had gone to Cruz, but only barely, with a mere six thousand votes separating him from the Manhattan billionaire; the latter had then come charging back, winning the next two contests decisively. Especially in New Hampshire, hard hit by the opioid epidemic, the wall had been a major selling point, proffered as a foolproof tool to keep heroin and other drugs out of the United States. But exploiting the pain of addiction-ravaged communities was only one part of the successful formula, with voters in the state citing their overwhelming support for another measure, announced in December following a deadly shooting perpetrated by two Pakistani Americans in San Bernardino, California. "Donald J. Trump is calling for a total and complete shutdown of Muslims entering the United States," declared the candidate himself, speaking in the third person, "until our country's representatives can figure out what the hell is going on." Once again, the technical merits and demerits of the wall were of less significance than the broader attitude of which it was a part.

With the primary wins—to say nothing of the bumper media coverage that followed every debate, every off-the-cuff remark, every rambling speech at every rally—the heretofore "quixotic" candidacy seemed more and more like a viable crusade. The first member of Congress to sign up to "Make America Great Again" was Chris Collins, the Republican representative from Upstate New York's 27th district; the area had benefited from an infusion of immigrants in recent years, and although Collins owned up to reservations about his endorsee's immigration politics he decided there were larger issues at stake. Next on the list of official congressional supporters was Senator Jeff Sessions of Alabama: Donning the red hat only four days after Collins, Sessions harbored no such qualms regarding immigration policy. In announcing his support, Sessions noted that "politicians have promised for thirty years to fix" the border problem and that it was time for a nonpolitician to try his hand. (The recipient of his praise hailed Sessions as "really the expert as far as I'm concerned on borders.") As the primary victories continued to mount, more endorsements came with them, including that of Chris Christie, who had previously criticized his new ally's strategy on Muslims and other immigrants, stating that "we don't need to be profiling in order to get the job done here."

All the while, so far as the national punditry was concerned, the Republican lather over immigration was much ado about nothing. Polling that appeared during the primary season suggested that immigration was not a particularly high-ranking concern, coming in at sixth after gun policy and health care. The candidates themselves, for all their frothing, scarcely spent any time at the border itself: "Trumpnado Hits Laredo," Politico.com had blared back in July, though the southwest sweep had lasted only four days and did not include a planned meeting with a group of border agents, who canceled at the last minute. Ted Cruz, who had never spent much time in his home state's southern tier, largely continued to keep his distance, while Rubio was hardly seen in the region at all. Perhaps the highest-profile visit was that of Senator Bernie Sanders, the independent-turned-Democrat from Vermont who visited in March to call for immigration reform and denounce further barrier-building. "We don't need a wall," said Sanders, "and we don't need barbed wire."

Both Sanders and Democratic frontrunner Hillary Clinton, who also declared her opposition to the proposal, enjoyed large leads in early general election polling over nearly the entire Republican field. Polls suggested that their immigration positions were politically prudent: A study by the Pew Research Center released in April showed that 62 percent of Americans were opposed to the wall, with only 34 percent claiming to support it. The numbers revealed a profound partisan divide—a nearly identical percentage of Republicans, 63 percent, were revealed to be wall-supporters, with 84 percent of Democrats anti-wall—suggesting that while Republican primary candidates could catch a tailwind with the idea, it might hurt them in the fall. These numbers should have been sobering to Republican hopefuls, especially for the one who continued to promise he would build the wall. Yet even as doubts lingered over his electability, he continued to lambast the insincerity of his fellow Republicans.

So why did he keep at it? Just after the New York primary, the editorial board of the *New York Times* held a meeting with their hometown's not-so-favorite son and asked him about his rallies. His response displayed a true showman's sense of the room. "You know, if it gets a little boring," he said, "if I see people starting to sort of, maybe thinking about leaving, I can sort of tell the audience, I just say, 'We will build the wall!' And they go nuts."

Indiana, West Virginia, Nebraska . . . One by one, the state primaries came and went in the spring of 2016, and with each passing vote the Republican field narrowed. First Jeb Bush and Ben Carson, then Marco Rubio all quietly bowed out. By then, there were no anti-wall candidates left among the Republicans. Nor was the frontrunner—increasingly referred to in the media as "the presumptive nominee"— showing any signs of tacking toward the middle on immigration, as might have been expected for a candidate gearing up for the general election. If anything, he was doubling down.

He could afford to, in part, because almost all the figures of the Republican establishment—those who might otherwise have been in a position to rein him in—were themselves hopelessly compromised by their own past statements. Mitt Romney could rail about the lack of civility creeping into political discourse; yet it was he, in 2012, who called for "an impermeable border fence" between the US and Mexico. Another former Republican standard-bearer, John McCain, would come to loggerheads with the party's new superstar; on immigration, however, they were not so unalike: In McCain's 2010 senate reelection bid—coming two years after his failed presidential candidacy, in the midst of the ultraconservative Tea Party insurgency—the four-term US senator shot a TV ad in which he walked side by side with a south Arizona sheriff, surveying landscape regularly traversed by border-crossing parties. What was his solution to the ongoing crisis? "Complete the danged fence," said McCain. (His previous support for barrier-building was now sufficiently embarrassing that his 2016 reelection campaign asked to have the six-year-old video blocked on YouTube.)

Sizing up the political novice who had suddenly taken their party by storm, many GOP stalwarts decided that he might make a useful tool. Even Rush Limbaugh, who sang the praises of the anti-immigrant platform throughout the campaign, admitted on air that "the thing is . . . I never took him seriously on this": Even if the wall was never built, the enthusiasm that the idea inspired in the conservative base could be used to advance causes—tax reform, deregulation, judges—nearer to the hearts of the Republican elite. This tactic, using anti-immigration rhetoric as a cudgel while still holding it at arm's length, was only a continuation of the same strategy that Republicans had pursued since the days of Proposition 187. What they did not recognize, even as the 2016 primary season progressed toward its inexorable conclusion, was that this time they were lashed to forces they could not control.

Whether the idea for the wall was gleaned from Miller or Nunberg, from the Minuteman movement, or someone else, the proposal only represented the tip of a far larger iceberg. "Borders, language, culture": This had long been the mantra of ultraconservative talking head Michael Savage, and in the furthest recesses of the right it was generally accepted that all three elements of nationhood were under systematic siege in the United States. Fed by philosophical streams very different from those of the mainstream conservative movement, the "alt right" that had been taking shape for years—primarily via the internet—drew on the cultural pessimism of philosopher Oswald Spengler, the "clash of civilizations" model favored by political scientist Samuel P. Huntington, and a grab-bag of exotic neo-Nietzschean thought. In this grim worldview, the post–Cold War order was led by a "globalist" elite who had "hijacked the country," in the words of conspiracy enthusiast Alex Jones; feminism, egalitarianism, and international business had sapped the national will and even corrupted American men, reducing them to "cucks," a crude term for cuckolds. It was the alt right that spoke through the comments section of websites like Breitbart.com, and the wall was the imminent distillation of their ideology, a giant thumb-in-the-eye to the forces of globalism and change.

Existential insecurity—a deep and abiding sense of economic and cultural marginalization—fed a growing anger that stretched well beyond the small circle of committed alt-right activists, reaching communities across the country. It was bolstered by a real-life demographic sea change: In 2015, census projections were released confirming that whites would comprise a minority of Americans aged under eighteen within five years. Illegal border crossing had never been a major contributor to the increasing size of the country's Latino community (17 percent in 2012, expected to rise to nearly 25 percent over the next three decades), which largely stemmed from legal immigration and natural increase. Building a wall was not going to stop it, and if the wall's enthusiasts imagined that their new political champion could somehow stand athwart the border holding back the immigrant hordes, they were sadly mistaken. But then this image—calling to mind the legend of King Canute, ordering the tides "not to rise onto my land"—did not necessarily hold much currency among the Republicans who were rallying under the pro-wall banner. A Fox poll in the runup to the election showed that only 66 percent of its supporters believed the wall would ever be built. What these voters wanted, apparently, more than results, was someone to echo their cultural anxieties. The alt right and its candidate gave it to them.

Nothing betokened the ascent of the movement so succinctly as the announcement, in mid-August 2016, that the campaign of the "presumptive nominee" would now be led by a new chief executive, Steve Bannon. After struggling through two managers since its inception, the campaign turned to Bannon to right the ship. The new director came straight from the staff of Breitbart.com, where he had stepped in as executive chair following the death of the site's founder; over the course of a checkered career that ran from Wall Street to Hollywood, Bannon had worn many hats, but one constant had been his attraction to the same blood-and-soil conservative thinkers who inspired the alt right. "I believe the world, and particularly the Judeo-Christian West, is in crisis," he had said in a 2014 speech, and he frequently name-checked obscure far-right theorists like Italy's Julius Evola and France's Charles Maurras. Organizationally, he proved no more effective than any of the previous directors, with the campaign continuing to demonstrate a lack of strategy and inconsistent messaging. Ideologically, he was the first to articulate a cogent notion of what the campaign and its signature issues were all about. As he had said of Breitbart, the vision was "center-right, populist, anti-establishment," and unquestionably anti-immigration.

Whatever it was, it appeared to be working. In May, John Kasich lost the Indiana primary and officially announced his withdrawal from the race. In the two months before the Republican National Convention, scheduled for August in Cleveland, there was much buzz in the media of a possible floor fight—"a convention coup," as media outlets called it—that might see GOP delegates turn to another, more conventional candidate. But while Kasich refused to attend the party's big event in his own home state, any organized opposition quickly fizzled. On Monday, July 18, Jeff Sessions appeared at the rostrum to make the nomination official. Four days later, as the Republican old guard stood aside helpless or stayed at home, the newly crowned nominee addressed the raucous crowd, promising once again "to make America great again." During the acceptance speech, he name-checked Kathryn Steinle only moments before reminding his audience that theirs would be a "great" wall: The implication, it seemed, was that this wall would do more than just prevent similar killings in the future; it would harrow up the soul of whomever saw it, redeeming the sadness and senselessness of Steinle's death by transmuting it into a monument 1,984 miles long.

After my afternoon in Juarez, I crossed the border back into El Paso, Texas. The two cities are as symbiotic as any in the region, yet despite the ongoing travails of its neighbor, El Paso is routinely named as one of the top-ten safest cities in the United States. It was election season again—a very different one—when I was there, and there were signs in the front yards; the streets were silent, and they only seemed to become more so in one of the poorer neighborhoods directly next to the border, where tiny houses flanked a narrow green mall. The city, 81 percent Latino as of the 2010 census, speaks more eloquently than any of the reams of reports and statistics, compiled over decades, demonstrating that neither Mexican Americans nor undocumented immigrants commit violent crimes at rates higher than those of other Americans. That point would be made over and over again during the 2016 general campaign, though like so many facts it seemed unable to gain traction with key parts of the electorate, confounding seasoned Democratic strategists. They would have done well to heed the words of Bannon's favorite reactionary author, Charles Maurras: "We must expect everything in politics, where everything is allowed, except to be surprised."

With election season in the United States having grown into a two-year-long slog, it is extraordinary to reflect that the general presidential campaign still lasts for only three months, between the end of the national conventions and the opening of the polls. As interminable as it felt, it was all over very fast.

After locking up the Democratic nomination—the first woman ever to do so for a major American political party—Hillary Clinton was the hands-down favorite throughout, and she fought a cautious, canny campaign rooted in her own and her allies' decades of political experience. The wall, like so many of the poll-tested policies of her opponent, was judged a losing position, one with which the Republicans should be allowed to hang themselves. It was discussed only glancingly during the presidential debates, most notably in the very last one on October 19, when the Republican nominee repeated his intention to build it: "Now, I want to build the wall," he said. "We need the wall. And the Border Patrol, ICE, they all want the wall. We stop the drugs. We shore up the border." Clinton responded by teasing him for failing to even mention the wall when he met with President Enrique Peña Nieto during a bizarre visit to Mexico in late August: "He choked, and then got into a Twitter war because the Mexican president said we're not paying for that wall," she said. In a line that seemed a reformulation of her husband's "bridge to the twenty-first century," Clinton repeatedly stated on the campaign trail that Americans "need to build bridges, not walls," as if to wave the matter away with a figure of speech.

On the whole, Mexico and the border played only a supporting role in a campaign where crises piled atop one another in constant succession, with a new one emerging almost every day. The first official television advertisement from the Republican side accused Clinton of wanting an "open" border, but abstained from directly mentioning the wall; Clinton's ads alluded to the subject, lambasting the recent suggestion of a "deportation force," but gave no more weight to the issue than to other hot-button topics and outrageous remarks made by her opponent and his proxies. In down-ticket races, the wall appeared sporadically. Otherwise, the "great, great" project largely faded into the background, its improbability submerged in the wider, wilder improbability of Clinton's loss.

Her mistake appears clear enough now. While serving up a sizable helping of misogyny ("nasty woman") and stoking long-simmering class resentments ("we're going to win"), the reality TV star succeeded in tapping into subterranean currents in the American psyche, ones that the alt right knew well but that long predated the movement. Along with anti-globalist sentiment, the shadows of the Zoot Suit riots, the anti-Chinese panic, the Mexican-American War, the Alamo—even, perhaps, of the beleaguered

New England settlers, surrounded by hostile natives—all of it seemed to be summoned forth by this man who, if pressed, would have had to admit he wasn't much aware of any of these historical events.

About walls in particular he understood nothing—not even how to build them, despite his insistence to the contrary—except for their most important use: as a political expedient. Whether or not the border wall would ever be effective as a tool of immigration enforcement, its quasi-subliminal sway over the minds of millions of voters proved its value as a means of getting and keeping power. There is no sure metric as to how much the wall figured in the decisions of voters on election day. An exit poll from a combination of news organizations showed that 86 percent of those who voted Republican favored the project, but this still only accounted for 41 percent of the overall vote. An unpopular policy, just as Clinton and the punditry had always maintained; but it didn't *have* to be popular. Clinton, after all, won the popular vote by nearly three million votes. If the exit polls are to be believed, wall-backing voters accounted for all but a small fraction of the winner's 46 percent vote share. The wall never enjoyed widespread support. It just had enough.

CONSTRUCTING THE NORMAL

BERLIN

The Berlin Wall was born at a garden party and died at a press conference. That the two events bookending its remarkable existence should be so banal in themselves has only tended to make those moments all the more intriguing: How could such a consequential structure have come about, and then suddenly ceased, attended by little or no ceremony, and at the will of such a small number of historical actors? No matter how often the stories are told and retold, they still seem incredible. They bear retelling at least once more.

Following the post–World War II partition of the country by the victorious Allies, there commenced a mass exodus of citizenry from the Soviet-dominated German Democratic Republic (GDR) to the US-aligned Federal Republic of Germany (FRG) via the nearly nine-hundred-mile inner German border, amounting to roughly three and a half million people by 1961. As that boundary had become increasingly fortified over the previous decade, almost 90 percent of those refugees were now crossing over from within the former Nazi capital, located wholly within the GDR but with one half of it occupied by the Western powers. Those fleeing cited various reasons for wishing to enter the *de facto* FRG exclave of West Berlin, ranging from economic opportunity to educational prospects to family ties, but all shared a similar profile, being predominantly young and high-skilled. Faced with a critical brain drain, GDR leader Walter Ulbricht made a drastic decision, calling together a group of his fellow functionaries at a small gathering in the backyard of his rural villa and announcing that he was permanently sealing off the western half of the city: "Better safe than sorry," as he told the Russian ambassador, and to be safer still he barred any of his houseguests from leaving until the process was underway. The group was detained there for the rest of the evening, as Erich Honecker—Ulbricht's trusted deputy, and later successor—carried out the detailed scheme, ordering sentries to erect road-blocks and unspool 150 tons of barbed wire, totally encircling West Berlin by the following morning, August 13, 1961. In the blink of an eye, and with a nuclear showdown between the global superpowers a very real possibility, the Iron Curtain, first mentioned by Winston Churchill in 1946, went from metaphor to a tangible thing. Meanwhile, the only people who knew what was going on were calmly knocking back beers and canapés in the forest.

Over the ensuing twenty-eight years, Honecker's ad hoc barrier evolved into an elaborate reinforced-concrete structure and a hated symbol of European division during the Cold War. Amid an atmosphere of increasing liberalization in the late 1980s, travel restrictions began to loosen throughout the Eastern Bloc and increasing numbers of East Germans slipped westward via other Soviet satellite states. The GDR leadership recognized that it had no choice but to permit its citizens to travel between the Berlins, but the details concerning the order were not fully disclosed to Günter Schabowski, an East German government spokesman who appeared in front of a gaggle of journalists on the evening of November 9, 1989, for what was meant to have been a routine (and routinely tedious) briefing. After the conference had formally ended, one of the journalists asked Schabowski to clarify the officialese surrounding when the restrictions would be lifted. The representative sputtered for a moment, having no firm idea when or how the policy was to be implemented. Acting without intelligence from his superiors, he stated simply, "*Ab sofort*"—immediately, suggesting East Berliners could enter the West as of that moment. Within hours, thousands of ecstatic easterners were shouting at confused and terrified guards, demanding to be let through. Their momentum proved irresistible, and the world awoke to televised images of people dancing atop the once-dreaded barrier and swinging at it with sledgehammers. It was a perfect media moment, a moving portrait of a world coming together, and it all happened thanks to an imperfect media messenger.

These two magic tricks—the wall appearing and then disappearing with a flourish, while everyone else seemed to be looking the other way—have tended to dominate in public memory and popular histories of the Wall. There are other stories as well, of course: stories of derring-do and heartbreak, of the attempts both successful and otherwise of the intrepid wall-jumpers, risking death at the hands of the East German border guards (bound by the infamous *Schießbefehl*, the order permitting them to shoot and kill any violator) for a chance at a life of freedom or at least for a moment in the spotlight. Their escapes and escapades are well known, and the castoff remains of their hang gliders and false-bottomed cars can be seen cluttering the Checkpoint Charlie Museum, the treasure-trove of Wall-iana that sits near the entrance to the erstwhile American sector.

But there was more to the Wall than these spectacular stories. Sometimes the madcap escapists were really just mad: Take poor Dieter Beilig, a thirty-year-old West Berliner and anti-Wall activist, possibly schizophrenic, who had been arrested in 1964 for going over the Wall—against the typical flow of traffic—into East Berlin. Seven years later, he breached the barrier from the West yet again, was immediately apprehended, and began ranting non sequiturs at his captors ("the curtain can be closed this afternoon . . . The slogan is Mao Zedong . . ."). During what may have been an abortive escape attempt through an interrogation-room window, he was shot in the back by a nervous GDR guardsman. While his disappearance was a close-kept secret in the East, it went completely unnoticed in the West, where Beilig's friends and family decided his erratic character was explanation enough. Like a thousand other episodes in the life of the Wall, this one was consigned to the shadows, just another murky melodrama between the Wall's nefarious beginning and its sensational end.

For as much high dudgeon as marked the Wall's nearly three decades in the global spotlight, there were also long years where little happened to it at all: years when the wall was simply *there*, a part of the landscape to which its human neighbors had grown largely indifferent, as neighbors will do once the obnoxious new arrival has become a regular part of the scenery. Even in the first tense hours of its construction, the builders of the Wall were at pains to make it appear that this disruptive entity was nothing out of the ordinary, broadcasting messages through GDR media that West German traffic was still moving easily in and out of West Berlin, claiming blithely that "nothing had changed." The Wall remained in place as long as it did thanks to a system—or several overlapping systems—designed to camouflage it, and which changed as circumstances demanded. Improvisation wasn't just the theme of the Berlin Wall's coming into being and its demise; it is also what sustained it for decades, allowing it to appear as an inconvenient but not unduly obtrusive presence, just another building in the crowded capital.

On September 13, 1966, a six-year-old boy named Andreas Senk was playing with a friend near the Oberbaum Bridge over the River Spree. The segment of the waterway running alongside Andreas's West Berlin neighborhood lay in East Berlin—but the Wall stood on the far side, and the boys were free to walk right down to the near bank. Six hundred feet away was an East German watchtower; since the guards' primary directive was to keep East Berliners from going westward, they did not notice the children, nor hear the splash as Andreas plunged headlong into the river. His friend had pushed him, apparently in a spirit of boisterous fun, which turned to panic when he realized what he'd done. Hours passed before the alarm finally went out and West Berlin firefighters arrived on the scene. They were able to pull the boy's body out with poles.

The rescuers would go on to claim that they had been actively impeded in their efforts by an East German patrol boat that had also been present, prompting an outraged response from the West: "Six-Year-Old Dies Before the Very Eyes of the Border Police," one headline ran. This would be disputed in the aftermath of the incident, but the same narrative would unfold repeatedly thereafter—in at least four additional incidents over the ensuing years, small children would fall to their death, inciting a hue and cry in the West about callous GDR soldiers watching impassively as helpless innocents drowned under their noses. The last of these episodes occurred in 1975, when five-year-old Çetin Mert, playing on the very same bridge as Andreas, went chasing after a lost ball. This time, however, something was finally done to put a stop to the recurring tragedies. Only months later, the two Berlins forged an agreement allowing for coordinated rescues along their mile-and-a-half riparian border, guaranteeing that no more children would drown in the Spree.

That instrument of interurban cooperation built on a growing sense of comity between the two Germanies, as both sides began to view their separation as a more or less permanent condition. After 1970, with the signing of international accords that recognized the de facto sovereignty of both nations, the governments of the GDR and FRG began to enter into a limited form of détente. Neither country quite accepted the existence of the other; but they and their respective international partners now saw fit to at least formalize the commerce, both economic and diplomatic, that had always taken place despite their mutual enmity. Extending a hand across the inner German border was in some ways easier than doing the same thing across the Wall: In Berlin, where the two systems lived in such unbearable proximity, there were endless opportunities for conflict. Yet the needless deaths of Andreas, Çetin, and others made clear that accommodation, if not amity, was necessary.

With the early-seventies thaw, West Berliners had been given blanket permission by the GDR to travel in East Berlin for limited periods, provided they secured the proper permits. They could enter via multiple routes: by way of select surface crossings, such as Ivalidenstraße and Bornholmer Straße, or courtesy of two transit lines that arced from the west into the east, arriving in the Friedrichstraße train station in East Berlin while bypassing the shuttered *Geisterbanhöfe*, the eerily vacant "ghost stations" removed from service when the Wall was built. The bureaucratic choreography required to operate these assorted connections was breathtaking, and it was carried out with stereotypically German precision—special crossings for waste disposal, walls between train platforms, trains managed by one government running over the other's territory. (The elevated S-Bahns in West Berlin were operated by the East German government; just to taunt the westerners, the cars were decked with Communist flags and slogans every May Day.) The arrangement even afforded opportunities for profit, as in the Friedrichstraße station, fully equipped with an East German duty-free store where westerners could make purchases on the cheap without passing through an East Berlin passport control. "Alcoholics from West Berlin populated the platform," recalled one observer. "Violent scenes that erupted between them were broken up by the patrolling GDR border personnel."

No more, as in the early days of the Wall, did parents have to stand on makeshift platforms on the western side, holding aloft their infant children so that their grandparents in the East could see them. This and other forms of protest were once common in West Berlin, tacitly sanctioned as part of the government's formal opposition to the Wall's existence; now that the Wall had achieved provisional acceptance as a fixture of east-west relations, such demonstrations were less popular. The FRG's minister for Intra-German Relations declared that "protests and proclamations" were no longer enough, and even as the east undertook the dramatic beefing-up of the border infrastructure, moving from brick and stone to concrete, commemorations of those killed on the Wall became less impassioned affairs. Publisher Axel Springer, whose office tower boasted a commanding view of the Wall's ragged course through the Mitte, Berlin's central district, remained one of the Wall's most outspoken critics, denouncing it regularly through the organs of his media empire—but he was viewed with barely more sympathy in the west than in the east, seen by many as an attention-seeking troublemaker. One West German magazine dubbed him the "Brandenburger Tor," a pun on the sealed-off triumphal arch, with the additional meaning of "Brandenburg Idiot."

The prevailing stasis did not mean that all was stable. Beginning in 1975, the Wall began to assume its final and most familiar form—the one that now exists in chunks, adorning mantelpieces around the world—a ninety-mile-long façade of concrete topped by a curved baffle, with guard towers and barracks at regular intervals along the route. The Grenzmauer 75, as it was known, faced West Berlin with vertical modules up to thirteen feet high, behind which lay a broad, clear path that could be as much as five hundred feet wide and that provided East German guards with a clear line of fire toward any prospective escapees. Backed up by a shorter wall facing East Berlin, the so-called death strip (*Todesstreifen*) entailed the demolition of thousands of structures in the historic center of the city, cutting a gruesome scar in the urban corpus, a no-man's-land populated only by anti-tank obstacles and patrol vehicles.

Still more disturbing, the East German leadership, with Honecker at its head after 1971, regularly shifted the rules of engagement, sometimes for no better reason than to demonstrate its authority. Documents from the GDR's archives showed that while the *Schießbefehl* was always theoretically in force, the government would periodically suspend it during the visits of prominent international guests, hoping to avoid the diplomatic embarrassment of a dead body. Just as rumors of its suspension began to circulate, the order would then be secretly reinstituted, keeping East Germans forever fearful and uncertain as to the actual perils of "desertion of the republic," as the regime dubbed it.

Yet despite the continuing danger, the Wall slowly receded into the urban background. It had become, before its final decade, an asset of sorts to the commercial life of West Berlin, the adjacent dead ends and grassy lots creating secluded spaces for bars and beer gardens. More than one company led guided tours of the Wall for crowds from all over Europe and beyond, curious to see the infamous structure in person; one Berliner recalled watching women from a French tour group leap from their motor coach to snap "photographs of each other ... in their hot pants," just in front of a memorial to a murdered wall-jumper. As the 1970s turned into the '80s, activist-minded artists began to cover the smooth outer face of Grenzmauer 75 with graffiti. "Overcoming the Wall by Painting the Wall," a 1984 program sponsored by the Checkpoint Charlie Museum, attracted participants from around the world, and in time the barrier became a veritable outdoor exhibition of slogans and images, including works by American painter Keith Haring. Even this, however, did not seem to portend any immediate change in the city's political predicament—even as their government began to wobble, East German border guards were still shouting at spray painters to stay away. Nature itself seemed to have adapted to the Wall, with the death strip becoming home to thousands of rabbits, who found a congenial habitat in the quiet, grassy margin.

Arriving in Berlin for the first time in many years, I came by way of the same route as generations of West Germans entering the capital when it was still "that isolated outpost" (as John F. Kennedy called it), crossing what was once the inner German border near Braunschweig. In those days, the train journey through East Germany took place in carefully marked stages: one crew change on entering the GDR, another at the West Berlin border, still another if the train was continuing on to East Berlin. Writer Stephen

Barber, a regular visitor to the city in the 1970s and '80s, described the process as an "infiltration," the train slipping from one world into the next "as though precipitating its passengers' bodies into unknown, vertiginous zones." No such thrills nowadays: Straight out of the station, bags in hand, I walked out of the Hauptbanhof, directly over the Spree and headed east.

*A moment out of time: the Berlin Wall Memorial
(Gedenkstätte Berliner Mauer)*

History has always had a place at the Wall, even when the Wall was still there. Both sides commemorated their honored dead with wreathes and placards placed alongside it; the GDR even commemorated the Wall itself, staging a grand twenty-fifth anniversary celebration of its construction, complete with parades. But today history lies far thicker upon the ground. Statuary and memorials abound, especially in the Mitte, addressing every aspect of the city's long-ago division, from the demolished houses and shops to the murdered escapees to the jubilant moment of reunification. This thicket of remembrance is made denser by the other histories receiving equal or greater attention: the somber field of concrete steles of architect Peter Eisenman's Memorial to the Murdered Jews of Europe sitting right in the former death strip; brass nameplates of deportees to concentration camps, embedded in the sidewalk by the riverbank; in front of the Reichstag building, a monument to German parliamentarians killed between 1933 and 1945, ninety-six cast-iron plates stacked untidily on their sides.

In place of the tense balance between separation and exchange, one now finds the anxious negotiation between memory and letting go. Even on the site of one of the largest state-sanctioned remembrance sites, the past and the present contend: The Berlin Wall Memorial (Gedenkstätte Berlin Mauer) is a nearly mile-long wedge of land along Bernauer Straße, a veritable museological sampler on wall themes, including sculptures, a viewing platform, minimalist sculptures, and the only fully-restored segment—two hundred feet long—of the wall as it actually stood, with death strip, guard tower, service road, and inner-wall all exactly as they were. But one portion of the park stands apart. At the time of the barrier's construction, the border between the two Berlins was partly defined by the northern wall of the Friedhof II der Sophiengemeinde, the cemetery of the nearby Sophienkirche. As the Wall expanded, it progressively swallowed much of the cemetery; graves were disinterred in the process, some as old as a century and more. When the Wall came down at last, and plans for the memorial began to gain traction, the church reasserted its claim to its erstwhile property. Ultimately, the solution was a compromise that allowed the churchyard to take up a bulge on one side of the memorial grounds and to mark the rest with a modest wooden cross. To signal its presence to passersby on the main road, the church was also permitted to build—of all things—a wall, made of brick and with a swinging gate.

"Paris is always Paris," quipped Jack Lang, France's former minister of culture, "but Berlin is never Berlin." Perhaps only a city visited by as many traumas as the German capital has been could recover and carry on so persuasively—not quite as though nothing had ever happened, but with a managerial attitude toward its own past at least equal to that with which it once managed its own division. Still the mystery persists: How did a system, once so thoroughly entrenched, suddenly cease to be so?

To imagine an unwalled Berlin in 1989 was all the more daunting since the structure, by that point, had grown into something more than a physical and procedural entity. As securely embedded as it was in the streetscape, it was even more so in the psychology of the East German people: The soldiers posted at the Wall who would later be abhorred (some of them tried in courts of law) for shooting dead more than a hundred individuals were lauded, during the lifespan of the GDR, as the guardians of socialism. Twenty-five of them, according to the regime, were killed in the line of duty, and their names were emblazoned on schools, streets, even campgrounds. On its construction, Honecker had dubbed the Wall the "Antifaschistischer Schutzwall"—the anti-fascist protection wall—and while this Orwellian turn of phrase may seem laughably transparent, the citizenry knew better than to laugh: By some estimates the ratio of agents of the State Security Service (counting informers) to citizens was nearly one to six. In East Germany, policing one's own thoughts was a habit of mind.

Self-interest of a different sort played a part as well. "Socialism means permanently rising living and cultural standards," declared GDR propagandists, and the regime could pride itself on telling at least a partial truth. Industrial production far outstripped that of other socialist nations, and East Germans enjoyed a comparatively high quality of life, with less of the grim scarcity common elsewhere in the Eastern Bloc. While the country's mini-miracle was dwarfed by the *Wirtschaftswunder*—West Germany's postwar boom, itself a contributing factor to East Germany's prosperity—it was enough to obscure the barbed wire and concrete behind a veil of material well-being. Ulbricht and Honecker's successful policy of "consumer-oriented socialism" had coincided with the advent of the Wall, and, though growth had slowed and the deficit skyrocketed by the eighties, the country was still a regional powerhouse, giving little hint of its imminent political peril (not even to Western intelligence agencies, who failed to predict it).

As the decade wore on, Honecker remained stalwart even in the face of Moscow's increasingly deferential attitude toward its satellite republics, still feeling a wind at his back despite General Secretary Mikhail Gorbachev's waning support. East Germany would go so far as to claim the Wall was a necessary instrument of world peace, a catalyst for the détente that followed its erection and that Gorbachev was now pursuing—as the Wall's twenty-eighth anniversary approached, the GDR's official news organ declared that

"13 August 1961 and the secure border are causally linked to the twenty-eight peaceful years since then." As perverse as the argument may appear, it was not without its defenders abroad. On first receiving word of its construction, President Kennedy's immediate response was that "a wall is a hell of a lot better than a war," and over time diplomats had grown still more habituated to the structure than Berliners, viewing it as a reliable constant in geopolitical calculations. In 1989, no less a Cold Warrior than Margaret Thatcher insisted (via Britain's ambassador to the FGR) that German reunification was "not currently on the agenda": For the sake of the balance of power, the Iron Lady was happy to leave the Iron Curtain just as it was. Her government had evinced no objections when, a few months earlier, the East German leader stated that the Wall would "remain so long as the conditions that led to its erection are not changed." The picture of confidence, Honecker added that the barrier "will be standing even in fifty years and even in a hundred years."

A slight exaggeration, in hindsight—but then posterity is not quite in a position to gloat. For not only did the wall fall, but it collapsed so completely that even the contemporary city's assiduous efforts to preserve its memory sometimes fall short. Heading east from the train station, I followed the cobbled strip of the Mauerweg, the marked path of the Wall installed by the city, to Sebastianstraße, site of a failed 1962 escape attempt by a group of tunnellers betrayed by a GDR mole and ultimately shot while still stuck underground. Their misfortune is related in one of the city-posted markers near their dig site, but the Mauerweg is lost, ending abruptly only a few steps away beneath a row of parked cars. The same thing happens near Alexandrinenstraße, as an enormous construction site all but swallows the wall route, and again near the Schillingbrücke, near the site of Andreas Sink's drowning, where the cobbles wander in and out of a re-paved section of roadway, then off at angle into weedy overgrowth that municipal services have not seen fit to tame. Though it would have been but cold comfort, Honecker might at least have consoled himself that his successors have been only slightly more effective in saving his Wall than he was.

How the byzantine ideological framework of the Berlin Wall, drummed into the minds of millions, should have given way (and given way as quickly it did) may never be adequately explained. Not that many haven't tried—claiming credit for the Wall's demise has turned into a perennial parlor game, with various candidates vying for the title of wall-buster. There was, of course, Ronald Reagan's celebrated 1987 speech: Though a bold diplomatic gesture, his famous demand was put to rather the wrong person, since it was Honecker, not Gorbachev, who was the Wall's chief protector. ("We really were not impressed," the Soviet leader later stated. "We knew that Mr. Reagan's original profession was actor.") A series of blockbuster rock concerts staged next to the Wall in the late 1980s (by David Bowie and Bruce Springsteen, the latter from within East Berlin itself) have also been cited as encouraging those in the East to think beyond the Wall. Western television, Western products, and Western literature all seeped through the barrier, and each can take some credit for awakening the dormant understanding that the Wall, despite appearances, was not a permanent fact of existence.

Where these explanations fall short is in what happened afterward. For the wall did *not* come down on the night of November 9, 1989, at least not all in one exultant blow. For months afterward, the GDR limped on as a political organism, with the new leadership of the former ruling party promising "a break with Stalinism and a serious new beginning." The government would eventually pledge to remove the Wall in its entirety—though not before trying to reinstitute some degree of border control, allowing official crossings only at specified points, part of a failing bid to stave off reunification. In a comical inversion of the old legal status quo, East Berliners briefly enjoyed more freedom of movement than their western counterparts, since Günter Schabowski's errant declaration had only granted cross-border access to residents of East Berlin. West Berliners were still technically bound by the same laws as before and were expected to respect the Wall even as thousands of so-called "wall-peckers" knocked it down with common garden tools.

When it did come, the GDR's official demolition of the Wall was undertaken less in a spirit of openness and reconciliation and more for the sake of economic cannibalism. Excised segments of the Wall were sold—mostly to international buyers—by the soon-to-be disbanded government, and the revenues pledged toward public projects in the forlorn hope of winning back the East German populace. As it progressed, the removal was also quite literally one-sided: Dismantling efforts focused predominantly on the west-facing slabs of Grenzmauer 75, the outer perimeter blocks best known to the non-Communist world. The inner wall, the barrier and central strip familiar to East Berliners, was left in place long after, leaving the view from that side all but unchanged. The media image of the fall only marks the triumph of the west; the liberation of the east was slower in coming.

Even with the Wall completely out of the way, the "Wall in [the] heads," as one writer put it, has taken "longer to tear down." *Ostalgie*, a longing for the simplicity and certainties of life under the GDR, began to set in only a few years after the Wall was removed, with the rebranded Communists making electoral gains in the 1990s. The movement persists today, often zeroing in on small but symbolically potent issues: The *Ampelmännchen*, the hat-wearing walk-signal figures on East Berlin traffic lights, have been preserved throughout the eastern half of the city thanks to a successful "Rescue the Little Traffic Light Man" campaign, launched by easterners loath to see him replaced by what critics derided as the "sexless beings with spherical heads" common in the west. This and other rearguard actions have proven the tenacity of the "Wall in the heads," still standing for those who recall that there was life, however difficult, under the Wall. Only lately has that mental Wall begun to truly collapse, and only as a result of a trauma comparable in size—though certainly not in human cost—to the traumas that put the Wall in place.

The radical transformation of Berlin, its history reduced to fragments, anodyne and remote, has taken place at breakneck speed, and it now appears nearly complete. The effacement of the past is nowhere more effective than where it hides in plain sight: One evening, I took a stroll with a friend who lives near the Gedenkstätte, walking from the memorial grounds through a portion of the death strip converted into a landscaped pedestrian passageway surrounded by new development. The decision to preserve the barrier—not as a means of dividing the city, but as an instrument to knit it back together—has to be reckoned a more than moderate success, and despite all the talk of *Ostalgie* the neighborhoods along much of the Mauerweg feel so totally and so artfully integrated that even another Honecker would be at pains to disentangle them a second time. And what Berliner (and what visitor) would want him to? On a warm night, with almost no one on the path, the parkway in the city seemed less vacant than tranquil, domestic, with silhouettes in the windows of the new houses.

Not all the recent changes, however, have been so innocuous. Veering off the Wall path near the Museumsinsel, I passed the busy construction site where the city is presently erecting an exact replica of the Stadtschloss, the eighteenth-century seat of the Prussian monarchs. In 1950, the GDR blew up this emblem of the hated imperial order—an act of historical vandalism that would seem more alarming if the city had not proceeded to do the same thing, in 2008, to the Palast der Republik, the glassy building the GDR put in place of the Stadtschloss. This was only one among numerous demolitions of East German buildings in Berlin, a determined bleaching of the very architecture that formed the proper context of the Wall. Surrounded by so many shifts and displacements, the Wall memorials scattered throughout Berlin come to appear increasingly abstract, divorced from the lived history of the city. The change points to the approach of a new temporality: a future in which the division between east and west is understood as *never* having seemed normal, as having *always* been aberrant, not a part of daily life for countless people for decades. "Man grows used to everything," wrote Dostoyevsky. He might have added that, once used to it, everything else has a way of becoming unthinkable.

The danger, as it occurred to me in Berlin, is that if the banal reality of the past is lost, the way could be open for its return. For one fleeting instant, I even thought I saw it come back. Standing outside the Ostbahnhof, I spotted an early-1970s model Peugeot 404 taxi, one of five remaining in what used to be a vast fleet in the city. Like a ghost, the vehicle glided up, and without particularly needing a cab I got in it, taking it back to the Gedenkstätte. The driver stopped curbside across the road from the restored Wall segment, and when I looked back I saw that the sidewalk opposite was empty save for a woman in a kerchief, hustling along a little girl in a frock dress. By the time I snapped a photo, the scene had changed, but it had all been there: Peugeot, kerchief, frock, Wall, guard tower—the age of the Wall had returned for a moment, as though it had never gone, as though there were nothing at all peculiar about its still being there. No one else even seemed to notice.

TAKEOVER

There was a lot of nervous talk about "normalcy" in the first frantic days following the 2016 election. A "new normal," or an aversion to allowing such a thing to set in, was a frequent topic of conversation among those who would come to form the opposition. For many of them, it seemed that nothing could ever be normal again: The widespread certainty, even among Republicans, that Donald Trump would never win lent a discomfiting, science fiction–like quality to ordinary experience. Every newspaper report seemed like a dispatch from an alternate universe.

No one, perhaps, was caught more unawares by this unforeseen turn of events than the president-elect himself. By most accounts, he and his senior advisers ranked the likelihood of victory as very low indeed; comparisons were made—by Stephen Colbert, among others—to "the dog who caught the car," and the transition process was marked by the same sense of careening unpreparedness that had characterized much of the campaign. Well after inauguration day, the administration had yet to name personnel to key posts. (Many have yet to be filled even years later.) How the new president would make good on his ambitious promises was anyone's guess, though the guessing game was shot through with worry.

On immigration at least, there did seem to be the rudiments of a strategy. Within days of the election, Stephen Miller was announced as the transition team's national policy director, putting the strident anti-immigration figure (and elementary school wall-builder) in a position to have an early and active influence. It was Miller who wrote the fiery inauguration speech, including the declaration that the United States had for too long "defended other nations' borders while refusing to defend our own," a situation the new administration swore to reverse. Of even greater import was the decision to establish Steve Bannon in the position of chief strategist. Carrying multiple portfolios, including an unprecedented advisory role on the National Security Council, Bannon would now have greater access to the levers of power than any of his alt-right friends would have dreamed possible only months before. With Bannon setting the pace, the White House seemed to take on a definitively nationalist cast. Surely the wall would not be long in coming.

Confirmation appeared to arrive early. Only five days after his January 20 inauguration, the president signed Executive Order 13767, stating that it was "the policy of the executive branch to ... secure the southern border of the United States through the immediate construction of a physical wall ... monitored and supported by adequate personnel." As with many such orders emanating from the White House, this one amounted to more of a notice of intent than anything else; the executive possessed no authority to fund any construction, though the document also stipulated that all branches of the federal bureaucracy were to "identify and quantify all sources of direct and indirect Federal aid or assistance to the Government of Mexico"—in theory, this would afford the White House the opportunity to make reductions in financial assistance, redirecting the funds to wall construction. Since so much of the foreign aid the United States sends to Mexico is devoted to military and anti-narcotics programs, such reductions would have been contrary to the purpose the wall was meant to serve. No substantial cuts were ever put into effect.

The same order called for an increase in CBP patrol officers by five thousand—also, two years later, largely unrealized—and was signed the same day as an additional order targeting so-called sanctuary cities that give safe harbor to undocumented immigrations—which would be declared unconstitutional later the same year. The logistical and legal hurdles to all of the administration's immigration efforts were evident from the start, and even before: The day after the election, the American Civil Liberties Union made plain its intent to combat any excesses carried out in the name of "law and order," putting up a website banner with the simple words "See you in court." Still, the White House appeared determined to move fast, and in the first anxious weeks it was hard to say how fast the opposition could mobilize in response.

Only two days after the wall order, both sides faced their first real test. In Executive Order 13769, the president announced the implementation of his promised "travel ban." Though it was extremely broad—barring entry to individuals from a list of seven majority-Muslim nations deemed sufficiently dangerous that even previously certified visa and green card holders could now be denied entry—the executive order was not as sweeping as suggested on the campaign trail, as it omitted the home nations of all of the 9/11 hijackers. The ban did apply to thousands who were in transit to the United States at the time of the announcement, with the effect that an unknown number of families were stuck in indefinite limbo. In the space of hours, crowds of protesters had gathered outside airports in New York, Los Angeles, and elsewhere. The frontline in the immigration battle had suddenly shifted from the borderlands to arrival halls and curbside pickup zones all over the country.

Inside, befuddled immigration officers found themselves saddled with vague and conflicting directives as to how to put the executive order into practice, leading to snafus up and down the bureaucratic ladder. So hasty had the new administration been to make good on its promise to shut the country off from the Muslim world, and so contemptuous was it of the ordinary processes of governance, that the ban had been subjected to only scanty legal review prior to its announcement. "The whole world will soon see," Stephen Miller told the media, that the president's authority on the issue "will not be questioned": It was evidently assumed that ban would simply *happen*, a frictionless process without a trace of bureaucratic or judicial interference. The shock value did cause immense consternation among immigrant advocates and the still nascent resistance movement. Yet in short order, it became evident that the White House had overreached. Less than twenty-four hours after the ban went into effect, a New York court issued a temporary restraining order that put things to a halt and allowed attorneys to step in; while the crowds at the airports rejoiced, the crisis only intensified, with some CBP representatives on the ground appearing to disregard the order—a constitutional breakdown happening in real time. Within a few days, however, the agency was toeing the line, just in time for another court to issue a more forceful injunction, suspending the ban nationwide.

The order was plainly meant to demonstrate the president's anti-immigration mettle, as well as his ability to manage the real-world operations of government. As to the latter, the failure to carry the policy through as drafted afforded some encouragement to pro-immigrant forces—though the chaos that attended this win could be in nowise comfiting: It was a sign that affairs were so out of control that there was no knowing where the next blow might land. The departures of high-ranking officials and the constant mixed signals about both policy and personnel prompted Senator John McCain to observe that "the whole environment is one of dysfunction." There was no clear path to the wall as yet. But amid so much confusion, and in a country where airports could turn overnight into battlegrounds, things could change very quickly.

Immediately after the election, Robert Ivy, the CEO of the American Institute of Architects, issued a statement on behalf of the building industry's most venerable trade group. "The AIA and its 89,000 members are committed to working with President-elect Trump to address the issues our country faces," Ivy wrote. "It is now time for all of us to work together to advance policies that help our country move forward." Ivy's intention, as the statement made clear, was to encourage the incoming administration to pursue the $500 billion infrastructure program that had been touted frequently during the campaign. His plea for cooperation was greeted with heckles from the profession. As one trade journal put it, "little mention was ever made by Trump, his surrogates, or his supporters for the 'investments in schools, hospitals, and other public infrastructure' that Ivy cites." The only specific infrastructure project the candidate had ever discussed was the wall. As design-build firms from all around the country made clear to the AIA, they wanted no part of it.

At least not at the time. Now that the new administration was in office, the chance that the wall might actually be built placed an uncomfortable moral onus on those who might be in a position to build it. On February 24, 2017, pursuant to the executive order from several weeks earlier, CBP posted a "pre-solicitation" for companies interested in securing contracts for "several prototype wall structures in the vicinity of the United States border with Mexico." Within days, the announcement elicited responses from nearly two hundred different architecture and construction firms, spread over almost every state in the union: For all the outrage directed at Ivy, rank-and-file contractors—most of them somewhat further down the professional food chain than the typical AIA membership—were evidently very willing to work on the project. Initial lists of the interested companies included mostly smaller outfits, some veteran-owned (a surprising number of them Latino-owned), some with extensive experience in defense-related work, others from well outside the government-contract mainstream. At least one name was well known in the industry, and within the AIA fold: Nebraska-based Leo A. Daly, a major player in public works for decades. The presence of the firm on the initial bidding lists was widely publicized, and it drew an outcry both from the media and from fellow professionals. Within days, the company's name had been withdrawn, along with that of another high-profile firm, defense contractor Raytheon.

Many other design companies expressed interest in the wall, albeit not in the way that CBP had intended. Miami architecture firm DOMO came out with a design for what it called a "sustainable, functional" wall, proposing the reuse of old shipping containers stacked in an artful jumble and enlivened with "fauna, flora, landscaping etc." The design team imagined housing and retail spaces occupying the structure, turning it from a barrier into an active space—not just a border, but a living part of the borderlands. "One of our goals was to not be like the Great Wall of China or the Berlin Wall or any of those typologies that represent division," the firm's Francisco Llado told Politico.com. The proposal was never formally submitted, after taking heavy flak from critics decrying any effort on the part of architects to "aestheticize" the wall.

The critiques did not put an end to such efforts. Throughout the spring of 2017, scads of fanciful proposals were turned out by architecture firms game to weigh in on the topic, and possibly even bid on the real contract. One imagined a futuristic "hyperloop" transit system (much like the one being pursued by SpaceX's Elon Musk) that would turn the border into a high-speed transit corridor; another envisaged two-way video feeds connecting people on either side. This was far from the first time that architects had trained their creative and critical faculties on the problem of the US-Mexico barrier: As early as 2006, during legislative debates over the Secure Fence Act, the *New York Times* canvassed ideas from thirteen architecture firms for a barrier with "more beauty" and "fewer barbs." While some prominent designers had sought to avoid the nettlesome issue altogether (Rick Scofidio, of celebrated New York firm Diller Scofidio + Renfro, told the *Times* that architects "might as well leave it to security and engineers"), others had made the border and its barriers their particular intellectual demesne, perhaps most prominently San Diego's Teddy Cruz, whose office had spent nearly a decade formulating various initiatives with an eye to creating a more humane, more culturally vibrant transnational zone.

Whether visionary or merely aestheticizing, few if any of these heady concepts would actually factor into the government's plan, which made little provision for careful, deliberative thinking. Working at a pace almost unthinkable for a government project (least of all one of this size), CBP's February 24 solicitation called for initial proposals to be submitted by March 10, with select firms to provide additional details including cost analysis only two weeks thereafter. A few weeks prior, Reuters had scored a sneak peek at an internal Department of Homeland Security report giving a projected completion date of 2020, with an expected total budget of $21.6 billion. While far over the $8- to $12-billion-dollar estimate thrown around the previous year by the then-candidate, the expedited timeline certainly made good on his insistence that his agenda would be executed "so fast." Even as opponents began to marshal their forces— the advocacy group Architecture Lobby organized a March 10 architects' walkout; even the AIA seemed to come around, condemning the partial Muslim ban—the wall's hasty production schedule seemed designed to keep it one step ahead of mounting protests.

If, that is, the schedule was kept. As the CBP's March 10 deadline rolled around, the agency announced it would be pushed back. Only the day before, the administration had revealed its first budget, requesting only $1.4 billion for the wall, enough to fund a hundred miles but little more; it also included a $560 million ask for improvements to existing fencing, a peculiar request if the much-derided barriers were soon to be rendered obsolete by a "great wall" (a phrase that appeared again in the first presidential address to Congress in late February). The project was simultaneously moving very fast and remaining stock-still.

At the border itself, things were quiet—quieter, it might be said, than they had been in a long time. While the disruptive new president wrought havoc in Washington, D.C., he could at least brag that his bull-in-a-china-shop routine appeared to produce a salutary effect on illegal immigration. By April 2017, monthly apprehension numbers at the border plunged from over sixty thousand to less than sixteen thousand, reaching their lowest levels in decades. "This is encouraging news," said then Secretary of Homeland Security John Kelly; whether it was attributable to the new administration was hard to quantify, but it did appear that would-be border crossers were thinking better of the journey in view of the political atmosphere on the other side. In a deeper sense, however, the bonds between the two countries only seemed to strengthen, with cross-border trade remaining robust amid the improving global economy. In Tijuana, the building of a brace of new condo developments to be aimed at price-weary San Diegans seeking cheaper accommodations south of the border was announced. "A lot of people are moving down," said the designer-developer of one of the largest projects, Alfonso Medina. The building opened as scheduled in 2017 and has been a resounding success.

One of the most anomalous spots on the US-Mexico border can be found near the foot of Mount Cristo Rey, in New Mexico, right by the western bank of the Rio Grande. There, in a sandy basin that used to be part of the river's (now much-reduced) floodplain, I found the pyramidal stump of Boundary Marker No. 1—the very first of the land monuments placed there in 1855 by the Emory-Salazar Commission. Refurbished in the twentieth century, it sits on a cement plinth next to the Casa de Adobe, the structure that served as the headquarters of anti-Díaz leader Francisco Madero in the early days of the Mexican Revolution. The house, preserved as a museum, lies on the Mexican side of the marker; on the American side, there is nothing, only a dirt road and a short slope with soft hills behind them. Although routinely patrolled by CBP, their presence was nowhere to be seen on a quiet weekday in October, and there was nothing to stop me from circling the monument, strolling in and out of the United States at will.

While this was once the customary state of affairs along most of the border, such spots—totally free of barriers, artificial or otherwise—are now very much the exception. A length of bollard fencing stops not far from the site, just across the river, and taking a train through the New Mexico desert I saw where it resumes, only a little way to the west, continuing in an unbroken line through the sable hills. This is what the "border" looks like now, and, even where it doesn't, the belief that it should is hard to shake: Walking around the marker, apparently unobserved, I felt a thrill of transgression each time I crossed and recrossed the line, the "unnaturalness" of such freedom thoroughly internalized.

Monument 1: Mexico in foreground; New Mexico at rear

Protests and marches notwithstanding, the American public had already come to accept the presence of a massive border barrier well before the wall, in its latest conception, had turned into an official policy point. In this regard, the Republican accusation frequently hurled at Democrats—that they had previously acquiesced to increased border infrastructure—

was entirely justified: The old fence had been a bipartisan venture and, having gone so far, there was some hypocrisy in trying to backpedal now. As if to concede the point, at least partially, the House of Representatives, with the votes of all but fifteen Democrats, agreed in early May 2017 to a Consolidated Spending Bill that included $1.5 billion for enhanced border security. It was enough to register as a qualified win, at least from the perspective of the soi-disant "winner." Via tweet, the president crowed that "we achieved the single largest increase in border security funding in 10 years."

It was a hollow boast. The money came with strings attached: It was explicitly earmarked for improvements to *current* infrastructures, not the building of a new one. The $20 million with which CBP was funding its prototypes had been drawn from existing departmental monies; with the congressionally imposed limits on how the new allocations were to be spent, CBP could not apply them to the prototype project. The spring spending fight inaugurated a pattern, one that would proceed to repeat itself over and over in different forms over the next year and beyond: Congress would engage in weeks of tedious back-and-forth over pending legislation, seeking compromise on various national priorities; the president would proceed to thunder that unless adequate wall funding were included, he would veto any bill, regardless of how laboriously assembled; Congress would then disregard these threats and send the bill to the White House undaunted. It would then be signed into law despite a modicum of grumbling from the signatory, mingled with claims that the setback was actually a victory.

The most formidable obstacle to financing the wall was not, as various conservative commentators insisted, "obstructionist Democrats." Within the Republican caucus itself, prominent legislators who had quietly declined to endorse the project were now digging in their heels. At what was described as a "binational, bilingual, and bipartisan" rally in the bordertown of Del Rio, Texas, in March, Republican Representative Will Hurd, whose district spans the longest stretch of border of any member of the House, spoke out against his party's officially stated border policy. "Building a wall from sea to shining sea is the most expensive and least effective way to do border security," said Hurd. He was not the only border representative to say so— regardless of party, borderland representatives were uniformly against the wall and declined to shut down the government in order to fund it. The inability of the Republicans to whip errant anti-wall members was consonant with their parliamentary struggles that spring and summer over repealing Obamacare, reducing spending, and increasing funding for infrastructure.

Failing with their own party, the White House in September sought to enlist Democrats, offering to restore the newly revoked Deferred Action for Childhood Arrival (DACA) program—the Obama-era initiative that provided prosecutorial relief to younger undocumented immigrants—in exchange for wall funding. As the negotiations dragged on, they widened to include possible legislation for a path to citizenship (the much-debated DREAM Act) as a trade-off for harsher enforcement against other undocumented immigrants; the compromise threatened to set one group of pro-immigrant forces against another, leaving anti-wall elements "divided and pitted against each other," as one Democratic legislator put it. Amid a flurry of near-deals, rumored deals, and retracted deals, the talks broke down in early autumn, followed by the familiar litany of recriminations as to why the consummate dealmaker-president had come up short yet again.

With the threat of a government shutdown ever present, the ongoing stalemate posed a legitimate danger, bringing the country to the edge of civic paralysis over and over. Yet the president's fulminations were so frequently shown up as pure theater that many doubted a shutdown over the wall would ever occur: "I don't think a government shutdown's necessary," House Speaker Paul Ryan stated in late August 2017, "and I don't think most people want to see a government shutdown, ourselves included." Republicans would eventually change their tune—though by the time the shutdown finally came four months later, the public had become so accustomed to the possibility that the fact had lost most of its dark novelty. Familiarity bred indifference, and, what with the interminable disarray on Capitol Hill and the stream of deceptive statements issuing from the Oval Office, the confusion surrounding the wall became almost routine.

This did not mean that the project was stalled (at least not yet). On the contrary, the repetitious and obscure brinksmanship over the wall's funding adhered to a certain political logic. "Confusion," in the words of political theorist Hannah Arendt, can "make possible swift and surprising changes in policy"—a diet of consistent inconsistency rendering "the body politic of the country . . . shock-proof." If the White House was deliberately pursuing what some termed a "chaos strategy," or if it had only happened on it by accident, the approach still gave them room to maneuver. Sufficiently acclimated to fear and arbitrariness, Americans might stop noticing that there was anything strange about what was happening with the border and border politics, or simply forget that things had ever been very different.

Flying in the face of critics wary of aestheticizing the wall project, artists of all descriptions continued to grapple with the subject. In the city, painter Enrique Chiu, who had already produced murals on fencing around Tijuana, vowed to do the same for the entire border should a two-thousand-mile wall be built: "If Trump gives me the canvas," Chiu told the media, "I will paint it." In Hollywood, on the Walk of Fame, a street artist with the moniker Plastic Jesus erected a tiny cement wall around the star belonging to the former reality TV personality. Another improbably named Angeleno, Phil America, traveled to El Paso, cut a hole in a section of chain-link border infrastructure, brought it home, and had it gold-plated, a tribute to the glitter-loving POTUS.

Were these acts of artistry effective forms of protest? Surely they were not likely to stop the wall from being built, and, however inadvertently, they may only have added another ring to the circus that border politics (to say nothing of American life in general) had turned into. There were real protests as well, including actions by figures in government: Several city councils, among them those of Berkeley and Oakland, California, passed statutes that forbade awarding any government contract to companies involved in the wall's construction; in El Paso, Mayor Oscar Leeser crossed the border to join a "human chain" with thousands of wall protesters. On the border, demonstrations were frequent—including one in Sunland Park, New Mexico, only a few minutes' drive from Border Monument No. 1, where activists and churchmen gathered for a demonstration in October 2017. One of them, Reverend Dr. William J. Barber II, had traveled there from North Carolina, and he told the crowd that the United States "had the nerve to go over to Germany, and rightfully so, and send the president there who said, 'Tear down this wall.' America loses her moral authority unless we unite together [to] say tear down this wall, as well."

Actions like these helped to fuel support for the legal challenges that had kept the Muslim ban at bay, and they swelled in attendance and frequency, with anti-wall messages cropping up in demonstrations not even directly connected with the project: At a rally shortly after the election, several attendees carried signs reading "Can't Build Wall, Hands Too Small"; another picket, at the massive Women's March the following January, blared "Build the Wall Around Trump." Over its first riotous year, the resistance, now fully gelled, had carried out a sustained campaign to amplify every break from White House precedent, every instance of erratic behavior. But the results were mixed. Even the Muslim ban had, by the fall of 2017, been re-crafted on narrower terms and was making its way through the courts again.

Autumn wore on with a benumbed sameness. Presidential approval moved little or not at all, as did support for the wall. Reports of accelerating deportations of longtime residents and sometimes inhuman treatment of apprehended immigrants did not seem to put a damper on the appetite of most Republicans for further crackdowns on immigration; neither did the by-now obvious fact that Mexico, as its former president Vincente Fox put it, was "not going to pay for that fucking wall" or that the price for American taxpayers would be cripplingly high, with some estimates pointing to a cost of nearly $25 million per mile. In November 2017, as off-year elections showed Republicans still rallying to the presidential banner, political pundit Andrew Sullivan declared in a *New York* magazine headline that "Democrats Are Failing the Resistance," with elected leadership either unable or unwilling to translate all the sound and fury into meaningful results. With DACA and the DREAM Act still being dangled as potential prizes, there were some signs of softening among segments of the Democratic coalition on the possibility of wall funding. Talking with his colleagues across the aisle, one Republican lawmaker insisted there "are a lot of positive conversations taking place. Are we there? No. Can we get there? We have to."

If the wall was becoming more imaginable, it was hard to see what further steps its enemies could take to reframe it as something beyond the pale. On a narrow party-line vote, the House Homeland Security Committee voted in October 2017 to provide $10 billion in funding for the wall; though the bill stood little chance of passage, it showed congressional Republicans were still prepared to go on the record in support of the project, leaving the panel's ranking minority member to fume that "there was a time in the not too far distant past when this committee cared for facts." While monthly border apprehensions still remained at historic lows, they began to creep back up from their post-election trough, and the small bump in numbers only served to fuel more fevered action from the executive branch, with Attorney General Jeff Sessions lobbying Congress in October to ask for increased authority to turn away asylum seekers and their families.

And still the critical artworks and satirical broadsides kept coming, each hoping to somehow prick the conscience of the nation and stop the momentum of events once and for all. Shortly after the one-year anniversary of the election, the makers of the popular board game Cards Against Humanity announced an initiative to buy land near the border, with the idea that they would then refuse to allow the wall to be built on it. (It wasn't much of a plan: Eminent domain and the original executive order would be able to override any such claims.) In December, joining the already-crowded field of outrageous conceptual hijinks—the Wall of Hammocks and Wall of Pipe Organs proposed by Pittsburgh's JM Design Studio; the suggestion from artist Luis Camnitzer that Christo and Jeanne-Claude be allowed to design the wall—Swiss-Icelandic artist Christoph Büchel began to petition the federal government to mark the site of CBP's wall prototypes as "a national monument under the Antiquities Act of 1906." Meant as a deadpan critique, the joke seemed to fall flat, though by that time all such intellectual exercises had been rendered moot. Nothing, no philosophical takedown or high-flown happening, could quite measure up to the imminent reality of the prototypes themselves, now complete and standing in the desert south of San Diego.

VI

THE RETURN OF THEM

WEST BANK

East Jerusalem, from the Mount of Olives

Ralph Bunche's first impression of Jerusalem was not a promising one. The city, he wrote, "is like an armed camp," with "troops, barricades, barbed wire" at every turn. It was June 1947, and Bunche, a forty-three-year-old American diplomat, among the first African Americans in history to occupy a senior diplomatic post, had come to participate in his first-ever peace mission abroad, taking up a diplomatic burden that had already been shrugged off by a mighty empire. Its most famous spokesman, the indefatigable Winston Churchill, had declared the entire enterprise nothing but "bloodshed, odium, trouble and worry."

The twenty-four-member United Nations Special Committee on Palestine (UNSCOP), to which Bunche was seconded as special assistant, was faced with an intractable dilemma. In a narrow strip of land between the Mediterranean and the Jordan River, governed (barely) as a British protectorate since the 1920s, two groups were facing off for control: On the one hand, more than half a million Jews, many of them refugees from Europe, increasingly well-armed and implacable in their national aspirations; on the other, more than a million Palestinian Arabs, most of whom had dwelled in the area for centuries under perpetual subjugation—first by the Ottomans, then by the British—and who were equally adamant in their demands for unfettered self-rule. With Britain looking to make an exit, Bunche and the UN team, which included representatives from eleven countries, were charged with designing a future for the troubled region. "One thing seems sure," Bunche wrote in his diary. "Reality is that both Arabs and Jews are here and intend to stay." His words seem prophetic.

Equally farsighted was Bunche's conclusion. "This problem can't be solved on the basis of abstract justice, historical or otherwise," the diplomat wrote, forecasting the UN team's ultimate approach to the situation—a tough-minded, technocratic solution that tried to deal fairly and frankly with the situation on the ground. Using recent British surveys of the population of Palestine, the UNSCOP team worked frantically to map out the disposition of cities and farms. Taking in the history, demographics, and economics of individual communities as well as of the territory as a whole, the group tried to reconcile the competing claims of the adversaries; they spoke or attempted to speak with leaders on both sides, finding themselves variously courted (primarily by Jewish settlers) and rebuffed (by Arab leadership) as factions in both camps sought to either win them over or send them packing. "The longer we stay here," Bunche wrote, "the more confused all of us get." Things only became more confusing as more and more Jews arrived from postwar Europe, and as political alliances in the Arab world fractured and re-formed. All through a hot Mediterranean summer, amid rising tensions and outbursts of sectarian violence, the UN team labored on.

In September, after only two and a half months, they presented their recommendations to the world. "Partition," declared the report written by Bunche, "is the only means available by which political and economic responsibility can be placed squarely on both Arabs and Jews." Of the eleven members, seven declared themselves in favor of separating the land of Palestine into two states under a common customs union. The physical outline of these twinned nations would be unlike almost any other in the modern world: Because Jewish settlement over the course of the foregoing forty years (and more) had occurred in fits and starts, according to no regular pattern, it was all but impossible to carve out contiguous, geographically separate spheres without massive displacements. Instead, the UNSCOP team proposed that the two countries occupy territories that wound through and around each other.

Based on the committee's study, with some emendations from another UN committee, a final map was proposed. The pockets of Jewish land in the far northwest near the Lebanese border, along the central western coastline, and the scattered communities throughout the south would be consolidated into a single state. The Palestinians, who enjoyed a larger but even more diffuse population, would maintain their traditional strongholds in Gaza, in the city of Jaffa near the new Jewish hub of Tel Aviv, and in the central swath from Jerusalem through the Judaean Hills to Jericho. Both would be obliged to abandon land they had hoped to claim as theirs—the Jews in the Jordan River Valley, the Arabs in the southern Negev Desert. Connecting the disjoined segments of each state would be extraterritorial roadways, available to both but belonging to neither, while Jerusalem, the great prize, was to be declared a separate body, governed under UN mandate. It was far from a simple solution. But for Bunche, who had been responsible for writing the initial draft report, it seemed enough to put the matter to rest. "The Palestine episode is over," he wrote.

On that score, he was tragically wrong. UN resolution 181(II) divided the former British protectorate of Palestine into what would become Israel and the Palestinian territories, setting off a conflict that would draw in the entire region. Notwithstanding the idealism of its framers, the partition was only the last in a long sequence of geopolitical gerrymanders that had seen the Middle East cut up into modern nation-states, a process that had produced at least as many problems as it solved, breeding new hostilities out of the old. In the postwar years, different kinds of national settlements (between India and Pakistan and between North and South Korea) would attempt the same thing elsewhere, yielding little better. None was to be so star-crossed as the division of Palestine, where geography, religion, and ethnic identity all conspired against the success of the two-state solution.

Over the following fifty years, through multiple wars, foreign interventions, failed peace initiatives, and atrocities on both sides, the state of Israel progressively expanded, while an independent Palestinian state failed to materialize—its territory whittled away, its people confined to towns and refugee camps in the western and eastern portions of the initial UNSCOP proposal. The former would be known as the Gaza Strip, a 140-square-mile corridor pressed hard against the Mediterranean seaboard; the other, the West Bank, assumed a more nebulous shape, a reversed *C* clamped around Jerusalem, the city claimed by Israel as its future capital. In the mid-1990s, under the terms of the Oslo Accords, the bulk of both areas was placed under the nominal control of the Palestinian Authority (PA), responsible for the civil affairs of the internal Arab population though still subject to the de facto military and commercial supremacy of Israel. This was understood to be a temporary condition only, pending a final resolution that would at last realize the dream of a sovereign Palestine living at peace alongside its Jewish neighbor. At the tail end of the Clinton years, it seemed that such a resolution really was imminent, with negotiations ongoing between the PA leader Yasser Arafat and Israeli prime minister Ehud Barack. Summoned to Camp David in 2000, the two appeared poised to put to rest the outstanding disagreements—Jewish settlements in Palestinian lands; the right of exiled Palestinians to return to the country; measures against anti-Israeli terrorists—that had so long divided them. The premature tickertape parade that had greeted Ralph Bunche on his return to New York would finally be qualified by success. And it very nearly was.

For a decade and more after the fall of the Berlin Wall, those who were (it was presumed) in a position to know were of the near-unanimous persuasion that the world was drawing closer together. Nations of both the East and West were hurtling along a trajectory that carried them further and further from any need to separate themselves by such clumsy instruments as physical barriers. Looking back at the millennial moment, one theorist would later write that "the common conviction is that globalization signifies the end of walls"—and indeed it briefly seemed that digital technology, together with what philosopher Francis Fukuyama deemed the "unabashed victory of economic and political liberalism," would make wall-building irrelevant. What few walls remained were bound to either fall or at the very most be enshrined, like China's and Britain's, as relics.

Three harried months in the Middle East were all it took to start unwinding that optimistic consensus. With the failure of the Camp David talks, hostilities between Palestinian militants and the Israel Defense Forces (IDF) escalated precipitously in the fall of 2000. The Second Intifada, a sequel to the Palestinian uprising of the previous decade, saw mass resistance against the Israeli occupation in both the West Bank and Gaza, with everything from stones to Qassam rockets striking both military and civilian targets throughout Israel. At the same time, the IDF launched airstrikes and special forces raids in the territories, all while imposing new restrictive measures upon millions of Palestinians. In the first month alone, nearly 150 Palestinians and a dozen Israelis died in a spasm of sectarian fighting. Vanished was the hope of the summer, swamped by the same tide of violence and recrimination that had engulfed every previous attempt at reconciliation since the days of Ralph Bunche and the UN.

Only this time there was a new element. Since the mid-1990s, a fence had divided the Gaza Strip from Israel; pursuant to the Oslo Accords, its intention was to create what then-Israeli prime minister Yitzhak Rabin had referred to as a "physical mechanism for peace." Sealing in all but the oceanfront and the border with Egypt, the fence would eventually grow to include two layers, one containing sensors and other "smart" features, the other a simple one of barbed wire; at thirty-two miles in length, it was easy enough to build, especially for a security apparatus as developed as Israel's. Rabin convened a team to explore the option of a similar barrier for the West Bank, but the idea was peremptorily dropped. The West Bank had a much longer border, 250 miles at the time of the Camp David talks, as well as a far larger population, nearly two million to Gaza's one. The difficulties of erecting such a barrier were obvious.

Now things were different. Under the pressure of the Second Intifada, the estimated $300 million cost of a West Bank barrier no longer seemed so daunting; neither did domestic opposition, which had previously been robust both on the left—where the idea provoked comparisons to repressive regimes like East Germany's—and on the right—where religious Jewish settlers feared a barrier as a potential impediment to further expansion. Barak had mooted the notion of a comprehensive West Bank border infrastructure during the Camp David talks, and in the wake of their collapse the prime minister embraced the idea outright (along with 84 percent of Israeli Jews, according to contemporary polling). In November 2000 the government authorized the construction of a barrier near the strategic hilltop of Latrun.

"When there are seventy dead Israelis, you can resist the fence," Barak told his successor, Ariel Sharon. "When there are 700 dead Israelis, you will not be able to resist it." Sharon had been among the right-wing critics of the idea, but on assuming office he began to embark on the total enclosure of the West Bank. By July 2003, the first eighty-five miles of infrastructure were complete, running from the town of Salem in the north to Elkana due east of Tel Aviv; within months, the government approved another 267 miles. In time, the barrier would run to almost twice that length, winding all the way around the territory to within striking distance of the Dead Sea. Its route was chosen by the IDF on the basis of what it deemed strategic necessity, a course that rarely cohered with the last mutually agreed-upon boundary, the line of the 1949 armistice that ended the First Arab-Israeli War. Over 14 percent of what had lately been Palestinian territory now sat on the west side of the barrier, creating a "seam" between the fence and the notional border—from which Palestinians were excluded barring special permission—along with assorted fingers of walled-off territory extending deep into the heart of the West Bank, usually for the defense of Israeli settlements.

Nowhere would this path be more tortuous and bewildering than in the areas around the sacred city of Jerusalem. It was here that the barrier took on its most iconic expression: Though much of the West Bank's infrastructure, like Gaza's, consists of various layers of metal fencing, the primary material found in the more populated sections is concrete, laid in thick vertical slabs up to twenty-seven feet high and four feet wide. Anxieties about sniper fire in Jewish-held communities around Israel's self-declared capital pushed the IDF to opt for the taller, less permeable structure; despite the added practical and financial hurdles (the modules are manufactured in the Negev Desert, trucked onto the site and then lowered in by crane), they would eventually come to account for at least 3 percent of the barrier. They have become a metonym for the whole enterprise of separation and occupation, an object of ire for Israel's critics around the world: "This ghastly racist wall," as the Palestinian-born critic Edward Said called it; "the menacing symbol of Israeli domination," according to border scholar Christine Leuenberger.

Just when the world had thought itself rid of walls, this new one showed that the idea still had life in it. Although President George W. Bush had originally rejected the idea—"It is very difficult to develop confidence . . . with a wall snaking through the West Bank," he said in 2003—within a year the official position of the United States had changed to one of acceptance. The United Nations remained opposed, but the Israeli High Court, after demanding changes to the wall's route to lessen its impact on Palestinians, ultimately found that the wall was, as the IDF insisted, a matter of domestic security, and therefore not subject to international adjudication. Bolstering the argument in the global arena, Israel could point to solid statistical evidence that its wall had worked: Between April and December of 2002, the Foreign Ministry stated that seventeen suicide bomber attacks had been launched from within the northern West Bank. In 2003, that number dropped to five.

Those figures would fluctuate from year to year. But for those Israelis who still had reservations about the wall, the change was enough to mollify most of them. The citizens of Israel enjoyed ancillary benefits as well: Alongside the walls, shielded by them in many places, a whole new set of roadways wound through the West Bank serving mostly (or exclusively) Israeli traffic, with only cars bearing the yellow-and-black Israel license plates allowed to travel on them. Together with the permit system that allowed Palestinians only limited access to their lands in the seam zone, the roadways became part of a vast new social and political superstructure that descended over the territory, fitted loosely to the framework of the Oslo Accords and creating a new kind of state-within-a-state, an Israel-in-Palestine. In its bureaucratic complexity, to say nothing of its geographical convolutions, this new system showed what was really possible for walls in the new millennium. It also brought with it a whole new nexus of contradictions and absurdities, supercharged for the twenty-first century, but recalling in many respects the paradoxes that have beset walls since time immemorial.

I had seen the West Bank barrier once before, on my first-ever trip abroad as a design journalist nearly a decade ago. Having been invited by the Israeli Foreign Ministry, I was then under the watchful eye of government minders who kept me far enough from the wall that I could not see any of the spray-painted slogans that already—only eight years after construction had begun—adorned the sides of structure, the work of protesters from both Palestine and abroad. This time, traveling on my own, I was determined to see it up close, all the more so since (as Israeli and American media had amply documented) so much of the recent graffiti has been aimed at the United States.

Pictures of Donald Trump and Israel's Benjamin Netanyahu locked in a fraternal kiss (recalling a famous work on the Berlin Wall featuring Honecker and Soviet premier Leonid Brezhnev); an image of the president reverently touching the wall, with a thought bubble declaring "I'm going to build you a brother" and another in which he appeared to be copulating with a guard tower: Anti-occupation activists perceived a clear link between the United States' border policy and Israel's—as well they might. In January 2017, Netanyahu had tweeted his approval of the American wall, saying that "President Trump is right. I built a wall along Israel's southern border. It stopped all illegal immigration. Great success. Great idea." (The "southern" wall he was referring to is a large fence between Israel and Egypt, completed in 2013.) Returning the compliment, the prime minister's American counterpart said on Fox News, "All you have to do is ask Israel. They were having a total disaster coming across and they had a wall. It's 99.9 percent stoppage." (Where the number came from, or which of Israeli's several barriers he had in mind, was not clear.) American and Israeli security forces have a long history of cooperation: Elbit Systems, an Israeli defense contractor, had been a player in fencing efforts on the US-Mexico border in the 2000s; at CBP's Otay Mesa border headquarters, I spotted mementos from a visit there by an Israeli border-enforcement delegation. Yet the affinity also invited an obvious, and to the administration unwelcome, comparison. Would the American wall, if built, become a similar lightning rod for discontent? How long before it too would be covered in graffiti?

All the more imperative, I thought, that I see the West Bank barrier up close, in all its paint-spackled wonder. I did see it, several miles of it—though not quite in the manner I'd meant to. Misunderstandings abound in the West Bank, and the one that interceded here was as telling, in its way, as anything that might be gathered from looking at the concrete slabs or the cartoons that cover them.

Only the day after my encounter at Jericho, I traveled to a town north of Ramallah. There I spent the better part of the evening negotiating with my Palestinian hosts to find a driver willing to take me up to and around the barrier outside East Jerusalem, only an hour's journey to the southwest. In the morning, my driver appeared and we set out. Only moments into our ride, he insisted on changing cars. It didn't occur to me to ask why.

The road between Ramallah and Jerusalem is sprinkled with concrete guard towers behind fenced-in enclosures and the elevated pillboxes used by IDF troops to track cars along the road. Most of these date to the years immediately following the outbreak of the Second Intifada; the reduction in terrorist attacks in the years since has meant that troops have been pulled back from some of these positions, leaving them temporarily idle. The empty installations, still marked with banners in Hebrew, have become just one more component in the defensive landscape that can be seen along the highways: landing strips and vehicle depositories, training areas and communication beacons. Most obtrusively, there are the Israeli settlements, banal-looking suburban developments with red-roofed houses, in many instances surrounded by portions of concrete wall.

It slowly dawned on me, as we approached Jerusalem, that the roads we were following south of Ramallah were better than the ones I had traveled up from Jericho and that the traffic was heavier. The surrounding hills were crowned with more and more settlements, and among the cars on the road there was an increasing number of IDF vehicles. I knew that there were different roads available to Palestinians and Israelis, but the lines between them, and between the different zones in the West Bank (three in all, as per the Oslo Accords, of which only two are open to Palestinians), are nearly impossible to discern in a fast-moving car. It wasn't until we reached the outskirts of Jerusalem that it became clear: My driver, though he kept a home in the West Bank, was not a Palestinian. As he presently (and haltingly) explained, he was born in East Jerusalem and held Israeli citizenship. In changing cars, we had cast aside the green-and-white PA tags for Israeli ones, and we were now hurtling down Israeli roads, threading our way through the dusty landscape by way of this unnatural circulatory system, this legal fiction made real. Against all my entreaties of the night before, he was driving me directly into Israeli-held East Jerusalem, in the mistaken belief that that was what I wanted to see.

The partition of Palestine, as chaotic in execution as it was problematic in conception, left over 150,000 non-Jews within the borders of the new nation, mostly Arab Muslim; tens of thousands more were added with the seizure of East Jerusalem during the 1967 Six-Day War. While the latter group was offered citizenship, few of them elected to take it, viewing it as an unseemly recognition of an invading power. My driver's family was among those who had, and he was therefore free to travel on whatever roads he wanted, to enter and leave Israel at will with no more scrutiny than any other citizen. This despite the fact that he shared the same faith, the same language, and much the same history as the millions of people against whom the wall had been built.

Such is the central paradox of Israel. The liberal and secular aspirations of its founders have always sat uneasily alongside the nationalist and religious impulses of their doctrine, and the contradiction has only become more jarring as the regional crisis has dragged on and as the Israeli security state has become more all-consuming. Today, despite the wall and all that has come with it, Arab Israelis (by whatever moniker they prefer to be called, be it Israeli Palestinian or Muslim Israeli) make up 20 percent or more of Israel's population. They participate in most aspects of Israel's national life; in Arab-majority cities like Umm al-Fahm, standing just on the Israeli side of the West Bank barrier, polling has suggested that 83 percent preferred to remain Israeli citizens rather than be traded to the PA as part of a comprehensive land-for-peace deal. Around the Holy City, the number of Arab residents of Israel are closer to 35 percent—though at present they receive a disproportionately small share of municipal services such as garbage pickup and street cleaning.

In both East Jerusalem and the surrounding West Bank, many residents now find themselves separated from their jobs and from family members by the barrier. And so, while that day thousands would try to pass through the wall at heavily guarded gates—some only to be turned away, others to be let through after an hours-long wait that could entail harsh treatment from IDF personnel with bulky machine guns—my driver and I cruised along a well-paved thoroughfare, past what looked like a small toll plaza, and into Israel, with soldiers waving at us. For all I saw of the wall from the West Bank side—curling around the hilltop settlements, looming over small Palestinian holdings and Bedouin camps—the closest I came was in passing through it. Closer than that, my driver would not go. Leaving Jerusalem the way we came in, I suggested over and over that we stop in one of the wall-adjacent Palestinian towns nearby; each time he turned the question aside with a squint. It is possible he didn't understand me. It is also possible that he did not wish to be seen in a Palestinian community behind the wheel of an Israeli car.

In the West Bank, every encounter is charged with some potential alternate meaning, some hidden significance that may or may not be waiting to disclose itself. Crossing the border from Jordan, a Ramallah-based businessman I'd befriended had had his luggage go temporarily missing while passing through the Israeli border crossing: It might have been an honest mistake on the part of the baggage handlers or it might have been a deliberate act of harassment by the IDF security personnel. And what about the traffic stop on the road near Ramallah? Two empty cars on the highway were sitting in the middle of an intersection, and armed IDF guards, as well as what appeared to be members of the Palestinian Security Services, were looking into every vehicle as it approached. Was this the scene of an accident or of an incident? Was it both? The night before I left the West Bank, I sat up late turning these mysteries over and over in my mind, along with what had happened in Jericho. The questions only dilated under scrutiny, the puzzle getting larger and larger, until it took in everything that had happened since 1947 and before. The scenes spun round and round, and they would not stop.

CONTROL

A few days after the official completion of the wall prototypes, I traveled to Southern California to see them for the first time. The somewhat understaffed CBP media apparatus had been racing to keep up with surging demand for access to the site, as journalists from all over the world rushed to get a glimpse of what the administration had wrought in a patch of brush thirteen miles from the Pacific Ocean. Around the building site, television crews bustled, drones buzzed, photographers crouched: The border agency had pulled off a true public relations coup, and the agents on hand exuded a cautious pride. Considering how the process had gone thus far, they could count themselves lucky for having anything to show at all.

They were faced from the outset with an awesome conundrum. Under the terms set out by Congress—first in the May 2017 appropriations bill and reiterated thereafter in subsequent legislation—the funds accorded to the agency for the construction of new infrastructure would, as one such bill asserted, "only be available for operationally effective designs deployed as of [January] 2017 . . . such as currently deployed steel bollard designs." This categorically ruled out any of the bold proposals, be it high-speed transit line or converted shipping containers, that had been circulated in the media by designers both serious and otherwise for the border. It also placed the agency in a statutory bind: On the one hand, CBP was obligated to carry out the executive order for "the immediate construction of a physical wall"; on the other, they were forbidden from claiming that the competition would produce anything that would result in such a wall being built. For official purposes, the prototypes were being constructed for no other purpose than to construct prototypes.

From there on out, nothing about the process was straightforward. In May, after weeks of delay, the agency at last declared that it had tapped approximately twenty finalists from among the two hundred competition entrants. The announcement was the first sign that the project was gaining traction in the real world, and the qualifying companies were slated to begin building the prototypes in a matter of weeks. Yet by July, CBP had disclosed no further information regarding the short-listed companies. The only name publicly associated with the project was that of Dennis O'Leary, the founder and CEO of DarkPulse Technologies in Scottsdale, Arizona. O'Leary had identified himself and his firm to local news outlets as being among the finalists, the sole individual to do so. Why DarkPulse (the makers of a fiber optic system used in one of the joint bids) had been selected, and what would happen next, was unclear, even to a finalist. "It's been—I don't want to say the word 'confusing,'" O'Leary said of the process.

No other word, however, seemed half as apt. The confusion was in no way dispelled by two other finalists who came forward shortly thereafter. The first was Jim Knott Jr., CEO of metals manufacturer Riverdale Mills, a Northbridge, Massachusetts, company specializing in the fabrication of wire mesh for lobster, crab, and oyster pots. Not the typical background for a future border-wall builder perhaps—though Knott would point out that his firm, like O'Leary's, was only one member of a larger collaborative team and that their proprietary material had been used in previous defensive walls, including ones in California and Arizona stemming from the 2006 Secure Fence Act. Having been elevated to the second phase of the border competition, Knott's firm was then trying to produce "a more in-depth proposal that includes production projections, a list of key personnel, pricing," he said. But even as Riverdale forged ahead, its chief remained unsure as to what CBP was truly looking for or when Riverdale might receive the green light to construct its prototype.

The other finalist, who asked that his name be withheld, was blunter by far. As he put it, "It's been a real mess." In more than three decades of soliciting and executing large-scale government construction projects, including multiple structures along the southern border, the anonymous contractor said he had never seen a bidding process so chaotic and rudderless.

"The lack of coordination, the lack of funding—they're just not ready for prime time."

First on the list of befuddlements: Why weren't the identities of all the finalists made public? In most government design-build competitions (particularly those held by the General Services Administration, responsible for most major federal building projects), transparency is key. The wall competition, by contrast, was taking place in a black box. According to CBP representative Carlos Diaz, this was mostly for the sake of fairness. "The companies are competing, providing designs that are going to be proprietary," Diaz said. "We want there to be equal opportunity for them to present without any intervention." But if that were so, why were O'Leary and Knott able to announce their status voluntarily—and why had no one else done the same? The anonymous stage-two bidder said the agency strongly hinted to him that silence would be "advisable," though CBP officials did not have contestants sign a formal nondisclosure agreement. O'Leary's decision to announce his status had made him the focus of a media maelstrom and put him on a bad footing with his hoped-for client. "I've been skirting the edge on this," he said.

The refusal on the part of Department of Homeland Security to issue a gag order was itself baffling. If the project was meant to be under wraps, why not say so to the participants? Then again, to do so would have flown in the face of the administration's bombastic pronouncements about their unstoppable progress on the border. Between a curious public and a demanding White House, CBP was left by itself to navigate the treacherous bureaucratic and economic waters.

All through the spring of 2017, the agency was still insisting on a June start date for construction. Come July, that date was jettisoned, with officials saying that ground would be broken before the end of the summer. Keeping to that schedule would largely hinge on how many prototype segments were actually going to be built—which was also still unknown, even mere weeks before the promised groundbreaking. While the twenty finalists from the initial list were still "under consideration," the agency was hoping to reduce that figure to "four to eight," according to Ronald Vitiello, deputy commissioner of the CBP.

That degree of selectivity did not mean that CBP was applying rigorous aesthetic or engineering standards. There were, as became evident, rather more mundane technical reasons for the rapid winnowing of entrants: The competition was split into two parts, one for concrete contractors and another for other material providers; some contractors had joined forces with like-minded competitors from the other category. The anonymous finalist pointed to still other, less routine factors. Among them, he said, "There have been threats"—the contentious character of the wall project had attracted intense criticism, and some of the twenty entrants backed out for fear of commercial or even physical reprisals. That, no doubt, was a further reason for CBP's secrecy, as was the potential embarrassment that might ensue once the press started looking into the finalists' backgrounds: One bidder, not in the finalist group (luckily, for the agency), was subsequently revealed to be a multiple felon and was implicated in the bombing of a Minnesota mosque later that year. (Notably, his firm's design had been an explicit homage to the Great Wall of China.)

The White House was the scene of a rolling staff crisis—in July, Chief of Staff Reince Priebus was replaced by John Kelly, and Press Secretary Sean Spicer stepped down after Anthony Scaramucci was named communications director, a position he would hold for only eleven days, during which he made a particularly vulgar on-the-record statement about Steve Bannon, who himself was fired on August 18. This instability, and the administration's frequent public embarrassments, cast a pall over the project, giving contractors more reason to worry about staying the course. The $20 million of CBP discretionary funds set aside for prototype construction meant that O'Leary, Knott, and their colleagues would likely see some compensation for their efforts; but the anonymous finalist was doubtful that the prototype fee would do more than stop his firm's financial bleeding. "I don't think we'll ever see a profit on this," he said.

So what would happen once the prototypes were complete? That was also a mystery. With no congressional funding, there was no promise that any of the eight finalists (or seven, or six, or however many it would be) would receive a fully funded contract for the border wall or that their prototypes would do anything but sit in the desert indefinitely, serving as a onetime photo-op for the president. The participants understood this, as did many figures in government, but the president, to all appearances, did not, and all summer long he sounded off on ambitious ideas that had already been removed from consideration. As the competition limped along, the president spoke out in favor of a solar panel–clad wall that could "pay for itself" by feeding energy back into the grid. Though he suggested he had had the idea himself, a similar proposal had been submitted in the competition, and it was not practicable: As the anonymous finalist observed, the cost of cleaning some three thousand linear miles of photovoltaics would be astronomical. So why was the president of the United States endorsing the idea? "Donald Trump," said the finalist, "is a fucking idiot."

"Obsession" may be the word that most accurately describes the feelings harbored for the wall by its most prominent supporter. Journalists aboard Air Force One could expect regular harangues on the topic; so too supporters at big arena rallies, golf partners, dining companions at Mar-a-Lago, and anyone else within earshot. As the construction of prototypes began in September 2017, the issue began to spill over into areas of policymaking far beyond immigration. During a White House meeting in September, a mixed group of Democratic and Republican politicians from around the New York area came to plead their case with the executive branch in support of the Gateway Program, a long-stalled effort to expand and renovate the dangerously decrepit railway corridor between Newark, New Jersey, and New York City. With senators, representatives, and governors in the room, the self-described "great builder" recommitted the federal government to funding the project—yet afterward, he asked Senate Minority Leader Chuck Schumer to stay behind, informing him that not a single dollar would go to Gateway until Democrats consented to additional wall funding. Schumer declined, and within weeks the White House launched an all-out assault on Gateway, trying to claw back money after the Republicans passed an appropriations bill that included it. "He thinks it would be a beautiful thing," remarked one source, "but only if it gets him the wall."

At last, on the final day of August 2017, CBP pulled the curtain back and disclosed the names of the firms selected to build the prototypes. There were only four to start, and those just for prototypes made of concrete; the following week, contracts were awarded to four mixed-material designs, two of them from the same firms as the first list, making a total of eight prototypes from six companies. It was reported that each received a payment of between $300,000 and $500,000 for the work—as modest a sum as the anonymous finalist had feared and which he himself would not actually receive: None of the finalists who had previously come forward were among the selected group.

The companies that did receive the nod were of comparable profile. First on the list was Caddell Construction of Montgomery, Alabama. One of the double-awardees, slated to produce prototypes in both categories, Caddell was far from a mom-and-pop operation, with more than three decades in the construction business and a portfolio that ranged from a desalination plant on a remote desert island to portions of the US embassy compound in Kabul, Afghanistan. The firm had also been the subject of multiple citations and reprimands, nearly facing formal debarment— permanent exclusion from government contracting—on several occasions; in one instance, the firm had fraudulently claimed additional payments due to Native American–owned contractors. Legal entanglements had also dogged a second competitor with a double bid, W. G. Yates & Sons Construction, a prolific public- and private-sector builder from Philadelphia, Mississippi: Among its embarrassments was one episode in which a scaffold in front of a hospital project collapsed and injured four workers. (When one of them sued, Yates claimed that the individual did not have standing because he was not a United States citizen. The court disagreed.) Then there was Fisher Sand & Gravel, winner in the concrete category, a vertically integrated, materials-and-machinery giant from Arizona that was identified by the independent Project on Government Oversight as the recipient of more than two thousand violation notices.

Rounding out the list were Texas Sterling Construction Company of Houston and, in the Other Materials category, Arizona's KWR Construction and Maryland's Elta North America. That last name is particularly eye-catching for those familiar with the tight-knit world of defense contracting. Elta's usual specialty is sophisticated systems like radar and surveillance, making their inclusion among so many brick-and-mortar construction companies somewhat surprising. As a category, "Other Materials" was willfully vague; was it possible Elta's design included embedded sensors or other high-tech gear? Even more remarkable is the company's provenance. Though its US offices are in Annapolis, Elta is actually an import: The company is a subsidiary of Israel Aerospace Industries, a major manufacturer of weapons and military technology headquartered in the city of Lod.

The fact that the company is, of all things, Israeli—the political significance of that choice, and its potential ramifications—went almost unnoticed in the ensuing rush to complete the prototypes. By the end of September, at the designated site in California, ground was broken—or rather opened: Most of the fabrication would be taking place offsite, with the modular units trucked to the desert where backhoes would excavate the foundations (as per the brief, prototypes had to be embedded no less than six feet beneath the ground); hefty buttress-like scaffolds would then brace the segments as they were lowered into the earth. As the work progressed, CBP continued to twist itself into verbal knots, stating that the prototypes would help "to deter illegal crossings in the area in which they are constructed." This implied that the models would be active deterrents, not merely test subjects, a rationale that was undermined somewhat when, during a visit by the media to the building site, a Mexican man jumped over the nearby landing-mat wall and made a beeline for the American side in full view of stunned onlookers. Undeterred by the wall segments, which could be easily run around, he was apprehended by CBP personnel who happened to be onsite. No sure date of completion had been discussed, though haste still seemed to be at a premium, given the directives coming from the top. One statement from the president suggested that major work on the full barrier would be complete "within the next six or seven months."

In the end, after all the wrangling and haggling over the competition, CBP got the job done, at least so far as the prototypes were concerned. Not to say the problems went away: Lawsuits were filed by spurned competitors; more legal action was threatened by advocacy groups and landowners; CBP officials could not specify what likely criteria they would apply in choosing the final winner from the current contestants, nor how testing would be conducted, nor precisely when an announcement would be made. Yet there the prototypes were, standing in the desert, as unnerving and perplexing an architectural spectacle as many people, myself included, had ever seen.

Otay Mesa was neither the worst nor the best town I would visit on the US-Mexico border. Still, on my first visit there, it instantly set me on edge: Although heavily trafficked by cross-border trucks, the town was very quiet, almost hushed; the sky was overcast and there was nothing on which to rest the eye, nothing picturesque in the scrubby mountains that ring the desert plateau. In Orson Welles's film *A Touch of Evil*, Mexican Narcotics officer Mike Vargas, portrayed (unconvincingly, caked in dark makeup) by Charlton Heston, tells his American bride, played by Janet Leigh, that bordertowns "always bring out the worst in a country." Whether or not there was any evil in Otay Mesa's chain restaurants and low-rise warehouses and offices, it struck me as place without welcome—a place where something was out of joint—where something was seething.

Just down the road, ferried there by CBP agents, I caught my first glimpse of the prototypes. For all the photographs that had circulated of them in the press, nothing could measure up to the experience of seeing them firsthand: in a patch of brush and sand, on sixty-five-foot square parcels, eight towering monoliths, all of them thirty feet by thirty feet and varying only in tone and the occasional detail. Standing just in front of the Vietnam-era metal slats, only a few yards away from the secondary fencing of the Bush era, the nearly identical structures did not resemble security systems of any kind, not individually and definitely not in the aggregate, ranging across the site in a regimented row with the mountains to the east and nothing behind them. All the artistic and architectural adventurers, the ones who had variously lampooned or reimagined the wall, could not have foreseen this: The most powerful nation on earth had created something that looked alarmingly like an architecture show.

The prototypes, seen from the Mexican side

Not that the walls were much to look at by themselves. Four of the slabs—two from W. G. Yates, one from Fisher, and the concrete proposal from Caddell—were little more than flat-out statements of the brief, unadorned blocks with hardly any surface treatment or other details save for a tubular baffle atop the first two and a fat, stabilizing bustle on one side of the fourth. Texas Sterling's was a singularly grim solution, a gray mottled elevation with a steel mesh rake on top, slanted southward; this was an intriguing touch, since CBP's experience with the mid-2000s barriers had shown that such slants could be used as an aid in scaling the fences. Only two prototypes would afford agents the ability to see through to the other side, an asset that one might have reckoned fairly essential for reasons of safety and reconnaissance: KWR's, a chrome multipede of tall metallic pillars beneath a metallic screen, and Caddell's multimaterial entry, its legs shorter and the screen larger, like the multipede's overweight cousin.

While all sported some manner of patina (if only incidentally) and most had vertical ridges to divide up their bulk (mostly, one speculated, for channeling water), Elta North America's was the sole model that boasted anything like color, with blue steel bars that emerged from a concrete foot-ing. The base was also adorned with rectangular blue panels, solely on the northern side, the side facing into the United States. That was as much self-conscious beautification as any of the teams was prepared to muster. If there was anything else that distinguished their designs one from the next—proprietary reinforcement bars in Caddell's perhaps or embedded sensors in Elta's—there was no way to know. Despite the strong public-relations push by CBP, none of the firms were fielding questions from the press, a proper nondisclosure agreement having been finally put into force. The policy would do nothing to endear the project to the media (though none of these structures were ever likely to grace the cover of *Architectural Digest*).

In any case, the prototypes achieved something different. "This odd open-air architecture gallery," as *Los Angeles Times* critic Christopher Haw-thorne called it, had an undeniable sway, a cumulative effect of looking at the slabs in ensemble over an extended period. The choice as to the thirty-foot building module was part of it: Any narrower and they would have lost their innate wall-ness, becoming mere towers; any wider and their height would have seemed less imposing; any bigger in either dimension and the sense of scale would have been lost altogether. They were also perfectly spaced, making for stunning photographs of the group in file. The appar-ently arbitrary distinctions between them made them seem like exercises in pure form as explored through iterative sequence, inviting the inevitable comparisons to the work of Donald Judd and other twentieth-century Min-imalist artists. Their strikingly artificial precision and monumental pres-ence made for comparisons to Michael Heizer and other pioneers of land art and site-specific installation.

Yet no land artist ever enjoyed a site quite like this one. Peeking over the top of the steel mats or between their joints, visitors could see the houses of the disheveled Mexican barrio of Escondido on the other side, while Tijuana residents often peered back, standing atop the dusty mound that ran along their side to catch a glimpse of these weird new monuments in their midst. The mountains crisscrossed by smuggler trails, the sound of distant helicopters, the enforcement officers patrolling the nearby brush on horseback—taken as a showcase of the border's future built environment, the wall prototypes were a mind-warping instance of idealized representation colliding headlong with messy reality.

As long as there have been architecture exhibitions, there has been the vexing matter of presentation. The mystique that can attach itself to even the most banal things the instant they're put in a museum (something related to critic Walter Benjamin's idea of "aura") is a serious problem for architecture, given its divers real-world responsibilities in shaping social life and the environment. The most any architecture exhibition can do is to somehow convey, not literally what a building might be "like," but—through suggestion, or through the evocation of a mood, in the way of paintings or sculpture—what the world of that architecture might feel like if realized. On this account, it was hard not to view the prototypes as a perverse sort of triumph, even if the mood they conveyed was far from triumphant.

Considering the return of tribalism in the twenty-first century, British philosopher John Roberts has warned against ascribing the phenomenon to "an external, monstrous force": "The reasoning of unreason," he has written, "is far more insidious and reasonable than that." The world has grown increasingly divided in the last decade, the old post–Cold War consensus torn asunder by economic and political change on an incomprehensible scale. What is happening in the United States is only one part of it, and those responsible, there as elsewhere, believe themselves to be acting on rational motives. Nonetheless, the structures in Otay Mesa seem to speak to something beyond the policies and politics that gave rise to them.

It isn't easy to discuss it. Mirroring the debate about anti-wall resistance art, there emerged in the wake of the prototypes' unveiling a new round of arguments about whether critiques of the structures risked taking them too seriously and thereby validating them. "Is It Inspired or Irresponsible to Call Donald Trump's Wall Prototypes 'Art'?" asked critic Carolina Miranda of the *Los Angeles Times*. In something of a riposte to the connoisseurial take of Christopher Hawthorne, her sometime colleague, she quoted local architect René Peralta: "It would be irresponsible, easy and lazy to consider it as an aesthetic object." No one had lavished this much attention on the fences that had been built in the mid-2000s. Why the sudden surge of interest now? Especially if they weren't going to lead to a real wall, granting the prototypes so much airtime would only be to carry the administration's water.

Theoretically, the prototypes were there to do more than just be seen. Over the next several months, the segments were subjected to a series of tests aimed at determining whether there was anything, any new insights, that could be gleaned from them and used by CBP for some future purpose, be it a contiguous wall or something else. It was reported that Special Forces teams had mounted assaults on the walls, assailed them with jackhammers and saws, attempted to climb them; analyses were made of the ease of construction and repair and of the soundness of the engineering behind them. All of this was documented in a report, completed in February 2018, that eventually found its way into the hands of San Diego's KPBS public radio and television station via a Freedom of Information Act request. Highly redacted, it left unclear the particulars of the testing process, though it did reveal that CBP had devoted inordinate energies to assessing one particular aspect: aesthetics.

A special team from Johns Hopkins University's Applied Physics Laboratory were commissioned by CBP to help devise a series of criteria that could determine which of the prototypes demonstrated the greatest visual élan. The February report laid out the aspects under consideration:

> Color—hue, intensity, brightness, depth
> Texture—look/feel of the physical surface, smoothness,
>   roughness, shape, configuration
> Pattern—large visual shape, arrangements, decorations
> Wall top style—appearance of top of the wall, top in relation to
>   rest of wall
> [. . .]
> Apparent difficulty to breach/scale—difficulty to get past the
>   wall, impenetrability
> Provision of situation awareness—ability to understand activity
>   near, around, by the wall

The method used to assign scores in these criteria, CBP explained, was "analysis of input from 72 participants on the aesthetics of each prototype"—interviews and surveys conducted with individuals in assorted fields. Many of these individuals, the report stated, did not see the prototypes themselves; rather, they were shown photographs of the prototypes and asked their impressions. While the authors concluded with a ranking of the prototypes' aesthetic value, which design was deemed most effective was among the extensively blacked-out segments of the report.

As the document put it, "The effective use of aesthetic choices can make a design resonate with a target audience." Truer words were never spoken (at least regarding the wall). It was only unfortunate that all the individuals who had to render aesthetic judgment on the prototypes were not obliged to see them in person.

Confronted not with digital renderings, not with pictures, but with the things themselves, the prototypes were sufficiently shocking that they put to rest, at least temporarily, every argument about the wall's morality or efficacy. The president of the United States had told many falsehoods about his signature project—that it would have solar panels, that it would be see-through, that Mexico would pay for it—but perhaps the most outrageous was his suggestion, a few weeks before the prototypes were unveiled, that he would be personally responsible for selecting the winner from the eight display samples. He would do nothing of the sort; he did not even visit the site until well after the tests had all been conducted. But at last, a man who had spent his whole life boasting of his accomplishments in the built environment could claim at least indirect responsibility for a genuine architectural sensation.

Whether it would do his reputation any good was another matter. Taken solely for what they are, symbols of an imagined architecture, the power of the prototypes is that they sound so clearly and so loudly such a stirring emotional note. That note is dread. The comparisons to land art or to late-modern sculpture had put the matter exactly backward: The works of Robert Smithson and his contemporaries were merely gestures toward sublimity; this was the reality, and it was chilling. As no other architectural initiative before that I know of, the prototype exhibition bodied forth an imminence of absolute doom, one that tainted everything around it in Otay Mesa—and, for some time after, everywhere else as well. Before I saw Israel, or China, or Berlin, I saw the prototypes. This was where my journey, such as it was, began, and the feeling it produced in me never really left, as if every wall I saw were casting the same shadow.

Of course, from the sublime to the ridiculous is but forty feet. In the opening sequence of *Touch of Evil*, the costars walk through the dodgy honky-tonk streets of the bordertown and then waltz across with scarcely a nod to the guards. Today, armed with only a passport, an American can walk into Mexico with only slightly greater official scrutiny—as I did—and then hop into a taxi and travel through the industrial suburbs of Tijuana to the exact other side of the fence, opposite the prototypes, only steps away but now in a different country. There, sitting on the ground right before the steel fencing, was where I found marker No. 252, the first I'd seen of the monuments set up by the old Border Commission a century and more ago. The amicability of that settlement was memorialized on the plaque on the little stone pile, set down in what was then an empty expanse of desert, a place where no one gave much thought to who went back and forth.

The marker hearkened back to a time of a border without bordertowns, a border whose existence as a spatial entity was to be regarded as a diplomatic fine point and occasional logistical hassle. The comedy (albeit a black one) came in seeing it so close to the prototypes, the totems of precisely the opposite disposition: a political order in which the country's physical boundary would be elaborated, at mammoth cost, into arguably the single most expensive public building in our history. If built, the wall would at once become the concentrated expression of our national values, surrounding us in every sense. Every single American city would then be turned into a sort of bordertown, full of shouts in the night and sordid official crimes, peopled by strangers and doubtful impostors who resembled no one so much as ourselves.

VII

THE WAY OF ALL WALLS

In the Koran, in Surah 18, it is related that Alexander the Great on his campaigns eastward toward the Indus paused among a distant people who "could scarcely understand [any speech]." They told him that they were being threatened by a people identified as Yajuj and Majuj—Gog and Magog in Arabic—and asked for his help. Alexander commanded them to gather up as much iron as they could find and to melt it down; they did so, and with the mass of ore they built a giant wall according to Alexander's design. So long as Yajuj and Majuj were kept behind it, the Koran claimed, the world would be safe. On judgment day, the wall would fall, and monsters would descend in hordes to drink away all the waters of the Tigris and Euphrates.

The Gates of Alexander are attested in multiple sources, including in the writings of the Judeo-Roman historian Josephus in his first-century *Wars of the Jews*, though most scholars today view the structure as having no basis in historical fact. It has been suggested that the tale is a mythical origin story for the Darial Gorge, a steep canyon in the northern Caucasus. More frequently, the gates are identified with the Great Wall of Gorgan on the eastern edge of the Caspian Sea in modern-day Iran: Though the real origins of that structure are unknown (some have dated it to the period of the Persian Sassanid Empire, others to the Parthian), the association with the illustrious Macedonian general is of ancient vintage, its common Persian name being Sadd-i-Iskandar, the Wall of Alexander. Buried beneath the hills of northern Iran, the wall can still be visited today.

I could not, unfortunately, see it myself. Relations between Iran and the United States worsened considerably between 2016 and 2018, especially since the latter's unilateral withdrawal (announced in May 2018) from the landmark nuclear agreement signed three years earlier. Curious Westerners now face considerable hurdles in obtaining visas; for journalists it is all but impossible, placing a bureaucratic wall between the two countries as daunting as Gorgan's ever was.

One Westerner who has been able to surmount it, and to see the real Gorgan, is Stuart Denison, a British-born artist based in Iran. "There's a mystique to the place," Denison told me, speaking from his home in Tehran. The mountains, he said, "come down to meet the coastal plain, stretching down to the Caspian." Turkic nomads still roam the steppes around the ridge of the wall. The structure itself, made largely of mud bricks, stretches 125 miles, longer, as Denison points out, than Hadrian's and the Antonine Wall combined. As for local beliefs about what the wall was and who built it, the Alexander connection is a popular one, but the stories vary from place and even person to person. "It all depends on what story you're trying to tell," says Denison.

Walls are often mutable in this way and, for centuries, the mythical Gates of Alexander afforded a convenient narrative: Among the medieval Germans, it was said that the gates kept out the *Rote Juden,* the hated Red Jews, who longed to break out and murder Christian children; Marco Polo claimed that they held back the Turkic hordes, cousins to the Ottomans who were the sworn enemies of his native Venice. Most of all, the gate and the stories told about it enhanced the legend of Alexander—the great conqueror out of Europe, tamer of the savage East—that remained a cultural common denominator in the West for centuries. The giant iron wall separated "them" from "us," if only in imagination. It didn't have to be real for people to believe in it; it was real so long as they did.

In our own time, we have borne witness to a resurgence in a related species of belief. As political theorist Wendy Brown has written, "the weakening of state sovereignty" in the global era has given rise to a new "tremulousness [and] vulnerability" in nations, with one after another seeking to reassert its sense of difference. Riding in on this insecurity, the old East-West enmity has come charging back, giving rise to America's new Iran policy; more generally, walls have come back, proliferating at a stunning pace. At least seventy walls, it is estimated, now zigzag across the surface of the Earth, most erected since the turn of the millennium: between Saudi

Arabia and Yemen; between South Africa and Zimbabwe; between India and Bangladesh; between Uzbekistan and Kyrgyzstan; between Hungary and Serbia . . . Ours is the moment of the wall, and there doesn't seem to be anything likely to check their continued growth.

Unless, that is, people stop believing in the stories behind them.

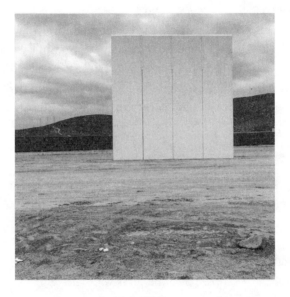

Prototype slab (Caddell Construction)

The last year in the life of Donald Trump's promised border wall was a hectic one. Nothing in it spelled the death of the project as such, and at times it seemed like it might be lurching forward despite all odds. More frequently, ostensible advances were revealed after the fact to be lateral moves or even setbacks, many of them self-inflicted.

The president of the United States finally undertook to see his "beautiful" prototypes about four months after I did. The visit, scheduled for the afternoon of March 13, 2018, should have been the ultimate photo op for the publicity-obsessed politician: If nothing else were ever to be built, the prototype tour represented a once-in-a-presidency chance to boast about something real, something tangible that emerged from all the administration's faltering efforts. But this was not to be.

Symptomatic of the White House's uniquely clumsy messaging strategy, the tour was effectively upstaged when, mere hours before it was set to begin, word reached media outlets that Secretary of State Rex Tillerson had submitted his resignation. The move was not unexpected: Tillerson had been among the most embattled members of a perpetually embattled cabinet and was rumored to have been contemplating stepping down since the previous July, only six months into his tenure. Nevertheless, the formal announcement of his departure, only the latest in a string of high-profile exits, consumed the public conversation that day and for much of the week. So far as public awareness was concerned, the prototypes slipped beneath the waves.

That may have been for the best, at least from the perspective of wall advocates. The arrival of the official tour group was attended by noisy crowds of protesters. There were supporters, too, railing against Mexican "murderers" and "rapists," but their arguments were undercut by CBP's announcement that, despite the bloodthirsty hordes supposedly lurking just to the south, all border crossings would remain open for ordinary business that day. The CBP site manager responsible for leading the agency's illustrious visitor through the area regaled the press with tales of unchecked illegal immigration at Otay Mesa—twenty and more years ago, when it was a dire problem there. Most of all, there were the remarks of the wall's number-one supporter. The president made a confounding comparison between would-be border crossers and "professional mountain climbers." He then repeated his insistence that the wall should be at least partially "see-through," despite the fact that most of the prospective designs standing directly next to him were completely solid. "We have a lousy wall over here now but at least it stops 90, 95 percent," said the commander-in-chief, figures that bear no resemblance to any documented data. He added, "We're going to stop 99 percent"—conceding, in effect, one of the arguments of the wall's opponents, that the proposed wall would produce diminishing returns at best.

The visit lasted only a few minutes before the presidential party sped on to an event at a nearby military installation. There a crowd of soldiers ("the

Marine Core," as they were dubbed in a presidential tweet) was treated to a breathless peroration about the recent defeat of ISIS (a victory already well in train during the Obama administration) and about the advantages of a putative extraorbital military branch, to be called the "Space Force" (an idea the administration had officially shelved, but that was now revived on the spot). Preempted by the Tillerson firing, the wall prototype visit was rapidly shoveled under with all the other issues of the day, just another below-the-fold story in a political age where only headlines seemed to count.

The next nine months would play witness to variations on the same theme, with the wall only an occasional leitmotif in the ongoing opera buffa of American political life. The same month that witnessed the ill-fated site tour also saw the last gasp of the DACA-for-wall deal, with the Democratic leadership offering up $25 billion for border infrastructure over ten years in exchange for a favorable settlement for younger undocumented Americans. The Senate had been poised to pass similar legislation a few weeks before, when the president unexpectedly announced his opposition; now Republicans insisted on a two-and-a-half-year sunset on Dreamer protections, robbing the bill of Democratic support. With no further quid pro quos on offer, subsequent budget negotiations would all be stalemated before they began, descending even deeper into the tiresome patterns of shutdown threats and last-minute funding resolutions.

Another recurring theme: the low-level jurisdictional warfare between the federal government and the state of California, where Governor Jerry Brown had made himself a persistent fly in the ointment. During the prototype site tour, Brown rebutted criticism by the president that he was doing "a terrible job" by noting via Twitter that "California remains the 6th largest economy in the world," having achieved this status thanks in part to its embrace of Mexican immigrants. Only two weeks before the Otay Mesa visit, California had lost a court battle to halt the barrier construction on the grounds that it swept aside too many state and local environmental regulations; in an almost Dickensian coincidence, the judge who issued the ruling in favor of the wall, Gonzalo Curiel of the Southern District, was the same who had declared Trump University to be fraudulent and had his objectivity questioned by the titular defendant on the grounds of his Mexican American heritage. (Curiel was born in Indiana.) Despite the judicial setback, the largest state in the union and its four-term governor continued to lobby against the wall, slow-walking an executive order to dispatch National Guard troops to the border and supporting the popular sanctuary city policies that made communities like Los Angeles and San Francisco a safe haven for the undocumented, and, proponents argue, safer for everyone.

The White House's response to Brown's obstructionism was to announce that no meaningful upgrades would be made to any existing fencing in California until the full wall was given the go-ahead by Congress. In May, however, that decision was reversed after the president claimed that officials in San Diego announced their support for the wall; the County Board of Supervisors later clarified that they had expressed no such support. The upgrades fell well short of full-bore wall construction, comprising mostly repair work, but they seemed increasingly urgent due to a recent, somewhat surprising, phenomenon. Despite all the bellicose rhetoric issuing from Washington, despite stepped-up ICE enforcement and the rising tide of deportations, the number of unauthorized border crossings was increasing at a statistically significant rate for the first time in years.

Underwritten by shared narratives—communal "psychic fantasies," to use Wendy Brown's phrase—walls collapse not when they cease to be of functional use, but when the narratives behind them give way, when a people loses sight of the conceptual foundation upon which walls are built. Narratives like these can take ages to form, to spread, and to gain currency before they decay. The length of the lifecycle is always different.

As the twenty-first century approaches its third decade, the decay seems long in coming. "You can follow the trends in the news in the US and across Europe," says Professor Reece Jones. The University of Hawaii political geographer has been studying walls and borders for fifteen years—since a time when "no one was talking about this," he jokes—and I spoke to him shortly after his return from the 2018 Borders and Border Walls conference in Montreal, a two-day academic summit exploring the explosion of physical barriers around the globe. At the conference, Jones told me,

the scholarly consensus held firm. "The tendency toward nationalist isola-
tion, closing off those connections in space," says Jones, is only accelerating.
In the middle of this worldwide pandemic, it is difficult to imagine, or to
recall, how such narratives of division can be unwound.

One could start at the beginning. Nine thousand years of continuous
habitation had seen Tell es-Sultan change hands countless times, invaded
and burned and destroyed by fire and earthquake. But its original wall-
building peoples, those intrepid inventors who first constructed the wall-
and-tower complex in the ninth millennium, may have faced a more
elemental problem.

Their structure was abandoned around 7800 BCE, five hundred years
and more after its completion. Though there is no persuasive explanation as
to why this should have happened, one hypothesis was favored by the site's
most famous interpreter: In the only complete account she ever composed
of her excavation, Kathleen Kenyon pointed to "increasing desiccation" in
the region as being a possible cause of a subsequent shift in settlement patterns on the Tell. The great glaciers of the last ice age had rolled back only
two thousand years before Jericho's founding; as warmer and drier weather
set in, finding provender would have become harder. Advanced irrigation
techniques would eventually increase the yield from the nearby spring and
more distant river—but not, conceivably, in time to save the first walled settlement. It would seem a poetic end to the ideological project of the wall's
creators. Having demonstrated their mastery over nature, they may have
succumbed to climate change.

"Cursed before the Lord be the man that rises up and rebuilds this
city," said Joshua, after his probably fictional battle was won. "At the cost of
his firstborn he shall lay its foundation, and at the cost of his youngest son
shall he set up its gates." This did not quite happen either: Long after Joshua
supposedly laid his hex upon it, the Tell was reoccupied, and in the Book
of Maccabees it is reported that the site was refortified as late as the second
century by Alexander's successors. Those who still yearn for pseudobiblical
explanations are not entirely without recourse. One epidemiological study,
dating to the 1970s, suggested that Joshua's curse really did blight the land,
coming in the form of a local infestation of schistosomiasis, a snail-born

parasite that made it impossible to live or build on the Tell for centuries. The theory has won few supporters.

It doesn't need any. Plagues, divine or otherwise, are not necessary to bring down walls or walled cities. In every age, in every place, they seem to collapse of their own accord. "The one thing that links them all together," says Reece Jones, "is that they all fail."

To seasoned border-watchers, the rise in illegal immigration came as no surprise. As early as October 2017, Steven Kopits, a prominent consultant and columnist on international affairs, had predicted that 2018 would be "a banner year for illegal immigration." The reasons, Kopits and others argued, would be the combination of a strong US economy with the inevitable tapering off the so-called Trump Effect, the temporary depression in immigration numbers resulting from the initial shock of the new administration. Bolstered by the seasonal spike occurring every spring, apprehensions in the CBP's southwest sector soared above the fifty thousand mark in April 2018, returning more or less to post-Great Recession norms and rising well above the rate for the last two years of the Obama administration.

The surge was cited as the primary rationale behind the mobilization of the National Guard that month. Yet by May, the numbers had scarcely budged, and talk of an incipient "crisis" began to fill the White House. In a cabinet meeting that month, DHS secretary Kirstjen Nielsen came in for a brutal dressing-down from her immigration-obsessed boss. Only weeks before, Nielsen had hovered in a Coast Guard helicopter over southern San Diego, scoping out the prototype site a day before the chief's arrival. Now rumors began to swirl that she had already penned a resignation letter. For the moment, she clung on.

True to form, Nielsen and her masters attempted to deflect criticism by insisting that the department's assorted non-wall projects—the expansion and reinforcement of existing fences—constituted wall construction. Yet even these projects were running into problems, as in South Texas, where a modest thirty-three-mile improvement project occasioned public outcry when CBP failed to abide by its own standards for community input, giving little or no notification to residents whose properties would be adversely affected by the work. Nor were human inhabitants of the borderlands the only ones complaining: More than a thousand plant and animal species inhabit the territory in the wall's path, some of them endangered and found nowhere else on earth. Environmental laws protecting them had been pre-empted, by the 2006 law and other measures, meaning that none of the customary ecological studies and regulatory review would halt either the wall or the pseudo-wall construction. In July, the conservation group Defenders of Wildlife circulated a paper cosigned by nearly three thousand scientists concerned about what one called the "massive blow" to the region's bio-diversity. Scientific groups would file multiple suits to slow or halt construction, the most recent in October 2018.

With more and more money going to enforcement rather than research, the atmosphere at the border has become increasingly hostile for the scientists who work there. In Arizona's Organ Pipe Cactus National Monument, ethnobiologist Gary Paul Nabhan was apprehended by CBP while performing a routine bird survey. "A rookie Border Patrol employee held us at gunpoint on our stomachs for one and a half hours," he said, "threatening to shoot us if we moved."

The collapse of Roman civilization may have taken away the raison d'être of Hadrian's Wall, but it did not quite mark the end of its military utility. This I discovered in a poorly considered wall-finding mission, chasing something billed on my hotel map as "Brunton turret," one of various Hadrianic structures that pop up in the middle of pastureland. The sole remaining Roman milestone in the area is no longer legible, thanks to cows rubbing up against it, and it can be difficult at times to tell the difference between the ancient wall and the more recent enclosures built by local farmers—the giveaway is the "dry stone" construction of the latter, as opposed to the lime-ground mortar that holds the stones of Hadrian's Wall together. Clear though the distinction is, I managed to mistake one for the other.

Once I had strayed from the wall path, I marched halfway up a hill onto private property, through another field, ankle-deep in grime and cow manure. It was only when I returned that I realized I'd gone over the verge of one century and into another—the area I'd entered was Heavenfield, the site where, in the early 630s, native Northumbrian and invading Welsh armies faced off in one of the obscure conflicts that beset Great Britain between the Roman departure and the Norman conquest. The Northumbrian leader Oswald arrayed his forces in a pocket of land, flanked by a steep crag to one side and the remains of Hadrian's Wall to the other. The tactic worked, delivering victory to Oswald.

Lost on the Hadrian trail—somewhere in Northumberland

In a limited sense, Oswald was only doing as the Romans had advised two centuries earlier. Thirty years after Britain's Great Conspiracy, the Romano-British people had turned one last time to their emperor for assistance. On this occasion they learned that no one would come to save them: As told by the sixth-century Greek historian Zosimus, the Emperor Honorius wrote "letters to the cities in Britain ordering them to guard themselves"—from one another, inevitably. With the letter, the empire officially bequeathed the island to its inhabitants, and with it the wall, drained now of its talismanic strength. After Oswald and his troops moved on, it was once again left in peace, sinking slowly into the mud.

* * *

Kirstjen Nielsen was subsequently readmitted to the administrative fold, becoming the official face of the detainee crisis that struck the White House in the early summer of 2018. In remarks from the presidential briefing room, Nielsen outlined a series of conditions in which Immigration and Customs Enforcement (ICE) retained the authority to "separate those who claim to be a parent and child"—circumstances that included such nebulous cases as "if the parent is a national security, public, or safety risk." Despite disturbing accounts of children kept in cages, Nielsen's advocacy of the family separation program continued in the weeks that followed, surprising many of those who'd known her as a dutiful public servant and earnest student of world politics: "That's not the Kirstjen we know," said one former Georgetown University classmate. The effect was quite the opposite at the uppermost levels of the Washington hierarchy, where talk of her removal ceased by midsummer.

Nielsen would again step to the front in the fall, with the impending arrival of the so-called migrant caravan, a column of displaced persons from Central America fleeing gang violence. Nielsen was as vocal as anyone in condemning the attempt on the part of the migrant train to seek political asylum in the United States. Though the outcry from the conservative circles about the caravan was conveniently timed to the upcoming national election, it was of a piece with the administration's general outlook on asylum seekers.

In Washington, I spoke with Adonia Simpson, the director of the Family Defense Program at Americans for Immigrant Justice. "Nationally, with changes in policy from the attorney general, we've been building a virtual wall for immigrants," says Simpson, who has watched as the administration has progressively weaponized law enforcement against immigrants, many of them long-term residents with previously protected status, turning ICE into a deportation machine. More and more, she says, her caseload is filled not with border-jumpers, but with legitimate asylum seekers, the 16 percent of undocumented immigrants to whom relief is available under current law. Many of them, she says, have been "surprised" to find that they've been targeted by the Justice Department's new and more stringent standards.

From Simpson's perch, the wall has been largely a sideshow, "a physical manifestation of the policies this administration has been implementing"; conversely, the new bureaucratic landscape could be seen as an attempt to compensate for the lack of meaningful progress on the border. Neither the enforcement regime nor the justice system seemed to benefit: Apprehensions fluctuated in 2018 but were mostly in line with seasonal expectations while the staggering backlog of cases referred to the Justice Department (in the administration's first nineteen months, the volume of unheard cases jumped by 38 percent) left the federal bureaucracy more or less back at square one, or worse. At the same time, the agency meant to be doing the enforcing was showing increasing signs of dysfunction. In September, in an echo of the hiring problems that had so long dogged CBP in the wake of its 2000s ramp-up, Juan David Ortiz, a ten-year veteran patrolman, was found to have murdered four women, all of them sex workers whom he drove outside Laredo, Texas, and then shot to death. Labeling him a serial killer, police suspected he had used his authority as an agent to track the investigation against him and attempt to elude it. Only months earlier, two other CBP agents had also been accused of serious crimes, one for demanding sex from an undocumented woman under threat of deportation, the other for killing his girlfriend and their year-old infant.

The "bad hombres," it seemed, were not only those trying to make their way northward. As if to underscore this fact, in the spring of 2018 a leading figure of the Mexican left launched a movement aimed at getting his national government to pursue a legal claim against the United States in the International Court of Justice. The lawsuit would allege that since the Treaty of Guadalupe Hidalgo, which ended the Mexican-American War, had been signed under duress, and since certain of its obligations were abrogated by the United States after its ratification, it was therefore null and void. The Republic of Mexico, it was argued, was therefore entitled to reparations up to and including the restoration of its lost territory. Although the case had "little chance of succeeding legally," as one Mexican editorialist admitted, it nonetheless served as a piquant reminder as to which country had invaded which.

* * *

When the Ming Dynasty entered its 276th year, warfare overtook the empire. Natural catastrophe and overtaxation prompted an internal revolt; at the same time, a group of familiar enemies massed outside the Great Wall—not the Mongols this time, but their occasional allies the Jurchen, a nation from the east and north in the region now known as Manchuria. Its leader, Dorgon, had set his sights on nothing short of complete control of China.

He was aided in this ambition by singular good fortune. Manning the Shanhai Pass where the wall met the sea were the armies of Ming general Wu Sangui. As rebel forces approached from his rear, Wu determined that the Manchu might be of good use in putting down the disturbance; once order had been restored, the invaders could be disposed of. Writing to Dorgon, Wu told him that the plight of his country had made him "weep tears of blood in search of help" and pledged to unite his forces with those of the Jurchen.

On May 27, 1644, on the same spot where Nationalists and the Japanese would fight it out three centuries later, General Wu raised the gate at Shanhai Pass. Moving through the open passage, the Manchu swept into China, routed the rebels, and reached the capital in less than two weeks. Dorgon claimed the Mandate of Heaven for his people and installed a young relative as the Shunzhi emperor, with himself as all-powerful regent. Forcing the native Han Chinese to adopt the traditional Manchu hairstyle—cropped close in front, with a long queue in back—the Manchu proceeded to rule over China as the Qing Dynasty for two and a half centuries, until the rise of the Nationalists and the collapse of the empire.

In all that time, the Manchu made no use of the wall whatsoever. Being from the north themselves, they could draw no strength, ideological or otherwise, from the idea that those beyond the wall were a dangerous Other: They *were* the other. They did build an unusual fortification between China and their own native Manchuria, but for the precise opposite reason: Known as the Willow Palisade, its intent was to keep their Han Chinese subjects out of the Manchu homeland, reserving it for themselves and their loyal bannermen. They maintained, just the same, a very skeptical view of walls in general. These were the words of the second Qing ruler of China, the Kangxi emperor: "At the end of the Ming, my grandfather led his great army, riding straight in, defeating all armies; nobody could stop him. It is obvious that the way to defend a state is really to promote good morality and let people live in peace."

On August 22, 2018, the very day that saw the conviction of Paul Manafort and guilty plea of Michael Cohen—the one a former Republican presidential campaign chairman, the other the personal lawyer of the president—it was revealed that Mollie Tibbetts, an Iowa college student, had been murdered by an undocumented immigrant. So far as the wall's supporters were concerned, this, not the simultaneous legal bombshells and their potentially impeachment-worthy implications, was the news of the day, a return to the same strategy they had been using since the 2016 campaign and the murder of Kathryn Steinle.

With the approach of the fall elections, there was even more reason to distract the public mind. That same August, the Government Accountability Office issued a report under the heading *Southwest Border Security: CBP Is Evaluating Designs and Locations for Border Barriers but Is Proceeding Without Key Information*. While the title seems to say it all, some of the study's more enlightening passages—the product of extensive interviews with DHS staff and review of agency records—were hidden in the dense document: that, according to the GAO, Border Patrol did not factor in the costs of building on sloping terrain when assessing the prototypes segments; that the two proposed initial locations for the wall had been chosen without any prior study, almost entirely at random; that no documentation existed as to what exactly, and how exactly, CBP intended to proceed with any future construction in the San Diego area. The most revealing item in the report, however, was the GAO investigators' recommendation that CBP "prioritize investments that allow the organization to obtain the greatest benefits for the least cost." In their official response to the report, DHS chafed at the suggestion. So long as the White House did not care about obtaining "the greatest benefits for the least cost," the agency claimed, they were obliged to follow suit.

They were, it should be said, in an impossible position. There are many ways by which to evaluate the cost-effectiveness of the wall, and the intensity of the debate has been fueled in part by competing data, with each side accusing the other of deploying biased analyses of the fiscal merits and demerits of immigration. To find a baseline relatively free of ideological taint, I sought out Alex Nowrasteh, an analyst with the Washington, D.C.-based Cato Institute. "I come from the Right," says Nowrasteh, who though affiliated with the libertarian think tank owns to having "some socially conservative bones." Despite this predisposition, his thorough combing of the available economic evidence yields no sound rationale for an anti-immigration investment on the order of the wall. "If the wall works, it makes the US poorer," Nowrasteh explains: On balance, the positive contributions of undocumented immigrants to the American economy—the labor they provide, the taxes they pay, the businesses from which they buy—balance or outweigh the negatives—use of public services, downward pressure on wages—typically imputed to them.

Most attempts to justify the expense of the wall entail some attempt to short the positive economic aspects of immigration while inflating the negative. Most galling, from Nowrasteh's perspective, is the persistence of some pro-wall groups such as Federation for American Immigration Reform (FAIR) in adding taxpayer money to the latter side of the ledger: By this logic, the wall's hefty price tag could itself be laid at the feet of illegal immigrants. "The FAIRs of the world are driving the costs they're complaining about," says Nowrasteh. Caught in the same contradiction, DHS could not hope to summon any fiscal rationalization for their actions, for the simple reason that there wasn't one.

On May 5, 1919, agreements between the French national government and Paris's civic administration finally went into effect, permitting demolition to commence on Adolphe Thiers's *enceinte*. A contemporary press photo shows "le premier coup de pioche"—the first strike of the pickax—being delivered at the Porte de Clignancourt just beyond Montmartre. The man doing the honors was Paul Chassaigne-Goyon, president of Paris's municipal council, and in the picture he wears a bowler and an impish smile beneath a decorous mustache, holding the ax high above his head. In a second photo, he lurches forward, as though tipped off balance by the strength of the blow.

The demolition of the primary fortifications took the better part of a decade, an undertaking as taxing and labor-intensive as the wall's construction had been sixty years earlier. The rude shock of the First World War— when the French were reminded, yet again, how useless such defenses were in modern warfare—did not quite disabuse them of some dearly held ideas about the power of fortifications. Only ten years after the demolition in Paris had begun, the government set to work on the most grandiose of their extra-urban defense projects, the Maginot Line, a perimeter of burrows and bunkers running the full length of the German border. Supposedly impregnable, its true strength was never really tested. In 1939, the invading Wehrmacht simply drove their tanks around it, through the seemingly impenetrable Ardennes forest.

Shattering one narrative can very easily give rise to another. The wild zone that had come to occupy the abandoned *enceinte*'s glacis was a font of urban fairy tales: A field "where the harvest was of broken bottles and shards of China," as one songwriter called it, it was filled with junkmen and flea markets, sought out by Surrealist painters, and rumored to be full of criminals whose reputed savagery led the Parisians to dub them *les apaches*. Beyond it, the city's immediate suburbs (*banlieues*) contained a different kind of threat—the *ceinture rouge*, the "red belt" of communities surrounding the capital whose working-class residents, it was feared, might rise in revolution against the bourgeois denizens of the city. Reconnecting these alienated strata to the city proper was the prime rationale for much of the furtive social engineering that went on in the former zone, the apartment blocks and community centers that have made it a playground for the architectural imagination ever since.

In the second decade of the twenty-first century, that imagination is still running riot, still responding to similar problems and similar anxieties. Neighborhood gardens, ad hoc municipal storage, parking of questionable legality: The disjecta membra of the metropolis float into the void left by Thiers's wall, slowly closing it. In the Parc de la Villette, superstar architect Jean Nouvel recently completed a controversial Philharmonic Hall that attempts to draw the suburbs and the city closer together with a series of ramps and sweeping gestural forms on the outward-facing side, as if beckoning to the modern-day *apaches*, inviting them in. Unfortunately, the building must contend with the Périphérique, the elevated roadway that cuts off the affluent city from the poorer *banlieues*, the inhabitants of which, many of them immigrants, are viewed by Parisians with the same suspicion they once bore the rag-pickers and seditious workers. The noisy and traffic-clogged highway has become a wall of its own—a frustrating circumstance, though a fitting one, given that the car has been getting the better of the zone's reformers since the beginning. In 1936, Paul Chassaigne-Goyon died after being struck down on the streets of Paris by a speeding automobile.

One of the most engaging voices on the culture of the border today belongs to Roger Hodge, an author and journalist who grew up in Del Rio, Texas. I spoke to him before I set out to see the border fences myself, and he was at pains to stress how differently the people of the borderlands view the history of the place and its present. "On the border it's so much more complicated," he told me. "People elsewhere are just clueless, they don't know how anything works down there." (I had to count myself in the latter category.) In his own conversations with his neighbors and family in the region, Hodge had found a relative uniformity in local attitudes toward the wall. "Most people," he said, "think it's ridiculous."

Of all the comic aspects of the wall, the most risible has been the matter of nomenclature, which has reached greater heights of absurdity as time has worn on. In the fall of 2018, Kirstjen Nielsen was on hand to unveil a new segment of bollard fencing in Calexico, California. It was, yet again, no different from the fencing that had been built elsewhere under previous administrations and that had been derided as inadequate by the then–Republican presidential candidate. Yet upon this new segment there was an engraved sign. *This plaque*, it read, *was installed on October 26, 2018, to commemorate the completion of the first section of President Trump's border wall*. "It's different than a fence in that it also has technology," Nielsen told the media. Pressed to elaborate, the secretary could only fall back on tautology. "It's a wall, this is what the president has asked us to do."

In the final round of budget negotiations of the congressional term, the semantic problem was everywhere. "It's just a matter of what you call it," said Roy Blunt: Along with his Republican colleagues, the senator from Missouri had been endeavoring to persuade the president that any increase in border-related funding, however small, *could* be considered as paying for the wall, if it pleased the president to think of it that way. Democrats could make the reasonable case that it was not, since none of it went toward a prototype-style wall—but why should that ruin a good tweet? "My understanding is it's for the wall," said another Republican, Senator Richard Shelby of Alabama. "Maybe other people's understanding is it's for border security." He reportedly smiled as he said it.

Set loose on the streets of East Berlin by Günter Schabowski's errant announcement, the hysteria of the populace was now the problem of the East German border guards. After years of training, and the threat of severe punishment for any soldier who failed to do his duty, the guards had to step carefully through a situation that was, for them and for the world, unprecedented. Forced to improvise, they made up their own story.

One of the chief authors was a forty-six-year-old East German border officer, Lieutenant Colonel Harald Jäger. As he would later tell the *New York Times*, Jäger was eating a late-night snack at his guard post at Bornholmer Straße when he heard the broadcast; it all but made him gag on his food. "Nobody had alerted us to any change of policy," he said. Seemingly out of nowhere, crowds began to form in front of the narrow viaduct over which Bornholmer passed from one Berlin to another; by eight o'clock, Jäger had all but given up on getting any change in orders from his superiors. At last, just after ten, he received a call encouraging him to allow through a few of the mob's more boisterous members, a maneuver meant to "let off steam" and calm the crowd. The move had the opposite effect, inciting still more enthusiasm, as well as outrage when some easterners attempted to come back and were told they were barred from reentry.

At last, at 10:30, Jäger made a bold decision. He ordered his men to open the gate at the base of the crossing and allow the entire assembly to pass through. He then called his superiors: "I am going to end all controls and let the people out," he told them and abruptly hung up. Not wanting to be seen by his subordinates, Jäger then ducked into a neighboring building and began to weep. Looking out, he discovered there was no reason to hide, since his soldiers were crying as well.

Included in the river of humanity who streamed past Jäger in the dark was one woman who had been relaxing at a spa when she stepped out and saw the crowds rushing west and fell in behind an older lady whom, she recalled, "had just thrown a coat over her nightdress." Angela Merkel, then thirty-five, would later claim that she did not remember much about that night—did not even notice, perhaps, the red-eyed guard with a half-eaten sandwich, standing to one side as she and the others strutted over the iron pedestrian bridge—except that she ended the night having beers in a stranger's apartment. It was, she told *Der Spiegel*, "one of the happiest moments of my life."

I came back to Otay Mesa for the second time almost exactly a year after my first visit. It was October again, and by some conspiracy of the weather it had clouded over once more, giving the place the same subdued menace it had had the last time. The building site, now devoid of any press, felt doubly forsaken, while the prototypes appeared the worse for wear, the testing process and the elements having taken their toll. The monoliths were stained in places, bleached in others, their façades pockmarked. And there was one additional difference, more outstanding than the rest. The mats were gone.

"It just happened a couple weeks back," said Agent Vincent Pirro, the CBP officer detailed as my escort. The Vietnam War surplus fence that had stood on the Tijuana border since the Clinton years had been replaced, just prior to my arrival, by a new line of beveled steel pikes topped by solid horizontal panels. Little different from the bollard fences I'd seen in South Texas, these were some of the 124 miles of new and improved fencing approved by Congress, the closest thing to a wall the administration had yet managed to finagle. Ostensibly they marked an improvement over the earlier model, taller by far and not so weather-beaten, while their transparency made them, if not quite inoffensive, at least less obtrusive. The open-work structure had produced one other effect: The stray dogs that I had previously spotted roaming the dusty road on the southern side were now able to slip through the verticals, and several of them frisked at the feet of the prototypes. "They would get through before, too," said Agent Pirro. "Just dig under."

They weren't the only ones. Driving westward in a departmental vehicle, following the track that runs between the primary fence (formerly the mats, now the pikes) and the secondary barrier (the loftier chain-link model, born of the 2006 law), Pirro pointed out a set of warehouses on the Mexican side directly adjacent to the Tijuana airport. He then traced his finger across a distance of a thousand feet to the American side: This was the length of just one of the tunnels that had run under the area and served the illicit drug trade. Since 2017, twelve such subterranean passages have been discovered in the sector, many as long as or longer than the airport tunnel; the primary fence, though improved, would still be of only limited utility against them. Continuing along the track, Pirro pointed to patch after patch on the secondary fencing where smugglers, of both human and material contraband, have vaulted the primary fence and cut through the chain link of the secondary. "They can do it in seconds," said Pirro; the perpetrators are so deft, and so brazen, that they can be spotted by CBP yet still slip away uncaught. The freshly installed slats might slow them a bit, but not much—in the little time they had been there, a few had already been damaged, and subsequent testing would prove they could be sawed through with common instruments.

For all that had changed about the border and border politics in the previous year, much was still the same. Mexico had elected a new president, Andrés Manuel López Obrador, a progressive populist who promised sweeping change; he was still less likely than his predecessor to obey American whims on wall funding, convinced that developing the Mexican economy would decrease immigration northward. NAFTA, against which the US president had spoken emphatically, had come within inches of death after protracted haggling, first between the United States and Mexico, then with Canada; in the end, pending congressional imprimatur, it survived with only superficial changes, including a name change, and with the endorsement of the incoming Mexican leadership. For all the hype about the approaching caravan of Central American migrants prior to the 2018 midterm election, the administration's subsequent attempt to limit the number of asylum seekers trying to enter at border checkpoints was set to be enmeshed in the same tangle of legal disputes that had slowed and weakened the Muslim ban.

A strong national economy, low rates of violent crime (which had dropped again in 2017), historically low levels of uninsured (8.8 percent, despite all the rearguard attacks on Obamacare): On its face, the outlook for incumbents on the eve of the midterms was rosy. But a presidency that had pledged itself to counter "American carnage" (as the Stephen Miller–penned inauguration speech dubbed it) could not long endure without some form of carnage to counter. The migrant caravan afforded a convenient target, and so immigrants—and the wall meant to stop them—were trotted out to stir up the conservative base, as they had been so many times since 2015. On this occasion, however, there were signs that fewer Americans were taking the bait. The president's approval numbers, never high, continued to hover in the upper thirties or low forties; the generic ballot for Democrats versus Republicans showed a strong preference for the opposition. "All of the indicators are, 'Boy, this is going to be really bad for Republicans,'" declared one prominent analyst, though talk of a "blue wave" seemed premature. Memories of 2016 were still fresh, and until election day there was no knowing whether the immigration issue had truly lost its sway.

Two years earlier, voters had been sold on the story of an out-of-control border where swarms of foreigners, bent on mischief, were pouring into the country from the hostile and primitive land beyond. It was a new narrative, based on one as old as the country itself, now being tested to see whether it would bear the weight of a wall—whether, after the revelations of the foregoing two years about its cost, its efficacy, and the political waywardness of its builders, the public would continue to endorse it. The reality of the border was still sufficiently remote from the experience of most Americans that the ancient narrative, clear and familiar, might yet be the surest thing they took with them into the voting booth.

And how could the reality ever be explained to them anyway? Even seeing the border, it was hard to believe: the rollercoaster hills west of Otay Mesa, where the fence stopped abruptly at a cliff; the smiles of small children nearby, sticking their hands through the fence and waving; the indulgent, frustrated half-smile on Agent Pirro's face as he waved back. The kids and their parents, it was rumored, had been reaching through and grabbing pieces of the stacked steel that were about to go into the new primary fence, using it to build out their houses on the other side or perhaps sell as scrap. Pirro related the story with a shrug, as if to say, "What can you do?"

Rawabi, a new Palestinian city in the West Bank

In a place like Israel, where the wall is still new, collapse may be a long way off. So deeply entrenched is the mutual contempt between Israelis and Palestinians that it seems unlikely to abate in the near future. Yet the West Bank barrier is also a symptom of a broader crisis, one that may foreshadow its own demise.

In Jordan, I talked to the Gaza-born American activist and writer Ahmed Moor. Israel's leaders, he notes, have a long history of making decisions "that are bad in the medium and long term," putting off a diplomatic endgame in favor of domestic political imperatives. Ignoring the obvious demographic threat to its Jewish identity, Israel has absorbed Palestinian territory and thwarted every effort at Palestinian statehood, becoming the reluctant legal guardian of the Palestinian population. "It's like the kid who gets into the candy store," as Moor puts it. "In the back of his mind, he's hoping someone would stop him from gorging." Thanks in no small measure to the wall, Israeli settlements will continue to expand in the West Bank; yet as they do so, they will make it progressively harder to see the wall as separating two nations. Rather, it will divide a single nation, with two peoples living in it. As the Israeli Arabs can attest, these two peoples could yet learn to live together—however uneasily—and the wall then lose its reason for being.

Precisely how that would happen is anyone's guess. Surveying the landscape of the West Bank—still, as when Ralph Bunche first saw it, marred by "troops, barricades, barbed wire"—it was impossible to imagine it cleared of all those impedimenta of hatred, returned to nature and to its rightful inhabitants, Jews and Arabs alike. I could not see it, and on my last, long night there I could conjure no other mental image than that of children with stones facing off against children with guns. But at least one person I spoke to was able to see something else.

The evening before I set out for my ill-fated drive south, I spoke with Bashar Masri, a Palestinian American investor and real estate developer. Masri told me about an encounter near his largest project to date, a planned city for forty-five thousand Palestinians called Rawabi. At the foot of the road leading to the hillside site, Masri had seen a group of IDF soldiers hammering a sign identifying the road as Area A territory, dangerous to Israelis; Masri objected to the sign, saying he welcomed Israeli visitors, but the IDF personnel hammered the sign in regardless.

"I said to them, 'What will you do to me if I pull this out?'" Masri told me. "'Will you shoot me?'" The soldiers glanced at one another—and then, in an instant, they simply wilted, shaking their heads and walking away. Before they were out of earshot, Masri noisily removed the sign and placed it in a warehouse that his construction crews had been using to store stones for Rawabi. "In the future," said Masri, "it will be the Museum of the Occupation."

The barriers that already exist between the United States and Mexico will doubtless stand for many, many years to come. Even for those who oppose the current fencing, the center of political gravity in the United States all but demands a "tough" stance against illegal immigrants. Just a few weeks before the midterm elections, I spoke to Democratic congressman Raúl Grijalva, the representative from Arizona's third district. "You have to look at the whole mission of how we deal with challenges both on the criminal and economic side," he said. Encompassing three hundred miles of the frontier, Grijalva's is one of the largest border districts, and he entertains few illusions about either the efficacy of barriers or the possibility of halting their growth altogether. "People's understanding of immigration, borderlands—it's shallow," he said. "They'll jump on walls as the end-all, be-all. It's a convenient and easy political posture."

For now, the wall-builders still have the wind at their backs, and not just in the United States. In 2016, France constructed (with funding from the UK) a wall at the city of Calais separating a local migrant camp from the nearest entrance to the Channel Tunnel. That same year, Tunisia began work on a multimillion-dollar wall to prevent any spilling-over of violence from neighboring Libya. On the northern coast of Africa, the Spanish enclaves of Ceuta and Melilla boast a fence system, renovated in 2005, that now stands nearly twenty feet high; although neighboring Morocco has lodged vociferous objections, that country is somewhat hamstrung by the fact that it still maintains a fortification of its own, nearly two thousand miles long, in the disputed territory of Western Sahara. Ecuador has attempted to build a wall on its border with Peru, and even Norway, at peace with neighboring Russia since 1905, has recently constructed a fence along its eastern border. In the years to come, increased migrant flows due to climate change and escalating wealth inequality—combined with the slow-motion breakdown of international institutions and collective-security arrangements—only threaten more trenches, more earthworks, more concrete and razor wire.

And yet there may be something—one hesitates to say "exceptional," but at least singular about the American case. For two years pro-wall forces had held a virtual monopoly on national power in the United States; they did not have a single mile of new border barrier to show for it, and now their time was up. The November 2018 elections, when they arrived, carried Grijalva's party back into the House majority by the highest voter turnout in any midterm for more than a century, as well as the highest-ever popular-vote margin for a minority party. Significantly, in district after district, the key element was not the wall: Exit polling pointed to health care, rather than immigration, as the top issue, while the gender gap (women broke for Democratic candidates by 19 percent, while men favored Republicans by 4) showed how much the #MeToo movement, together with the president's personal comportment and the rightward tilt of the judiciary, had turned female voters away from the incumbent party. Though not dispelled, the actuating narrative behind the wall had been overwhelmed at least for the present cycle by other, more pressing considerations. Following the election, a pro-wall group announced plans to crowdfund the wall by raising $1 billion in private donations, only to be forced to offer refunds a month later, having collected only $20 million and with no clear notion as to how it could be legally used for construction. The idea of the wall was once enough to stand up an unpopular candidate for president and get him elected. Now it looked like it had failed, no longer able to capture the imagination of fearful American voters. The wall had fallen before it was even built.

Less than a month later, with Congress barreling toward shutdown once more, Senator Chuck Schumer and Representative Nancy Pelosi—set to become the majority leader in the next session—were summoned to the Oval Office. In front of the gathered press—despite Schumer's suggestion that they "debate in private"—their host insisted, as he had for months, on at least $5 billion in additional border-security funding, most of it for additional infrastructure. He proudly proclaimed his willingness to shut down the government and berated the two Democrats who sat smiling stiffly into the cameras. It availed him nothing; nor did the shutdown that followed, even when it grew to become the longest in American history; nor did the purported concession, during the first Oval Office address of the administration, that the White House would be happy to accept a steel rather than a concrete structure, "at the request of Democrats." Given that no such request had been made, this last bout of lexical gamesmanship seemed especially pointless: At a single stroke, it simultaneously disregarded the proven failings of the newer steel fences, while officially throwing the much-ballyhooed prototypes under the bus.

On January 25, 2019, the two-year anniversary of the executive order commanding the "immediate construction" of the wall, the second shutdown ended with no additional wall funding, prompting jeers from the conservative critics who had egged on the White House during the thirty-five-day ordeal. With that, the federal purse strings were drawn closed for the duration of the 116th Congress. Minor improvements to current fencing there might be, and potentially a few dozen miles of new fences as well, but nothing on the order of what had been promised, or even what had been built under the previous administration. While declaring an emergency to fund the wall remained a presidential prerogative, the long delay in making such a move, as well as the uncharacteristic sheepishness with which it was finally debuted in February, was a good augur of its likely course: stymied in courts, whittled away by future congressional action, thwarted by landowners and protesters and bureaucratic mismanagement. Not to say that that, or anything else, would alter the determination of Donald Trump to build it. The economic and cultural divide that had brought him to power, and the existential angst that accompanied it, was still present, and his

Wall's end: the fence in the surf, California

reelection would hang on his ability to fill his sails once again with those same winds. In any other instance, continuing to push the wall might be seen as a simple political calculation; but here it resembled something else—an individual psyche merged seamlessly with the greater psychosocial forces at large in the country. Following the contentious December meeting, Pelosi offered her diagnosis of the pathology that has made the wall such a critical issue to the president and led to his public outburst. "It's like a manhood thing for him," she said. "As if manhood could ever be associated with him."

"A city will be well fortified which is surrounded by brave men and not by bricks." Those words of the lawgiver Lycurgus of Sparta might give a special jolt to the modern wall-men—most of whom are men, and self-styled manly men at that—all the more so since Sparta, a city that eschewed walls, was famed for its strength. One might stand that Spartan ideal beside the wall idea, that profoundly insecure "manhood thing" that has gripped the American psyche for three years, and discover that a whole host of promising comparisons present themselves to the mind: against an insecure and chimerical manliness, an expansive, forthright humanity; against a state of walls, a state of confidence; against Otay Mesa, an open city on an upland plain, surrounded by groves of olive and orange. Alongside the study of walls, there must be a study of all the places that have thrived without them; to trace the absence of walls might prove still more valuable than to trace their presence. It might even be found that, just as the history of walls is marked by recurrences and coincidences, so the history of not-walls is marked by a convergence—and that it lies somewhere just up ahead, in the future.

ACKNOWLEDGMENTS

Most of the histories presented here—like the borderlands themselves—are well-trod terrain. Subjects that I dealt with only in passing have been the subjects of whole books, and researchers and writers have devoted entire careers to working out fine points that I've dispatched in the space of a paragraph. I am deeply indebted to the work of all those whose names appear in the footnotes and bibliography, but in particular to Kathleen Kenyon, Ran Barkai, and Roy Liran on Jericho; Anthony Everett on Hadrian; Carlos Rojas on China; Jean-Denis G. G. Lepage on Paris; Pertti Ahonen on Berlin; and Visualizing Palestine and Tami Amanda Jacoby on the West Bank.

With regard to the current wall debate, I wish to express my gratitude to all of the interview subjects—not all of whom I was able to quote here—who agreed to speak with me when so many both inside and outside government refused. Having to rely, perforce, on secondary reporting to keep pace with events as they happened, I'm particularly thankful to the reporters and editors of the *Washington Post*, the *New York Times*, *The Hill*, and *Politico* who have covered every twist and turn in the now three-year wall saga. For the deeper background on the US-Mexico borderlands, I also wish to single out the writings of Francisco Cantú, Roger Hodge, and Ronald Rael, as well as Wendy Brown, Reece Jones, and Élisabeth Vallet, whose scholarship gave me some much-needed grounding in the broader conceptual issues at play.

To weave the contemporary and historical material into something like an original synthesis, it was essential that I see in person the borders and barriers about which I was writing. For that, all credit belongs to the subjects, editors, and publications for whom I traveled on assignment to over half a dozen countries spread across three continents: Ma Yansong of MAD

Architects; Sam Cochrane of *Architectural Digest*; Dallas Contemporary; Fan Zhong of *W*; Julie Coe of *WSJ: The Wall Street Journal Magazine*; Dan Rubinstein of *Departures*; Kendra Nichols of the *Washington Post*; Henry Muñoz and the staff at Muñoz & Co.; Cameron Abadi of *Foreign Policy*; Katie Gerfen and Eric Wills of *Architect*; and Kelsey Keith of *Curbed*. Special appreciation goes to the latter three, who granted permission to republish portions of articles originally written for them.

Lastly, I want to acknowledge the friends and family who have helped me in countless ways through a very challenging year. These include but are not limited to: Andrew Ayers; Éva Calon; Rachel Gracey; Kat Harriman; Angelica Hicks; Michael and Lily Idov; Greg Lindsay and the staff at ReSite Prague 2018; Henry Lyon; Esther Park; Jon Reinish; Abigail Shaw; Joel Stein; Jim and Ashley Turner; Theresa Veltri; Ian and Martha Volner; Matthew Volner; and Mildred Weisz, my grandmother, who sadly passed away before this book went to press. And needless to say, endless thanks to my agent, Nicole Tourtelot of De Fiore & Co., to fact-checker Lian Rangkuty, to my editor, Jamison Stoltz, and to the whole staff at Abrams Press, without whom none of this would have been possible.

SELECTED BIBLIOGRAPHY

WALL OF JERICHO

Barkai, Ran and Roy Liran, "Midsummer Sunset at Neolithic Jericho." *Time and Mind: The Journal of Archaeology, Consciousness and Culture* 1, no. 3 (November 2008): 273–284.

Bar-Yosef, Ofer. "The Walls of Jericho: An Alternative Interpretation." *Current Anthropology* 27, no. 2 (April 1986): 157.

Davis, Miriam C. *Dame Kathleen Kenyon: Digging Up the Holy Land*. Walnut Creek: Left Coast Press, 2008.

Hulse, E.V. "Joshua's Curse and the Abandonment of Jericho." *Medical History* 15, no. 4 (October 1971): 376–386.

Kenyon, Kathleen. *Digging Up Jericho*. New York: Frederick A. Praeger, 1957.

Nigro, Lorenzo. "The Archaeology of Collapse and Resilience: Tell es-Sultan/ancient Jericho as a Case Study." In *Overcoming Catastrophes: Essays on Disastours Agents, Characterization, and Resilience Strategies in Pre-Classical Southern Levant*, edited by Lorenzo Nigro, 55–85. Rome: La Sapienza Studies on the Archaeology of Palestine and Transjordan, 2014.

———. *Tell es-Sultan/Jericho in the Early Bronze II (3000–2700 BC): The Rise of an Early Palestinian City*. Rome: La Sapienza Studies on the Archaeology of Palestine And Transjordan, 2010.

Ruby, Robert. *Jericho: Dreams, Ruins, Phantoms*. New York: Henry Holt and Company, 1995.

Scheffler, Eben. "Jericho: From Archaeology Challenging the Canon to Searching for the Meaning(s) of Myth(s)." *HTS Teologiese Studies* 69, no. 1 (2013): 1–10.

Wood, Bryant G. "Dating Jericho's Destruction: Bienkowski Is Wrong on All Counts." *Biblical Archaeological Review* 16, no. 5 (1990): 45–49, 68–69.

HADRIAN'S WALL

Atkins, Jed W. *Roman Political Thought*. New York: Cambridge University Press, 2018.

Beard, Mary. "A Very Modern Emperor." *The Guardian*, July 18, 2008.

Everett, Anthony. *Hadrian and the Triumph of Rome*. New York: Random House, 2015.

Hughs, Ian. *Imperial Brothers: Valentinian, Valens and the Disaster at Adrianople*. Barnsley, UK: Pen & Sword, 2013.

Laycock, Stuart. *Britannia, the Failed State: Tribal Conflicts and the End of Roman Britain*. Stroud, UK: The History Press, 2008.

Mathisen, Ralph W. "Peregrini, Barbari, and Cives Romani: Concepts of Citizenship and the Legal Identity of Barbarians in the Late Roman Empire." *The American Historical Review* 111, no. 4 (October 2006): 1011–1040.

Murphy, Cullen. "Roman Empire: Gold Standard of Immigration." *Los Angeles Times*, June 16, 2007.

Rizzi, Marco, ed. *Hadrian and the Christians*. New York: De Gruyter, 2010.

Rushworth, Alan. *Housesteads Roman Fort: The Grandest Station*. London: Historic England Publishing, 2014.

Stout, S.E. "Training Soldiers for the Roman Legion." *The Classical Journal* 16, no. 7 (April 1921): 423–431.

UNESCO World Heritage List. "Frontiers of the Roman Empire." Accessed January 12, 2019. https://whc.unesco.org/en/list/430.

GREAT WALL OF CHINA

Billé, Franck, Grégory Delaplace, and Caroline Humphrey, eds. *Frontier Encounters: Knowledge and Practice at the Russian, Chinese and Mongolian Border*. Cambridge: Open Book Publishers, 2012.

Campanella, Thomas J. *The Concrete Dragon: China's Urban Revolution and What It Means for the World*. New York: Princeton Architectural Press, 2008.

Christian, David. *A History of Russia, Central Asia and Mongolia, Volume 2: Inner Eurasia from the Mongol Empire to Today, 1260–2000*. Hoboken, NJ: Wiley, 2018.

Elverskog, Carl Johan. *Buddhism, History & Power: The Jewel Translucent Sutra and the Formation of Mongol Identity*. Bloomington: Indiana University Press, 2000.

Jiaxin Du. "Last Battle on the Great Wall." *Military History* (January 2017): 30–39.

Kafka, Franz. "The Great Wall of China." In *Selected Short Stories of Franz Kafka*. Translated by Will and Edwin Muir. New York: Modern Library, 1952.

Man, John. *The Great Wall*. Cambridge, MA: Da Capo Press, 2008.

Rojas, Carlos. *The Great Wall*. Cambridge, MA: Harvard University Press, 2010.

Shu-Yun Ma. "The Role of Power Struggle and Changes in the 'Heshang Phenomenon' in China." *Modern Asian Studies* 30, no. 1 (February 1996): 29–50

Waters, Dan. "Foreigners and Feng Shui." *Journal of the Hong Kong Branch of the Royal Asiatic Society* 34 (1994): 57–117.

THIERS WALL

Cannon, James. *The Paris Zone: A Cultural History, 1840–1944*. London: Routledge, 2015.

Dass, Nirmal, ed. *Viking Attacks on Paris: The Bella Parisicae Urbis of Abbo of Saint-Germain-des-Près*. Translated by Nirmal Dass. Paris: Peeters, 2007.

Haughton, J. "The Fortifications of Paris." *The Lakeside Monthly* 4 (1870): 407–412.

Higonnet, Patrice L. R. *Paris: Capital of the World*. Cambridge, MA: Belknap Press, 2002.

Hugo, Victor. *Les Misérables*. Translated by Isabel F. Hapgood. Minneapolis: First Avenue Editions, 2015.

Le Goff, François J. *The Life of Adolphe Thiers*. Translated by Theodore Stanton. New York: G. P. Putnam, 1879.

Lepage, Jean-Denis G. G. *The Fortifications of Paris: An Illustrated History*. Jefferson, IA: McFarland & Company, 2006.

Lissagaray, Prosper-Olivier. *History of the Commune of 1871*. Translated by Eleanor Marx Aveling. London: Reeves and Turner, 1886.

Sante, Luc. *The Other Paris*. New York: Farrar, Straus and Giroux, 2015.

Vidler, Anthony. "The Rhetoric of Monumentality: Ledoux and the Barrières of Paris." *AA Files* 7 (September 1984): 14–29.

Wright, George Newenham. *Life and Times of Louis Philippe, King of the French: Volume 1*. London: Fisher, Son, & Co., 1848.

BERLIN WALL

Ahonen, Pertti. *Death at the Berlin Wall*. New York: Oxford University Press, 2011.

Barber, Stephen. *Berlin Bodies: Anatomizing the Streets of the City*. London: Reaktion Books, 2017.

Baron, Udo. *The Victims at the Berlin Wall 1961–1989: A Biographical Handbook*. Berlin: Ch. Links Verlag, 2011.

Dodds, Laurence. "Berlin Wall: How the Wall Came Down, As It Happened Twenty-Five Years Ago." *The Telegraph*, November 9, 2014.

Hodgin, Nick, and Caroline Pearce. *The GDR Remembered: Representations of the East German State Since 1989*. New York: Camden House, 2011.

Katona, Marianna S. *Tales from the Berlin Wall: Recollections of Frequent Crossings*. Berlin: Anotam, 2003.

Kotkin, Stephen. *Uncivil Society: 1989 and the Implosion of the Communist Establishment*. New York: The Modern Library, 2010.

Meyer, Michael. "Günter Schabowksi, the Man Who Opened the Wall." *New York Times*, November 6, 2015.

Smyser, W. R. *Kennedy and the Berlin Wall*. New York: Rowman and Littlefield, 2009.

ISRAEL-WEST BANK BARRIER

Backmann, René. *A Wall for Palestine*. Translated by A. Kaiser. New York: Picador, 2010.

Bard, Mitchell. "West Bank, Gaza and Lebanon Security Barriers: Background & Overview." Jewish Virtual Library. Accessed January 12, 2019. https://www.jewishvirtuallibrary.org/background-and-overview-of-israel-s-security-fence.

Ben-Dror, Elad. *Ralph Bunche and the Arab-Israeli Conflict: Mediation and the UN, 1947–1949*. Translated by Diana File and Lenn Shramm. London: Routledge, 2016.

Catignani, Sergio. *Israeli Counter-Insurgency and the Intifadas*. London: Routledge, 2008.

Jacoby, Tami Amanda. *Bridging the Barrier: Israeli Unilateral Disengagement*. London: Routledge, 2007.

Leuenberger, Christine. "Maps as Politics: Mapping the West Bank Barrier." *Journal of Borderlands Studies* (2016): 1–26.

Makovsky, David. "A Defensible Fence: Fighting Terror and Enabling a Two-State Solution." Monograph for the Washington Institute for Near East Policy, April 2004.

Said, Edward. "A Road Map to Where?" *London Review of Books* 25, no. 12 (June 19, 2003): 3–5.

United Nations Special Committee on Palestine. "Report to the General Assembly Vol. 1." Official Records of the Second Session of the General Assembly, 1947. Accessed January 12, 2019. https://unispal.un.org/DPA/DPR/unispal.nsf/0/07175DE9FA2DE563852568D3006E103.

Urquhart, Brian. *Ralph Bunche: An American Life*. New York: W. W. Norton, 1993.

Weizman, Eyal. *Hollow Land: Israel's Architecture of Occupation*. London: Verso, 2012.

AMERICA, MEXICO, AND THE BORDER,
1519–1992

Briscoe, Edward Eugene. "Pershing's Chinese Refugees in Texas." *Southwestern Historical Quarterly* 62, no. 4 (April 1959): 467–488.

Burt, Kenneth. *The Search for a Civic Voice: California Latino Politics* (Claremont: Regina Books, 2007).

del Castillo, Bernal Díaz, *The True History of the Conquest of New Spain*. London: The Hakluyt Society, 1908.

Gallay, Allan. *Colonial Wars of North America, 1512–1763*. New York: Routledge, 1996.

Greenberg, Amy S. *A Wicked War: Polk, Clay, Lincoln and the 1846 Invasion of Mexico*. New York: Vintage Books, 2012.

Hansen, Todd. *The Alamo Reader*. Mechanicsburg: Stackpole Books, 2003.

Heer, Jeet. "Operation Wetback Revisited." *The New Republic*, April 25, 2016. Accessed January 12, 2019. https://newrepublic.com/article/132988/operation-wetback-revisited.

Hernández, Kelly Lytle. *Migra! A History of the U.S. Border Patrol*. Berkeley: University of California Press, 2010.

Hodge, Roger. *Texas Blood: Seven Generations Among the Outlaws, Ranchers, Indians, Missionaries, Soldiers, and Smugglers of the Borderlands*. New York: Alfred A. Knopf, 2017.

International Boundary Commission, United States and Mexico. *Report of the Boundary Commission*. Washington: Government Printing Office, 1896.

Jencks, Tudor. *Captain Myles Standish*. New York: The Century Company, 1905.

Joseph, Gilbert M., and Timothy J. Henderson, eds. *The Mexico Reader: History, Culture, and Politics*. Durham, NC: Duke University Press, 2002.

Matthews, Matt M. *The U.S. Army on the Mexican Border: A Historical Perspective*. Fort Leavenworth, KS: Combat Studies Institute Press, 2007.

Rippy, J. Fred. *Joel R. Poinsett, Versatile American*. Durham, NC: Duke University Press, 1935.

St. John, Rachel. *Line in the Sand: A History of the Western U.S.-Mexico Border*. Princeton, NY: Princeton University Press, 2012.

AMERICA, MEXICO, AND THE BORDER,
1992–2019

Cantú, Francisco. *The Line Becomes a River: Dispatches from the Border.* New York: Riverhead Books, 2018.

Customs and Border Protection. "Design Build Structure, Solicitation." Number: 2017–JC-RT-0001." Federal Business Opportunities, February 24, 2017. Accessed Janaury 12, 2019. https://www.fbo.gov/index?s=opportunity&mode=form&tab=core&id=b8e1b2a6876519ca0aed748e1e491cf&_cview=0.

Customs and Border Protection, Office of Acquisition. "Border Wall Mock-Up and Prototype Test Final Report [Redacted]." Doc. no. ENT12–BW-14-000004 Revision A, February 23, 2018.

De Leon, Jason. *The Land of Open Graves: Living and Dying on the Migrant Trail.* Oakland: University of California Press, 2015.

Everett, Burgess and Marianne Levine. "Senators Bicker Over Definition of Trump's Wall." *Politico,* December 6, 2018. https://www.politico.com/story/2018/12/06/congress-border-wall-trump-funding-government-shutdown-1046169.

Freedlander, David. "Sam Nunberg Is Still Talking." *Politico,* March 23, 2018. Accessed January 12, 2019.https://www.politico.com/magazine/story/2018/03/23/sam-nunberg-donald-trump-217697.

Government Accountability Office. "Southwest Border Security: CBP Is Evaluating Designs and Locations for Border Barriers but Is Proceeding Without Key Information." GAO-18-614, July 2018.

Hattam, Victoria. "Imperial Designs: Remembering Vietnam at the U.S.-Mexico Border Wall." *Memory Studies* 9, no. 1 (Spring 2016): 27–47.

Miller, Meg. "Please Do Not Aestheticize the Wall." *Fast Company,* March 13, 2017. Accessed January 12, 2019. https://www.fastcompany.com/3068888/architects-please-do-not-aestheticize-the-wall.

Nevins, Joseph. *Operation Gatekeeper: The War on Illegals and the Remaking of the U.S.-Mexico Boundary.* New York: Routledge, 2002.

Nixon, Ron and Linda Qiu. "Trump's Evolving Words on the Wall." *New York Times,* January 18, 2018.

Press, Robert L. et al., "In the Shadow of the Wall, Part I: Borders, Wildlife, Habitat and Collaborative Conservation at Risk." Report for Defenders of Wildlife, 2018.

Rivas, Jorge. "The Companies Vying to Build the Border Wall Seem Shady as Hell." *Splinter*, April 18, 2018. Accessed January 12, 2019. https://splinternews.com/the-companies-vying-to-build-the-border-wall-seem-shady-1825356649.

Trump, Donald J. "Executive Order: Border Security and Immigration Enforcement Improvements." The White House, January 25, 2017. Accessed January 12, 2019. https://www.whitehouse.gov/presidential-actions/executive-order-border-security-immigration-enforcement-improvements/.

Volner, Ian. "The Trump Administration Doesn't Want a Winner for Its Wall Competition." *Foreign Policy*, July 12, 2017. Accessed January 12, 2019. https://foreignpolicy.com/2017/07/12/the-trump-administration-doesnt-want-a-winner-for-its-wall-competition/.

Wroe, Andrew. *The Republican Party and Immigration Politics: From Proposition 187 to George W. Bush*. New York: Palgrave MacMillan, 2008.

WALLS AND BORDERS: IN THEORY AND AROUND THE WORLD

Ballif, Florine and Stéphane Rosière, "The Challenge of 'Teichopolitics': Analyzing Contemporary Border Closures." *L'Espace géographique* 38, no. 3 (2009): 193–206.

Brown, Wendy. *Walled States, Waning Sovereignty*. New York: Zone Books, 2010.

Chaichian, Mohammed. *Empires and Walls: Globalization, Migration, and Colonial Domination*. Boston: Brill, 2014.

Coutin, Susan Bibler. "Borderlands, Illegality and the Spaces of Non-Existence." In *Globalization Under Construction: Government, Law and Identity*, Richard Perry and Bill Maurer, eds., 171–202. Minneapolis: University of Minnesota Press, 2003.

Jones, Reese. *Violent Borders: Refugees and the Right to Move.* New York: Verso, 2016.

——. *Border Walls: Security and the War on Terror in the United States, India and Israel.* New York: Palgrave Macmillan, 2012.

Martin, Marijke and Judith Smals. *Wall House #2: John Hejduk in Groningen.* Groningen, Netherlands: Platform Gras, 2001.

Mattelart, Armand. *Networking the World, 1794–2000.* Translated by Liz Cary-Libbrecht and James A. Cohen. Minneapolis: University of Minnesota Press, 2000.

Nail, Thomas. *Theory of the Border.* New York: Oxford University Press, 2016.

Rael, Ronald. *Borderwall as Architecture: A Manifesto.* Oakland: University of California Press, 2017.

Roberts, John. *The Reasoning of Unreason: Universalism, Capitalism and Disenlightenment.* London: Bloomsbury, 2018.

Savage, Michael, *Government Zero: No Borders, No Language, No Culture.* New York: Center Street, 2015.

Vallet, Élisabeth, ed. *Borders, Fences and Walls: State of Insecurity?* London: Routledge, 2016.

NOTES

INTRODUCTION

vi "Life has to do with walls": Marijke Martin and Judith Smals, *Wall House #2: John Hejduk in Groningen* (Groningen, Netherlands: Platform Gras, 2001), 41.

2 "7 quarts per day for the men": *Report of the Boundary Commission* (Washington, DC: Government Printing Office, 1896), 32.

4 "our associates of the Mexican Commission": Ibid., 4.

4 "the president expressed a desire": "In Territories," *Indianapolis Journal*, May 7, 1901.

5 "commercial well-being and good understanding": Quoted in Stephen Kinzer, *The True Flag: Theodore Roosevelt, Mark Twain, and the Birth of American Empire* (New York: Henry Holt, 2017), 205.

9 "immediate past": Robert Maxwell, Introduction, *The Journal of Architecture* 1 (Spring 1996): 3.

I. THE INVENTION OF DIFFERENCE

13 "as the sand of the sea": Revelation 20:8.

13 "set [his] face": Ezekiel 38:2.

14 "Now Jericho was straitly": Joshua 6:1.

17 "ideological reasons": Ran Barkai and Roy Liran, "Midsummer Sunset at Jericho," *Time and Mind: The Journal of Archaeology, Consciousness and Culture* 1, 3 (November 2008): 276, 279.

18　"Our theory would appear less daring": Gaston Bachelard, *The Psychoanalysis of Fire*, trans. Alan C. M. Ross (Boston: Beacon Press, 1968), 27-28.

18　"The initial wall of circa 8300 BCE": For descriptions of the oldest wall and corresponding community see Kathleen Kenyon, *Digging Up Jericho* (New York: Frederick A. Praeger, 1957), 67-76, 113; Robert Ruby, *Jericho: Dreams, Ruins, Phantoms* (New York: Henry Holt, 1995), 124-26; Ofer Bar-Yosef, "The Walls of Jericho: An Alternative Interpretation," *Current Anthropology* 27, 2 (April 1986): 157.

19　"The Great *Sitt*": For a thorough account of Kenyon at Jericho see Miriam C. Davis, *Dame Kathleen Kenyon: Digging Up the Holy Land* (Walnut Creek, CA: Left Coast Press, 2008), 101-54.

25　"The fog of cultural conflict": The felicitous phrase is from Dan Kahan's blog, www.culturlacognition.net/blog; for a more in-depth take, see his article "Vaccine Risk Perceptions and Ad Hoc Risk Communication," *CCP Risk and Economic Studies Report* 17 (January 2014). The 1954 study was the Robbers Cave experiment, while the University of Sheffield experiment was published as "Three-month-olds, but not newborns, prefer own-race faces," *Developmental Science* 6, 5 (November 2005): F31-36.

27　"All the houses have flat roofs": Bernal Díaz del Castillo, *The True History of the Conquest of New Spain* (London: The Hakluyt Society, 1908), 220.

28　"Arrows in a snakeskin quiver": John S. C. Abbot, *Miles Standish the Puritan Captain* (New York: Dodd & Mead, 1874), 179-81. For the description of the fence, see Allan Gallay, *Colonial Wars of North America, 1512-1763* (New York: Routledge, 1996), 569.

29　"Only a month after the wall's completion": Tudor Jencks, *Captain Myles Standish* (New York: The Century Company, 1905), 178.

31　"to explain the practical operation": Quoted in J. Fred Rippy, *Joel R. Poinsett, Versatile American* (Durham, NC: Duke University Press, 1935), 106. Much of the information on Poinsett came from the same source.

32   "ambitious people, always ready": Quoted in ibid., 106.

32   "to compare [Mexicans]": Quoted in Gilbert M. Joseph and Timothy J. Henderson, eds., *The Mexico Reader: History, Culture, and Politics* (Durham, NC: Duke University Press, 2002), 12.

32   "all intercourse with foreigners": Quoted in ibid., 14.

35   "ordered every one of the Americans": Quoted in Todd Hansen, *The Alamo Reader* (Mechanicsburg, PA: Stackpole Books, 2003), 483.

36   "disguised in a blue cottonade": Quoted in Stephen L. Moore, *Eighteen Minutes: The Battle of San Jacinto and the Texas Independence Campaign* (Dallas: Republic of Texas Press, 2004), 379.

37   "savage fiend": "Natchez," *Fayetteville Weekly Observer*, April 21, 1836.

37   "tumble headlong": "General Houston and Santa Anna's Former Friendship," *Selma Daily Reporter*, June 11, 1836.

37   "too lazy to advance": "Texas," *The Daily Picayune*, May 16, 1839.

37   "not the slightest reliance": "Texas," *Democratic Free Press*, July 6, 1836.

37   "wicked barbarians": Quoted in John S. D. Eisenhower, *So Far from God: The U.S. War with Mexico* (Norman: University of Oklahoma Press, 2000), 86.

37   "These Mexican savages": "Dow, Jr., On War," *Louisville Daily Courier*, June 6, 1846.

38   "Spartan-like defense of the Alamo": Quoted in Eisenhower, *So Far from God*, 87.

38   "young infantrymen waiting in San Antonio": Letter from Colonel John Hardin, cited in Amy S. Greenberg, *A Wicked War: Polk, Clay, Lincoln and the 1846 Invasion of Mexico* (New York: Vintage Books, 2012), 137.

38   "the soulless butcheries": Quoted in Robert W. Merry, A *Country of Vast Designs: James Polk, the Mexican War and the Conquest of the American Continent* (New York: Simon & Schuster, 2009), 153.

39   "American blood": Quoted in Spencer Tucker, ed., *The Encyclopedia of the Mexican-American War*, Vol. 1 (Santa Barbara, CA: ABC-CLIO, 2013), 959.

II. BORDER AS FORGE

43 "the border is in between": Thomas Nail, *Theory of the Border* (New York: Oxford University Press, 2016), 2.

45 "Graeculus": Anthony Everett, *Hadrian and the Triumph of Rome* (New York: Random House, 2015), 15. The same source furnished much of the background on Nerva, Trajan, and Hadrian's life in general, as did Mary Beard, "A Very Modern Emperor," *The Guardian*, July 18, 2008.

45 "three thousand miles long": UNESCO World Heritage List, "Frontiers of the Roman Empire," https://whc.unesco.org/en/list/430.

47 "Son of all the deified emperors": Roman Inscriptions of Britain, "Rib. 1051. Imperial Dedication," https://romaninscriptionsofbritain.org /inscriptions/1051.

47 "explorer of all things interesting": Tertullian, quoted in Marco Rizzi, ed., *Hadrian and the Christians* (New York: De Gruyter, 2010), 15.

47 "wild": Jordanes, *The Origins and Deeds of the Goths*, trans. Charles C. Mierow (Princeton, NJ: Princeton University Press, 1908), 5.

48 "up to the waist": This and other descriptions of Britain and Scotland taken from Herodian, Cassius Dios, and Procopius, quoted in "Roman Perceptions of Britain," http://penelope.uchicago.edu/ ~grout/encyclopaedia_Romana/britannia/miscellanea/geography .html.

50 "Hadrian can offer anything": The slogan is that of Hadrian Valeting, of Haltwhistle.

51 "ten thousand Roman auxiliary troops": Mohammed Chaichian, *Empires and Walls: Globalization, Migration, and Colonial Domination* (Boston: Brill, 2014), 39.

51 "I mean your magnificent citizenship": Quoted in Jed W. Atkins, *Roman Political Thought* (New York: Cambridge University Press, 2018), 65-66. Additional information on Roman citizenship and status of immigrants from Ralph W. Mathisen, "Peregrini, Barbari, and Cives Romani: Concepts of Citizenship and the Legal Identity of Barbarians in the Late Roman Empire," *American Historical Review* 111, 4 (October 2006): 1011-40; Ancient History Encyclopedia, "Roman

Citizenship," https://www.ancient.eu/article/859/roman-citizenship/; Cullen Murphy, "Roman Empire: Gold Standard of Immigration," *Los Angeles Times*, June 16, 2007.

52 "who have served twenty-five years": British Museum Online Collection, "Military Diploma," https://www.britishmuseum.org/research /collection_online/collection_object_details.aspx?objectId=810661 &partId=1&object=33809&page=5.

53 "Training was arduous": On Roman military training, see S. E. Stout, "Training Soldiers for the Roman Legion," *The Classical Journal* 16, 7 (April 1921): 423-31.

53 "*Maurorum Aurelianorum*": David Derbyshire, "Border Folks May Be Descended from Africans," *The Telegraph*, June 11, 2004.

53 "Cohors I Tungrorum": Alan Rushworth, *Housesteads Roman Fort: The Grandest Station* (London: Historic England Publishing, 2014), 243, 283.

54 "to the spirits of the departed": Roman Inscriptions of Britain, "RIB 1065. Funerary Inscription for Regina," https://romaninscriptionsof britain.org/inscriptions/1065.

55 "Seventy miles long, most of it in stone": Tony Wilmott, ed., *Hadrian's Wall: Archaeological Research by English Heritage 1976–2000* (London: English Heritage, 2009), p. 137. Mary Beard also points out that nearly a third of the structure was not, in fact, constructed of stone, but of turf. Beard, "A Very Modern Emperor."

57 "the Romans could no longer regain Britain": Procopius, quoted in Lara Bishop, "The Transformation of Administrative Towns in Roman Britain," unpublished master's thesis, University of Victoria, British Columbia, Canada, 2011, 53.

57 "to hasten about hither and thither": Ammianus, quoted in ibid., 28.

57 "The Great Conspiracy": This account is largely drawn from Ian Hughs, *Imperial Brothers: Valentinian, Valens and the Disaster at Adrianople* (Barnsley, UK: Pen & Sword, 2013), 56-60, 69-72, 84.

57 "Cohors I Cornoviorum": Stuart Laycock, *Britannia, The Failed State: Tribal Conflicts and the End of Roman Britain* (Stroud, UK: The History Press, 2008), 129.

58 "whom they were forced to abandon": Bede, *The Miscellaneous Works of Venerable Bede* (London: Whitaker & Co., 1843), 65.

58 "spaces of non-existence": Susan Bibler Coutin, "Borderlands, Illegality and the Spaces of Non-Existence," in *Globalization Under Construction: Government, Law and Identity*, eds. Richard Perry and Bill Maurer (Minneapolis: University of Minnesota Press, 2003), 171–202.

58 "To ravage, to slaughter, to usurp": Cornelius Tacitus, *Germany and Agricola of Tacitus: The Oxford Translation* (New York: Translation Publishing Company, 1922), 88.

60 "Let there be a desert": Quoted in Matt M. Matthews, *The U.S. Army on the Mexican Border: A Historical Perspective* (Fort Leavenworth, KS: Combat Studies Institute Press, 2007), 46.

60 "twenty-three times between 1873 and 1882": Ibid., 48.

60 "Every Mexican schoolboy": T. R. Fehrenbach, quoted in ibid., 49.

61 "It is almost too much to hope": Ibid., 59.

62 "alien immigration": Robert DeC. Ward, "National Eugenics in Relation to Immigration," *North American Review* 192, 1 (1910): 63.

62 "twenty thousand legally admitted persons annually in the 1910s": Cited in Jason Steinhauer, "The History of Mexican Immigration to the U.S. in the Early 20th Century," John W. Kluge Center at the Library of Congress, March 11, 2015, https://blogs.loc.gov/kluge/2015/03/the-history-of-mexican-immigration-to-the-u-s-in-the-early-20th-century/.

63 "At any truck concentration point": Quoted in L. A. Shively, "'Pershing's Chinese Leave Mark on History," *San Antonio Express News*, May 26, 2011. The comprehensive history from which the line is drawn is Edward Eugene Briscoe, "Pershing's Chinese Refugees: An Odyssey of the Southwest," unpublished master's thesis, St. Mary's University, San Antonio, TX, 1947.

63 "I cannot commend too highly": Quoted in Andrew Carroll, *War Letters: Extraordinary Correspondence from American Wars* (New York: Scribner's, 2001), 140.

64 "kind remembrances to all refugees": Quoted in Edward Eugene Briscoe, "Pershing's Chinese Refugees in Texas," *Southwestern Historical*

Quarterly 62, 4 (April 1959): 481. The article is an extract from an unpublished thesis.

65 "Blackjack Wong": News staff, "Talk to Highlight 'Pershing's Chinese,'" *Albuquerque Journal*, February 13, 2007.

65 "I shall ask for adequate and decent laws": Quoted in Jonathan Daniels, *The Man of Independence* (Columbia: University of Missouri Press, 1950), 356.

65 "the dead hand of the past": *Public Papers of the Presidents: Harry S. Truman, 1952–1953* (Washington, DC: Government Printing Office, 1966), 182.

66 "unworthy of our traditions": Ibid., 443.

67 "*Yo quiero Ike*": Kenneth Burt, "Latinos con Eisenhower," http://kennethburt.com/blog/?p=436. The same author has also written an extensive study on the development of the West Coast Latino electorate, *The Search for a Civic Voice: California Latino Politics* (Claremont, CA: Regina Books, 2007).

68 "1.25 million individuals": Jeet Heer, "Operation Wetback Revisited," *The New Republic*, April 25, 2016.

68 "penal hell ship": Ibid.

68 "Republican conscience and Republican policy": Quoted in Marc Fisher, "GOP Platform through the Years Shows Party's Shift from Moderate to Conservative," *Washington Post*, August 28, 2012.

68 "beneficial both to the Mexican nationals": Stephen Shadegg, quoted in Micaela Larkin, "Southwestern Strategy: Mexican-Americans and Republican Politics in the Arizona Borderlands," unpublished conference paper, 2009, 13.

68 "Our ties with Mexico": Quoted in Matt Novak, "Senator Barry Goldwater Imagines Arizona in the Year 2012," *Smithsonian Magazine*, December 7, 2011.

69 "Brother of the Month": Larkin, "Southwestern Strategy," 12.

70 "It never even occurred to me": Quoted in John R. Burch Jr., *The Great Society and the War on Poverty in Essays and Documents* (Santa Barbara, CA: Greenwood, 2017), 327.

70   "The day is not far off when the population explosion": Quoted in Sam Peak, "We Already Tried Trump's Immigration Plan, and It Created Today's DACA Crisis," *Washington Examiner*, February 6, 2018.

71   "like the boom of a cannon": Quoted in Paul Kramer, "A Border Crosses," *The New Yorker* online, https://www.newyorker.com/news/news-desk/moving-mexican-border.

71   "They have a heritage": Quoted in James Warren, "Nixon on Tape Expounds on Welfare and Homosexuality," *Chicago Tribune*, November 7, 1999.

72   "May there never be a wall": Quoted in Yanan Wang, "At One Border Park, Separated Families Hug Across a Steel Divide," *Washington Post*, May 1, 2016.

72   "Located on landscaped grounds": Portions of this paragraph are adapted from reporting conducted in the fall of 2018 and appear courtesy of *Architect*: see Ian Volner, "The Activism of Henry Muñoz," *Architect*, December 5, 2018, https://www.architectmagazine.com/practice/the-activism-of-henry-munoz-iii_o.

74   "not so bad as the Negroes": Quoted in Kelly Lytle Hernández, *Migra!: A History of the U.S. Border Patrol* (Berkeley: University of California Press, 2010), 30.

74   "The Democratic party . . . no longer can take Mexican Americans": Quoted in Martin Waldron, "Chicanos in Texas Bid for Key Political Role," *New York Times*, August 2, 1970.

75   "a better understanding and a better relationship": "George H. W. Bush and Ronald Reagan Debate on Immigration in 1980," YouTube, https://www.youtube.com/watch?v=YsmgPp_nlok.

75   "preserve the value of one of the most sacred": Quoted in Robert Pear, "President Signs Landmark Bill on Immigration Law," *New York Times*, November 7, 1986.

76   "an estimated 1.5 million family members of qualified immigrants": Cited in Marvine Howe, "New Policy Aids Families of Aliens," *New York Times*, March 5, 1990.

76   "It certainly did not originate with anyone": David Bier of the Cato Institute, quoted in Dan Nowicki, "Did Ronald Reagan Regret

1986 Immigrant 'Amnesty' Law?," *Arizona Republic*, February 11, 2018.

III. UNSTABLE WALLS

79   *"If it were not for a bone-chilling spell"*: Feng Menglong, *Stories to Awaken the World*, trans. Shuhui Yang and Yunqin Yang (Seattle: University of Washington Press, 2009), 365.

81   "the many legends which have arisen about the structure": Franz Kafka, "The Great Wall of China," *Selected Short Stories of Franz Kafka* (New York: Modern Library, 1952), 130.

83   "Some of the wealthiest and best-known capitalists": Quoted in Carlos Rojas, *The Great Wall* (Cambridge, MA: Harvard University Press, 2010), 38. Rojas's book was a key source concerning the hoax and much else besides.

83   "Will China's Wall": Quoted in Thomas J. Campanella, *The Concrete Dragon: China's Urban Revolution and What It Means for the World* (New York: Princeton Architectural Press, 2008), 110.

84   "cut through the veins": Quoted in Dan Waters, "Foreigners and Feng Shui," *Journal of the Hong Kong Branch of the Royal Asiatic Society* 34 (1994): 60.

84   "Four decks, with a tonnage comparable": For details on the treasure voyages, see Joseph Needham, *Civilization in China Volume 4: Physics and Physical Technology* (London: Cambridge University Press, 1971), 480.

85   "barbarian regions": Excerpted in Stephen Morillo and Lynne Miles-Morillo, *Sources for Frameworks of History*, Vol. 2, *Since 1350* (New York: Oxford University Press, 2014), 7.

85   "These dogs and sheep": David Christian, *A History of Russia, Central Asia and Mongolia, Vol. 2: Inner Eurasia from the Mongol Empire to Today, 1260-2000* (Hoboken, NJ: Wiley, 2018), 100.

86   "In the White Ox Year": Quoted in Carl Johan Elverskog, *Buddhism, History and Power: The Jewel Translucent Sutra and the Formation of Mongol Identity* (Bloomington: Indiana University Press, 2000), 66.

88 "One night, the Kwantung garrison commander": Most of this account is drawn from Jiaxin Du, "Last Battle on the Great Wall," *Military History* (January 2017): 30–39.

89 "really didn't need the coat": Quoted in Neil A. Hamilton, *The 1970s* (New York: Facts on File, 2006), 119.

89 "appropriation of this morsel": Armand Mattelart, *Networking the World, 1794–2000*, trans. Liz Cary-Libbrecht and James A. Cohen (Minneapolis: University of Minnesota Press, 2000), 121.

90 "As we look at this wall": Quoted in Hamilton, *The 1970s*, 118.

90 "in reality . . . it has never served": Quoted in Rojas, *The Great Wall*, 129–30.

90 "And yet, if the great wall could speak": Quoted in Franck Billé, Grégory Delaplace, and Caroline Humphrey, eds., *Frontier Encounters: Knowledge and Practice at the Russian, Chinese and Mongolian Border* (Cambridge: Open Book Publishers, 2012), 38. A full chronicle of the *Deathsong* affair appears in Shu-Yun Ma, "The Role of Power Struggle and Changes in the 'Heshang Phenomenon' in China," *Modern Asian Studies* 30, 1 (February 1996): 29–50.

91 "good architecture": Andrew Leach, "Huh? Wow! ≠ Wow! Huh?" *OASE Journal* 90 (2013): 32.

92 "From 900,000 in 1980, the numbers of apprehensions": Ana Gonzalez-Barrera, "Apprehensions of Mexican Migrants at U.S. Borders Reach Near-Historic Lows," *Pew Research Center*, http://www.pewresearch .org/fact-tank/2016/04/14/mexico-us-border-apprehensions/.

92 "*They keep coming*": Quoted in Andrew Wroe, *The Republican Party and Immigration Politics: From Proposition 187 to George W. Bush* (New York: Palgrave MacMillan, 2008), 47.

92 "Of course I do. Do I think there were some": Quoted in Mark Z. Barabak, "Pete Wilson Looks Back on Proposition 187 and Says, Heck Yeah, He'd Support It All Over Again," *Los Angeles Times*, March 23, 2017.

93 "President Bill Clinton ordered a twofold increase": For details on Clinton-era immigration policies, see Joseph Nevins, *Operation*

Gatekeeper: The War on Illegals and the Remaking of the U.S.-Mexico Boundary (New York: Routledge, 2002).

93 "The front line was nowhere and everywhere": General William C. Westmoreland, *A Soldier Reports* (New York: Da Capo Press, 1989), 299.

94 "In the face of American airpower": Quoted in Isaac Keister, "Technology and Strategy: The War in Vietnam," unpublished master's thesis, Western Oregon University, Monmouth, Oregon, 2016, 11.

94 "Millions more simply moldered": Bulk of facts and figures about the Marston fence from Victoria Hattam, "Imperial Designs: Remembering Vietnam at the U.S.-Mexico Border Wall," *Memory Studies* 9, 1 (Spring 2016), 27–47.

94 "40 percent decrease in illegal traffic": "Government Claims Partial Victory in Struggle Against Illegal Immigration," *CNN* online, October 8, 1997, http://www.cnn.com/US/9710/09/operation.gatekeeper/.

95 "to create the illusion that Operation Gatekeeper": Office of the Inspector General, "Operation Gatekeeper: An Investigation into Allegations of Fraud and Misconduct," US Department of Justice, https://oig.justice.gov/special/9807/gkp02.htm.

96 "Illegal aliens should not receive public benefits": Quoted in "Excerpts from Platform Adopted by Republican National Convention," *New York Times*, August 13, 1996.

96 "Still, as late as 2014, a majority of Latinos": Gary Segura, "Reviewing the Evidence, Part 2: CIR Failure and Political Fallout," *Latino Decisions*, http://www.latinodecisions.com/blog/2014/08/29/reviewing-the-evidence-part-2-cir-failure-and-political-fallout/.

97 "little brown ones": "Bush Introduces Grandchildren as 'Little Brown Ones,'" *Associated Press*, August 16, 1988.

97 "why the Democrats are so wholeheartedly": Quoted in Kristina Torres, "Did Dems Vote for a Border Wall in 2006?," *Atlanta Journal-Constitution*, April 26, 2017.

97 "the same imprisonment term": H.R. 4437, "Border Protection, Antiterrorism, and Illegal Immigration Control Act of 2005," 109th Congress, Sec. 205.

97 "There should be 700 miles": Quoted in Editorial, "How Congress Prevented Border Fence Law's Implementation," *Investor's Business Daily*, November 12, 2015.

98 "appropriate for fencing and barriers": Lisa Seghetti, *Border Security: Immigration Enforcement Between Ports of Entry, Prepared for Members and Committees of Congress* (Washington, DC: Congressional Research Service, December 18, 2014), 17.

98 "The 'sand dragon,' as some called it": "Beloved Parts of U.S.-Mexican Border Changed Almost Overnight," Associated Press, February 19, 2009.

99 "All the stuff they asked for": "Remarks by the President on Comprehensive Immigration Reform in El Paso, Texas," The White House, Office of the Press Secretary, May 10, 2011, https://obamawhite house.archives.gov/the-press-office/2011/05/10/remarks-president -comprehensive-immigration-reform-el-paso-texas.

99 "Between 2009 and 2014, the total number of Mexican nationals": "More Mexicans Leaving than Coming to the U.S.," Pew Research Center, http://www.pewhispanic.org/2015/11/19/more-mexicans-leaving -than-coming-to-the-u-s/.

101 "It's going to be ugly": Quoted in "Texas: A Border Clash over a Mexico Border Fence," *Newsweek*, April 26, 2008, https://www.newsweek .com/texas-border-clash-over-mexico-border-fence-86193.

102 "All this history": Eloisa Tamez, quoted in Kevin Sieff, "Borderlands," *Brownsville Herald*, December 9, 2007.

102 "The ramping up of border security": "Border Patrol Agent Nationwide Staffing by Fiscal Year, 1992–2017," US Customs and Border Protection, December 12, 2017,https://www.cbp.gov/document/stats /us-border-patrol-fiscal-year-staffing-statistics-fy-1992-fy-2017.

103 "radiant, confident, poised": "Border Patrol Agent Gets Five Years in Prison for Immigrant Smuggling," Associated Press, July 28, 2006.

103 "In Matamoros, just a few miles": Oscar Cáseras, "How Crossing the Bridge to Matamoros Got Complicated," *New York Times*, February 7, 2018.

103 "a prime destination for investors": Eduardo Bolio, Jaana Remes, et al., "A Tale of Two Mexicos: Growth and Prosperity in a Two-Speed Economy," McKinsey Global Institute, March 2014, https://www.mckinsey.com/featured-insights/americas/a-tale-of-two-mexicos.

103 "at least 750,000 American jobs were lost as a result of NAFTA": Quoted in Gene Epstein, "Mr. Dobbs' Whacky World," *Wall Street Journal*, August 14, 2006.

104 "studies suggested that for every 10 percent increase": Jesús Cañas, Roberto A. Coronado, et al., "The Impact of Maquiladora Industry on U.S. Border Cities: Research Department Working Paper 1107," Federal Reserve Bank of Dallas, May 17, 2011, 5.

104 "Brownsville's destiny has changed": City Commissioner Jessica Tetreau-Kalifa, quoted in Alyssa Newcomb, "How SpaceX Is Changing the 'Destiny' of Brownsville, Texas," ABC News, August 4, 2014, https://abcnews.go.com/Technology/spacex-changing-destiny-brownsville-texas/story?id=24844569.

106 "While no one was watching": H. Ross Perot and Pat Choate, *Save Your Job, Save Our Country: Why NAFTA Must Be Stopped—Now!* (New York: Hyperion Books, 1993), 92.

106 "Nobody would be tougher on ISIS": "Here's Donald Trump's Announcement Speech," *Time*, June 16, 2015, http://time.com/3923128/donald-trump-announcement-speech/.

IV. THE ART OF THE WALL-ABLE

111 "a population of 800,000": "La croissance de Paris," *Atlas Historique de Paris*, http://paris-atlas-historique.fr/8.html.

111 "The modern Babylon": Alfred de Musset, *Confession of a Child of the Century*, trans. Robert Arnot (New York: Current Literature Publishing, 1910), 142. The anecdote about his cigarette butts appears in Francine du Plessix Gray, *Rage and Fire: A Life of Louise Colet* (New York: Simon & Schuster, 1994), 223.

112 "harmful miasmas": Alexandre Parent du Châtelet, quoted in David S. Barnes, *The Great Stink of Paris and the Nineteenth-Century Struggle*

Against Filth and Germs (Baltimore: Johns Hopkins University Press, 2006), 70.

112 "the true capital of Europe": Quoted in Patrice L. R. Higonnet, *Paris: Capital of the World* (Cambridge, MA: Belknap Press, 2002), 7.

112 "In a contemporary engraving": "The 1st Gaslamp in Paris at Place du Carrousel in 1818," engraving, Bridgeman Images/Musée de la Ville de Paris, image no. CHT276309.

112 "Citizens,": Quoted in George Newenham Wright, *Life and Times of Louis Philippe, King of the French*, vol. 1 (London: Fisher, Son, & Co. 1848), 551.

113 "On the walls, the towers": Nirmal Dass, ed. and trans., *Viking Attacks on Paris: The Bella Parisiacae Urbis of Abbo of Saint-Germain-des-Près* (Paris: Peeters, 2007), 77.

114 "To augment its salary": Quoted in Anthony Vidler, "The Rhetoric of Monumentality: Ledoux and the Barrières of Paris," *AA Files* 7 (September 1984): 15. The translations of both poems—with apologies to Professor Vidler, with whom I studied—are mine.

115 "careful of his health, of his fortune": Victor Hugo, *Les Misérables*, trans. Isabel F. Hapgood (Minneapolis, MN: First Avenue Editions, 2015), 749.

115 "the great handwriting of the human race": Victor Hugo, *The Hunchback of Notre Dame*, trans. Isabel F. Hapgood (Auckland, NZ: The Floating Press, 2009), 331.

115 "Fascinating": Quoted in Graham Robb, *Victor Hugo: A Biography* (New York: W. W. Norton, 1997), 452.

115 "Its presumed cost ran to thirty-five million francs": Cited in "The Fortifications of Paris," *The London Quarterly Review* 77, no. 156 (October 1846): 146.

116 "Plunder Master General": For a full account of Soult's career see Sir William Stirling Maxwell, *Annals of the Artists of Spain* (London: John C. Nimmo, 1891), 1034.

116 "It is a plan to put down liberty": J. Haughton, "The Fortifications of Paris," *Lakeside Monthly* 4 (1870), 410.

116 "in politics, we must repair the evils": Adolphe Thiers, *Histoire de la révolution française*, vol. 2 (Brussels: Belgian Typographical Society, 1840), 112. Translation is mine.

117 "old umbrella": François J. Le Goff, *The Life of Adolphe Thiers*, trans. Theodore Stanton (New York: G. P. Putnam, 1879), 90.

117 "overseeing a workforce that eventually grew to 21,600": Jean-Denis G. G. Lepage, *The Fortifications of Paris: An Illustrated History* (Jefferson, NC: McFarland & Company, 2006), 178. Many details on the wall's construction were likewise drawn from Lepage's book.

119 "a dimwit whom we will lead": Quoted in Jean Dautry, *1848 et la Deuxième République* (Paris: Éditions Sociales, 1957), 228. Translation is mine.

119 "parody of restoration of empire": Karl Marx, *The Eighteenth Brumaire of Louis Bonaparte* (New York: International Publishers, 2008), 117.

120 "plaything . . . that will never carry voyagers": Quoted in Antoine Bouruilleau, "Comment est née la SNCF," *Slate FR*, March 2, 2018, https://www.slate.fr/story/158311/naissance-sncf?amp. Translation is mine.

120 "You are not ready": Gustave Ducoudray, *Histoire de France et histoire contemporaine de 1789 à la constitution de 1875* (Paris: Librairie Hachette, 1888), 798.

122 "forces numbering only about six thousand": Prosper-Olivier Lissagaray, *History of the Commune of 1871*, trans. Eleanor Marx Aveling (London: Reeves and Turner, 1886), 305.

122 "we had only [one] cannon": Ibid., 304.

122 "You can enter": Ibid., 307.

122 "gate of St. Cloud has fallen": Ibid., 310.

122 "Citizens," said the conductor: Ibid., 307.

123 "troops had worked their way along the wall": Contemporary maps show the precise patterns of troops as they entered the city and how they were able to take advantage of the enceinte: see L. Meunier and P. Rouillier, "Paris en mai 1871: Plan indiquant les operations de

l'armée contre l'insurrection," Historical Library of the City of Paris, G 305.

123 "their numbers were proved": W. Pembroke Fetridge, *The Paris Commune in 1871* (New York: Harper & Brothers, 1871), 440.

123 "army transformed . . . into a vast platoon": Lissagaray, *History of the Commune*, 383.

123 "cause of justice, order, humanity": Ibid., 321.

125 "a circular enclosure in which the imagination": Louis Cheronnet, quoted in James Cannon, *The Paris Zone: A Cultural History, 1840–1944* (London: Routledge, 2015), 1.

127 "something had taken place": Sargeant Michael Andraychak, quoted in Kate Pickles and Alexandra Klausner, "Suspect in Woman's Death of San Francisco Pier Claims Gun Went Off Accidentally," *Daily Mail*, July 6, 2015, https://www.dailymail.co.uk/news/article-3150736/Kathryn-Steinle-s-SF-pier-suspect-Francisco-Sanchez-claims-gun-went-accidentally.html.

128 "Another victim of the war": Comments on Joel B. Pollack, "Kathryn Steinle, 32, Killed by Illegal Alien, Laid to Rest," *Breitbart*, July 10, 2015, https://www.breitbart.com/local/2015/07/10/kathryn-steinle-32-killed-by-illegal-alien-laid-to-rest/.

128 "Electrified razor wire is a good start": Comments on Bob Price, "Video Shows Prototypes of the Border Wall," *Breitbart*, June 28, 2017, https://www.breitbart.com/border/2017/06/28/watch-video-shows-prototypes-border-wall/. The commenters are not expressly remarking on the Steinle case, rather on the "invasion" as a whole.

128 "We are going to build a big, beautiful, powerful wall": Interview on *The O'Reilly Factor*, "Trump on Immigration Plan," August 18, 2015, YouTube, https://www.youtube.com/watch?v=80cY76l-pMQ.

128 "Beautiful Kate": "Presidential Candidate Donald Trump at the Family Leadership Summit," July 18, 2015, C-SPAN, https://www.c-span.org/video/?c4557271/presidential-candidate-donald-trump-family-leadership-summit.

129 "Spandex bodysuit": Yoav Gonen, "This Trump Supporter Wore a Mexico Wall Costume to Rally," *New York Post*, March 5, 2016.

129 "SECURE THE BORDER!": Quoted in Ron Nixon and Linda Qiu, "Trump's Evolving Words on the Wall," *New York Times*, January 18, 2018. My chronology hews closely to theirs.

129 "must cover the entirety of the southern border": Quoted in Jeremy W. Peters, "Republican Platform Defends 'Traditional Marriage,' a Border Wall and Coal," *New York Times*, July 18, 2016.

130 "wouldn't stop a tricycle": Quoted in Stephen Lemons, "Chris Simcox's Life Mirrors the Nativist Movement's Demise," *Phoenix New Times*, September 5, 2013.

130 "spend hours building mock walls out of tape and glue": Related in John F. Muller, "I Sat on the Other Side of Stephen Miller's First Wall," *Politico*, June 22, 2018, https://www.politico.com/magazine /story/2018/06/22/i-sat-on-the-other-side-of-stephen-millers-first -wall-218886.

130 "Maybe we do this, maybe we do that": Quoted in David Freedlander, "Sam Nunberg Is Still Talking," *Politico*, March 23, 2018, https://www.politico.com/magazine/story/2018/03/23/sam-nunberg -donald-trump-217697.

130 "the (much briefer) prepared version": See "Trump's Prepared Remarks." Scribd, https://www.scribd.com/document/268863888 /Trump-s-prepared-remarks#from_embed.

131 "For Donald Trump, we were just what he needed": Quoted in C. W. Nevius, "Steinle's Parents: No Room for Angry," *San Francisco Chronicle*, September 24, 2015.

131 "That's the Donald being the Donald": Quoted in Ryan Parry West and Joanne Clements, "'Help Me, Dad': Heartbroken Father Describes the Final Moments of Daughter," *Daily Mail*, July 5, 2015.

132 "We cannot deny the humanitarian crisis": Quoted in Jim Yardley and Azam Ahmed, "Pope Francis Wades into U.S. Immigration Morass with Border Trip," *New York Times*, February 17, 2016.

133 "a very political person": Quoted in James Carroll, "The Radical Meaning of Pope Francis's Visit to Juárez," *The New Yorker*, February 18, 2016, https://www.newyorker.com/news/news-desk/the -radical-meaning-of-pope-franciss-visit-to-juarez.

133 "We don't have to spend hundreds of billions": Quoted in Jon Keller, "On the Issues: Building a Wall Along the Mexico Border," CBS Boston, February 2, 2016, https://boston.cbslocal.com/2016/02/02 /donald-trump-immigration-mexico-wall-ted-cruz-marco-rubio -hillary-clinton-bernie-sanders-wbz-jon-keller-at-large/.

134 "[It's] more of a slogan": Ibid.

134 "chose . . . to stand with Obama": Quoted in Priscilla Alvarez, "A Telling Confrontation Between Ted Cruz and Marco Rubio," *The Atlantic*, December 16, 2015, https://www.theatlantic.com/politics /archive/2015/12/a-telling-confrontation-between-ted-cruz-and -marco-rubio/420762/.

134 "If he builds the wall the way he built Trump Towers": Quoted in Jacob Brogan, "The Best Lines of the CNN GOP Debate," *Slate*, February 25, 2016, https://slate.com/news-and-politics/2016/02/these -are-trump-rubio-and-cruz-best-quotes-and-lines-of-the-cnn-gop -debate.html.

135 "Donald J. Trump is calling for a total and complete shutdown": Quoted in Jenna Johnson, "Trump Calls for Total and Complete Shutdown," *Washington Post*, December 7, 2015.

135 "politicians have promised for thirty years": Quoted in Jeremy Diamond, "Sen. Jeff Sessions Endorses Donald Trump," CNN, February 29, 2016, https://www.cnn.com/2016/02/28/politics/donald-trump -jeff-sessions-endorsement/index.html.

135 "we don't need to be profiling": "Chris Christie Responds to Trump," *Face the Nation*, December 6, 2015, https://www.cbsnews.com /news/face-the-nation-transcripts-december-6-2015-trump-christie -sanders/.

136 "We don't need a wall": Quoted in Danny Freeman, "Bernie Sanders Calls for Immigration Reform," NBC News, March 20, 2016, https:// www.nbcnews.com/politics/2016-election/bernie-sanders-calls -immigration-reform-during-u-s-mexico-border-n542091.

136 "a study by the Pew Research Center": "Americans' Views on Immigrants Marked by Widening Partisan, Generational Divides," April 15, 2016, http://www.pewresearch.org/fact-tank/2016/04/15/americans

-views-of-immigrants-marked-by-widening-partisan-generational
-divides/.

136 "You know, if it gets a little boring": Editorial, "A Chance to Reset the Republican Race," *New York Times*, January 30, 2016.

137 "an impermeable border fence": Quoted in Edgar Munoz, "Meet the Romneys of Mexico," PRI, October 30, 2012, https://www.pri.org /stories/2012-10-30/meet-romneys-mexico.

137 "Complete the danged fence": Quoted in Rafael Bernal, "McCain Campaign Blocks Own Ad," *The Hill*, May 19, 2016, https://thehill.com /latino/280524-mccain-campaign-blocks-mccain-ad-on-youtube.

137 "thing is . . . I never took him seriously": "The Primaries Are Over," Rush Limbaugh, August 29, 2016, https://www.rushlimbaugh.com /daily/2016/08/29/the_primaries_are_over_and_now_we_must _stop_hillary_to_save_the_country/.

138 "Borders, language, culture": See for example Michael Savage, *Government Zero: No Borders, No Language, No Culture* (New York: Center Street, 2015).

138 "a 'globalist' elite who had 'hijacked the country' ": Quoted in Liam Stack, "Globalism: A Far-Right Conspiracy Theory Buoyed by Trump," *New York Times*, November 15, 2016.

138 "a minority of Americans aged under eighteen within five years": "Projecting Majority-Minority," United States Census Bureau, 2015, https://www.census.gov/content/dam/Census/newsroom/releases /2015/cb15-tps16_graphic.pdf.

138 "the increasing size of the country's Latino community": "Facts on U.S. Latinos, 2015," Pew Research Center, September 18, 2017, http:// www.pewhispanic.org/2017/09/18/facts-on-u-s-latinos/.

139 "only 66 percent of its supporters believed the wall would ever be built": Cited in Jenna Johnson, "Many Trump Supporters Don't Believe His Wildest Promises—and They Don't Care," *Washington Post*, June 7, 2016.

139 "I believe the world, and particularly": Quoted in Thomas J. Main, *The Rise of the Alt-Right* (Washington, DC: The Brookings Institution, 2018), 216.

139 "center-right, populist, anti-establishment": Quoted in Aaron Blake, "It's Official: The Chief of Breitbart News Is Headed to the West Wing," *Washington Post*, November 13, 2016.

140 "We must expect everything in politics": Charles Maurras, "La Politique," *L'action française*, February 22, 1918. Translation mine.

141 "He choked": "The Third Presidential Debate," YouTube, October 19, 2016, https://www.youtube.com/watch?v=smkyorC5qwc.

141 "need to build bridges, not walls": See for example Clinton's tweet of July 25, 2016, https://twitter.com/HillaryClinton/status /757813382636380160.

142 "An exit poll from a combination of news organizations": Jon Huang, Samuel Jacoby, et al., "Election 2016: Exit Polls," *New York Times*, November 8, 2016, https://www.nytimes.com/interactive /2016/11/08/us/politics/election-exit-polls.html.

V. CONSTRUCTING THE NORMAL

145 "roughly three and a half million people by 1961": Cited in Pertti Ahonen, *Death at the Berlin Wall* (New York: Oxford University Press, 2011), 11. I rely heavily on Ahonen's research throughout this chapter.

145 "Better safe than sorry": Quoted in W. R. Smyser, *Kennedy and the Berlin Wall* (New York: Rowman and Littlefield, 2009), 100.

146 "*Ab sofort*": Quoted in Michael Meyer, "Günter Schabowksi, the Man Who Opened the Wall," *New York Times*, November 6, 2015.

147 "the curtain can be closed this afternoon": Ahonen, *Death at the Berlin Wall*, 182.

147 "nothing had changed": Ibid., 18.

148 "Six-Year-Old Dies Before the Very Eyes": Quoted in Udo Baron, *The Victims at the Berlin Wall 1961–1989: A Biographical Handbook* (Berlin: Ch. Links Verlag, 2011), 244.

149 "Alcoholics from West Berlin": Marianna S. Katona, *Tales from the Berlin Wall: Recollections of Frequent Crossings* (Berlin: Anotam, 2003), 33.

150 "protests and proclamations": Quoted in Ahonen, *Death at the Berlin Wall*, 187.

150 "Brandenburger Tor": Cornelia Krause, "Publisher's Crusade for Reunited Germany on Exhibit," Reuters, March 9, 2007.

151 "photographs of each other": Quoted in Ahonen, *Death at the Berlin Wall*, 186.

152 "infiltration": Stephen Barber, *Berlin Bodies: Anatomizing the Streets of the City* (London: Reaktion Books, 2017), 208.

153 "Paris is always Paris": Quoted in Jesse Rhodes, "Berlin, Alive Again," *Smithsonian Magazine*, July 27, 2011. Accessed January 12, 2019, https://www.smithsonianmag.com/travel/berlin-alive-again-37313631/.

154 "agents of the State Security Service (counting informers) to citizens": Cited in John O. Koehler, *Stasi: The Untold Story of the East German Secret Police* (Boulder: West View Press, 1999), 9.

154 "Socialism means permanently rising living": Quoted in Stephen Kotkin, *Uncivil Society: 1989 and the Implosion of the Communist Establishment* (New York: The Modern Library, 2010), 45.

155 "13 August 1961 and the secure border": Quoted in Ahonen, *Death at the Berlin Wall*, 237.

155 "a wall is a hell of a lot better": Quoted in Smyser, *Kennedy and the Berlin Wall*, 106.

155 "not currently on the agenda": Quoted in Carsten Volkery, "The Iron Lady's Views on German Reunification," *Der Spiegel*, September 11, 2009.

155 "remain so long as the conditions that led to its erection": Quoted in Kotkin, *Uncivil Society*, 44.

156 "We really were not impressed": Quoted in Kate Thayer, "During Elgin Visit, Gorbachev Recalls Being 'Not Impressed' by Reagan's Berlin Wall Speech," *Chicago Tribune*, April 21, 2012.

156 "a break with Stalinism": Quoted in Franz Oswald, *The Party that Came Out of the Cold War: The Party of Democratic Socialism in United Germany* (Westport, CT: Praeger, 2002), 5.

157 "Wall in [the] heads": Peter Schneider, quoted in Nick Hodgin and Caroline Pearce, *The GDR Remembered: Representations of*

the East German State Since 1989 (New York: Camden House, 2011), 133e.

157 "sexless beings with spherical heads": Quoted in Olga Khazan, "The 'Little Traffic Light Man' that Could," *The Atlantic*, September 25, 2013, https://www.theatlantic.com/international/archive/2013/09 /the-little-traffic-light-man-that-could/279968/.

158 "Man grows used to everything": Fyodor Dostoevsky, *Crime and Punishment*, trans. Constance Garnett (New York: Dover, 2001), 22.

159 "the dog who caught the car": Colbert added: "Remember, we're in the backseat of a car being driven by a dog now." *The Late Show with Stephen Colbert*, March 22, 2017, https://www.youtube.com /watch?v=hzAFOLToeCA.

159 "defended other nations' borders while refusing": "The Inaugural Address," The White House, January 20, 2017, https://www.white house.gov/briefings-statements/the-inaugural-address/.

160 "the policy of the executive branch to . . . secure the southern border": "Executive Order: Border Security and Immigration Enforcement Improvements," The White House, January 25, 2017, https:// www.whitehouse.gov/presidential-actions/executive-order-border -security-immigration-enforcement-improvements/.

160 "See you in court": Quoted in Rebecca Kheel, "ACLU to Trump: See You in Court," *The Hill*, November 9, 2016, https://thehill.com /policy/defense/305216-aclu-pledges-to-use-full-firepower-if-trump -pursues-deportations-muslim-ban.

161 "The whole world will soon see": Quoted in Molly Redden, "Trump Powers 'Will Not Be Questioned' on Immigration," *The Guardian*, February 12, 2017.

161 "a more forceful injunction, suspending the ban": Judge James Robart, State of Washington v. Donald Trump, 2:17-cv-00141, February 3, 2017.

162 "the whole environment is one of dysfunction": Quoted in David Smith and Ben Jacobs, "Chaos in the White House," *The Guardian*, February 18, 2017.

162   "The AIA and its 89,000 members are committed": Quoted in Editorial, "AIA Pledges to Work with Donald Trump, Membership Recoils," *The Architect's Newspaper*, November 11, 2016.

162   "little mention was ever made by Trump": Ibid.

162   "several prototype wall structures in the vicinity": CBP, "Design Build Structure, Solicitation Number: 2017-JC-RT-0001," Federal Business Opportunities, February 24, 2017, https://www.fbo.gov/index?s =opportunity&mode=form&tab=core&id=b8e1b2a6876519ca0aedd 748e1e491cf&_cview=0

163   "One of our goals was to not be like the Great Wall": Quoted in Katelyn Fossett, "The Great Green Wall of America," *Politico*, March 8, 2017, https://www.politico.com/magazine/story/2017/03/beautiful -border-wall-214882.

163   "aestheticize": See for example Meg Miller, "Please Do Not Aestheticize the Wall," *Fast Company*, March 13, 2017, https://www.fastcompany .com/3068888/architects-please-do-not-aestheticize-the-wall.

164   "more beauty": William L. Hamilton, "A Fence with More Beauty, Fewer Barbs," *New York Times*, June 18, 2006.

164   "completion date of 2020, with an expected total budget of $21.6 billion": Cited in Julia Edwards Ainsley, "Trump Border Wall to Cost $21.6 Billion, Take 3.5 Years to Build," Reuters, February 9, 2017.

165   "apprehension numbers at the border plummeted from over sixty thousand": "Southwest Border Migration FY2017," CBP Newsroom, https://www.cbp.gov/newsroom/stats/sw-border-migration.

165   "This is encouraging news": Quoted in Tal Kopan, "Does Borer Drop Mean Trump's Tough Talk Is Working?" CNN online, March 9, 2017, https://www.cnn.com/2017/03/08/politics/border-crossings-huge -drop-trump-tough-talk/index.html.

165   "A lot of people are moving down": Interview, Alfonso Medina, February 23, 2018.

167   "with the votes of all but fifteen Democrats": "Final Vote Results for Roll Call 249, HR 244," May 3, 2017, Office of the Clerk of the House of Representatives, http://clerk.house.gov/evs/2017/roll249.xml.

167 "we achieved the single largest increase in border security": "Remarks by President Trump at the Presentation of the Commander-in-Chief Trophy to the United States Air Force Academy," The White House, May 2, 2017.

167 "binational, bilingual and bipartisan": Quoted in Mariana Alfaro, "U.S. Representatives Hurd, Castro Rally for Bipartisanship on the Border," *Texas Tribune*, March 25, 2017.

167 "Building a wall from sea to shining sea": "Rep. Will Hurd: 'Building a Wall from Sea to Shining Sea' Least Effective Way to Do Border Security," Rep. Will Hurd official website, April 26, 2017, https://hurd .house.gov/media-center/in-the-news/gop-rep-will-hurd-building -wall-sea-shining-sea-least-effective-way-do.

168 "divided and pitted against each other": Rep. Karen Bass, quoted in Michael D. Shear and Yamiche Alcindor, "On 'Dreamers' Deal, Democrats Face a Surprising Foe: Dreamers," *New York Times*, October 1, 2017.

168 "I don't think a government shutdown's necessary": Quoted in Lisa Mascaro, "McConnell Pushes Back on Reports of Discontent with Trump," *Los Angeles Times*, August 23, 2017

168 "Confusion": Hannah Arendt, *The Origins of Totalitarianism* (New York: Harcourt, 1976), 409.

169 "If Trump gives me the canvas": Quoted in Brian Boucher, "One Mexican Artist Is Already Planning to Paint the World's Largest Mural on Trump's Wall," *Artnet*, July 31, 2017, https://news.artnet.com /art-world/donald-trump-border-wall-mural-1035635.

169 "had the nerve to go over to Germany": Quoted in Angela Kocherga, "Rights Advocates Protest Plan to Build Border Wall," *Albuquerque Journal*, October 23, 2017.

170 "not going to pay for that fucking wall": "Former Mexican President to Trump," YouTube, February 25, 2016, https://www.youtube.com /watch?v=x4OwJOVi0ec.

170 "Democrats are Failing the Resistance": Andrew Sullivan, "How the Democrats Are Failing the Resistance," *Intelligencer*, November 3,

2017, http://nymag.com/intelligencer/2017/11/how-the-democrats
-are-failing-the-resistance.html.

170 "are a lot of positive conversations taking place": Rep. Mario Díaz-
Balart, quoted in Brian Bennett, "DACA Negotiations Slow as Trump
Demands More than Democrats Will Give," *Los Angeles Times*,
November 17, 2017.

171 "there was a time in the not too far distant past": Rep. Bennie Thompson, quoted in Rafael Bernal, "House Panel Approves $10 Billion for
Border Wall," *The Hill*, October 4, 2017, https://thehill.com/home
news/house/353904-house-panel-approves-10b-for-border-wall.

171 "a national monument under the Antiquities Act of 1906": Quoted
in Sarah Cascone, "Art Provocateur Christoph Büchel Wants to Turn
Trump's Border Wall Models into Land Art," *Artnet*, January 4, 2018,
https://news.artnet.com/exhibitions/christoph-buchel-trump-wall
-art-1191518.

VI. THE RETURN OF THEM

175 "is like an armed camp": Quoted in Elad Ben-Dror, *Ralph Bunche and
the Arab-Israeli Conflict: Mediation and the UN, 1947–1949*, trans.
Diana File and Lenn Shramm (London: Routledge, 2016), 14.

175 "bloodshed, odium, trouble and worry": Quoted in Brian Urquhart,
Ralph Bunche: An American Life (New York: W. W. Norton, 1993),
140.

176 "One thing seems sure": Quoted in ibid., 146.

176 "This problem can't be solved": Quoted in ibid.

176 "The longer we stay": Quoted in ibid.

176 "Partition": United Nations Special Committee on Palestine, "Report
to the General Assembly Vol. 1," Offical Records of the Second Session of the General Assembly, 1947, https://unispal.un.org/DPA
/DPR/unispal.nsf/0/07175DE9FA2DE563852568D3006E10F3.

177 "The Palestine episode is over": Quoted in Urquhart, *Ralph Bunche*,
149.

NOTES

178 "the common conviction": Technically a pair of theorists: Florine Ballif and Stéphane Rosière, "The Challenge of 'Teichopolitics': Analyzing Contemporary Border Closures," *L'Espace géographique* 38, no. 3
(2009): 193. Translation mine.

179 "unabashed victory of economic and political liberalism": Francis
Fukuyama, "The End of History?" *The National Interest*, no. 16 (Summer 1989): 3.

179 "nearly 150 Palestinians and a dozen Israelis died": Cited in Sergio
Catignani, *Israeli Counter-Insurgency and the Intifadas* (London:
Routledge, 2008), 105.

179 "physical mechanism for peace": Quoted in Tami Amanda Jacoby,
Bridging the Barrier: Israeli Unilateral Disengagement (London: Routledge, 2007), 21.

179 "the estimated $300 million cost of a West Bank barrier": Cited in
ibid., 22.

180 "84 percent of Israeli Jews, according to contemporary polling": Cited
in ibid., 38.

180 "When there are seventy dead Israelis": Quoted in David Makovsky,
"A Defensible Fence: Fighting Terror and Enabling a Two-State Solu-
tion," monograph for the Washington Institute for Near East Policy
(April 2004): 7.

180 "the first eighty-five miles of infrastructure": Cited in Jacoby, *Bridging
the Barrier*, 26.

180 "the government approved another 267 miles": Cited in René Backmann, *A Wall for Palestine*, trans. A. Kaiser (New York: Picador,
2010), 221.

180 "Over 14 percent of what had lately been Palestinian territory":
Makovsky, "A Defensible Fence," 24.

181 "at least 3 percent of the barrier": Cited in Mitchell Bard, "West
Bank, Gaza and Lebanon Security Barriers: Background & Overview, "Jewish Virtual Library, https://www.jewishvirtuallibrary.org
/background-and-overview-of-israel-s-security-fence.

181 "this ghastly racist wall": Edward Said, "A Road Map to Where?" *London Review of Books* 25, no. 12 (June 19, 2003): 4.

181 "the menacing symbol of Israeli domination": Christine Leuen-
     berger, "Technologies, Practices and the Reproduction of Conflict:
     The Impact of the West Bank Barrier on Peace Building," in Elisabeth
     Vallet, ed., *Borders, Fences and Walls: State of Insecurity?* (London:
     Routledge, 2016), 225.

181 "It is very difficult to develop confidence": Quoted in Makovsky, "A
     Defensible Fence," 8.

181 "Between April and December of 2002, the Foreign Ministry stated":
     Cited in "Saving Lives: Israel's Anti-Terrorist Fence," Israel Ministry
     of Foreign Affairs, https://mfa.gov.il/MFA_Graphics/MFA%20Gallery
     /Documents/savinglives.pdf.

181 "roadways wound through the West Bank serving mostly (or exclu-
     sively) Israeli traffic": For an in-depth exploration of the West Bank's
     byzantine legal-infrastructural system, see Visualizing Impact, "Seg-
     regated Roads," Visualizing Palestine online, accessed January 12,
     2019, https://visualizingpalestine.org/visuals/segregated-roads-west
     -bank.

182 "President Trump is right": Benjamin Netanyahu, Twitter, Janu-
     ary 28, 2017, https://twitter.com/netanyahu/status/82537179597282
     5089?lang=en.

182 "All you have to do is ask Israel": Quoted in Isabel Kershner, "Trump
     Cites Israel's Wall as Model. The Analogy is Iffy," *New York Times*,
     January 27, 2017.

184 "20 percent or more of Israel's population": "Vital Statistics: Latest
     Population Statistics for Israel," Jewish Virtual Library, https://www
     .jewishvirtuallibrary.org/latest-population-statistics-for-israel.

184 "83 percent preferred to remain Israeli citizens": Cited in Leon Hadar,
     "Israel's Arabs: Not Zionists, but Israelis," *The National Interest*,
     January 15, 2014, https://nationalinterest.org/commentary/israels
     -arabs-not-zionists-israelis-9711.

185 "a disproportionately small share of municipal services": For the chal-
     lenges faced by Jerusalem's Arab population, see Netta Ahituv, "Fif-
     teen Years of Separation: The Palestinians Cut Off from Jerusalem by
     the Wall," *Haaretz*, March 10, 2018.

186 "only be available for operationally effective designs": 115th Congress, H.R. 1625, Consolidated Appropriations Act of 2018, §230(b).

187 "It's been—I don't want to say the word 'confusing' ": Interview, Dennis O'Leary, June 6, 2017. The following passage is based on reporting conducted in the summer of 2017 and appears courtesy of *Foreign Policy*: see Ian Volner, "The Trump Administration Doesn't Want a Winner for Its Wall Competition," *Foreign Policy*, July 12, 2017, https://foreignpolicy.com/2017/07/12/the-trump-administration-doesnt-want-a-winner-for-its-wall-competition/.

187 "a more in-depth proposal": Email interview, Jim Knott/Jane Lanzillo, July 11, 2017.

187 "It's been a real mess": Anonymous finalist interview, June 30, 2017. As of January, 2019, the subject with whom I spoke has not made himself available again for further interviews concerning the competition. I have decided therefore to leave him unnamed.

188 "The companies are competing, providing designs": Interview, Carlos Diaz, May 19, 2017.

188 "I've been skirting the edge": O'Leary interview.

188 "under consideration": CBP wall press conference, No. 062717, US Department of Homeland Security, June 28, 2017.

189 "There have been threats": Anonymous finalist interview.

189 "The $20 million of CBP discretionary funds": Cited in Julia Edwards Ainsley, "Trump Administration Has Found Only $20 Million in Existing Funds for Wall," Reuters, March 1, 2017.

190 "pay for itself": Quoted in Maggie Haberman, "Trump Turns an Iowa Rally into a Venting Session," *New York Times*, June 21, 2017.

190 "'Donald Trump,' said the finalist": Anonymous finalist interview.

190 "He thinks it would be a beautiful thing": Quoted in Michael Grunwald, "The Tunnel That Could Break New York," *Politico*, July 6, 2018, https://www.politico.com/magazine/story/2018/07/06/gateway-tunnel-new-york-city-infrastructure-218839.

191 "each received a payment of between $300,000 and $500,000": Cited in Callum Patton, "Trump Wall: Israeli Company to Make Prototype for his Mexico Border Wall," *Newsweek*, September 14, 2017, https://

www.newsweek.com/trump-wall-israeli-company-make-prototype
-200000-mile-long-mexico-border-wall-664968.

191 "the recipient of more than two thousand violation notices": Cited
in Jorge Rivas, "The Companies Vying to Build the Border Wall
Seem Shady as Hell," *Splinter*, April 18, 2018, https://splinternews
.com/the-companies-vying-to-build-the-border-wall-seem-shady
-1825356649. The article includes a general overview of the competitors' assorted legal woes.

192 "to deter illegal crossings in the area": "Construction Begins on Wall
Prototypes," CBP Newsroom, September 26, 2017, https://www.cbp
.gov/newsroom/national-media-release/construction-begin-wall
-prototypes.

192 "a Mexican man jumped over the nearby landing-mat wall": "Watch:
Illegal Immigrants Jump Fence During MSNBC Report on Border
Wall," Fox News, October 24, 2017, https://insider.foxnews.com/2017
/10/24/illegal-immigrants-jump-border-wall-during-msnbc-report.

192 "within the next six or seven months": Quoted in Calvin Woodward
and Elliot Spagat, "AP Fact Check: How's Trump's Border Wall Coming Along?" Associated Press, September 26, 2017.

193 "Otay Mesa was neither the worst nor the best": The following section is adapted from reporting conducted in the fall of 2017 and
appears courtesy of *Curbed*: see Ian Volner, "Prototypes of Trump's
Wall Offer Chilling Lesson in the Power of Architecture," *Curbed*,
November 28, 2017, https://www.curbed.com/2017/11/28/16705202
/trump-wall-mexico-border-prototypes.

195 "This odd open-air architecture gallery": Christopher Hawthorne,
"Trump's Border Wall Through the Eyes of an Architecture Critic,"
Los Angeles Times, December 30, 2017.

196 "an external, monstrous force": John Roberts, *The Reasoning of
Unreason: Universalism, Capitalism and Disenlightenment* (London:
Bloomsbury, 2018), 7.

196 "Is It Inspired or Irresponsible": Carolina Miranda, "Is It Inspired
or Irresponsible to Call Trump's Border Wall Prototypes 'Art'?" *Los
Angeles Times*, February 8, 2018.

197   "Color—hue, intensity, brightness, depth": CBP Office of Acquisition, "Border Wall Mock-Up and Prototype Test Final Report [Redacted]," Doc. no. ENT12-BW-14-000004 Revision A (February 23, 2018): 166, https://www.documentcloud.org/documents/4891728-Border-Wall -Mock-Up-and-Prototype-Test-Final.html#document/p26/a454445.

198   "The effective use of aesthetic choices": Ibid., 165.

VII. THE WAY OF ALL WALLS

203   "could scarcely understand [any speech]": Koran, 18:93.

204   "There's a mystique to the place": Interview, Stuart Denison, October 10, 2017.

204   "the weakening of state sovereignty": Wendy Brown, *Walled States, Waning Sovereignty* (New York: Zone Books, 2010), 36.

204   "At least seventy walls, it is estimated": Cited in interview, Reece Jones, 10.22.18.

206   "professional mountain climbers": Quoted in Kaila White, "Trump: Some Immigrants Crossing Border Are Like 'Professional Mountain Climbers,'" *The Arizona Republic*, March 13, 2018.

206   "We have a lousy wall over here now": Quoted in Priscilla Alvarez, "What's Next for Trump's Border Wall," *The Atlantic*, March 16, 2018, https://www.theatlantic.com/politics/archive/2018/03/trump-border -wall-san-diego/555698/.

207   "$25 billion for border infrastructure over ten years": Cited in Sahil Kapur and Steven T. Dennis, "How Trump Let His Goal of Building a Border Wall Slip Away," *Bloomberg*, December 13, 2018, https://www .bloomberg.com/amp/news/articles/2018-12-13/how-trump-let-his -goal-of-building-a-border-wall-slip-away

207   "California remains the 6th largest economy in the world": Jerry Brown, Twitter, March 13, 2018. Accessed January 12, 2019. https:// twitter.com/jerrybrowngov/status/973668776993439744.

208   "psychic fantasies": Brown, *Walled States*, 121.

208   "You can follow the trends in the news": Reece Jones interview.

209   "increasing desiccation": Kenyon, *Digging Up Jericho*, 76.

209 "Cursed before the Lord": KJV, 6:26.

209 "One epidemiological study, dating to the 1970s": E.V. Hulse, "Joshua's Curse and the Abandonment of Jericho," *Medical History* 15, no. 4 (October, 1971): 376–86.

210 "a banner year for illegal immigration": Steven Kopits, "Expect Illegal Immigration Across the Mexican Border to Double Next Year," *The Hill*, October 27, 2017, https://thehill.com/opinion/immigration/357381-expect-illegal-immigration-across-the-mexican-border-to-double-next-year.

210 "apprehensions in the CBP's southwest sector soared above the fifty thousand mark": "Southwest Border Migration FY2018," CBP Newsroom.

211 "massive blow": Ecologist Gerardo Ceballos, quoted in Kate Furby, "Thousands of Scientists Object to Trump's Border Wall," *Washington Post*, July 24, 2018.

211 "A rookie Border Patrol employee held us at gunpoint": Quoted in Robert L. Press et al., "In the Shadow of the Wall, Part I: Borders, Wildlife, Habitat and Collaborative Conservation at Risk," report for Defenders of Wildlife (2018), 8.

212 "letters to the cities in Britain": Quoted in E. A. Thompson, "Zosimus 6. 10. 2. and the Letters of Honorius," *The Classical Quarterly* 32, no. 2 (1982): 445.

213 "separate those who claim to be a parent and child": Transcript, "Kirstjen Nielsen Addresses Family Separation at Border," *New York Times*, June 18, 2018, https://www.nytimes.com/2018/06/18/us/politics/dhs-kirstjen-nielsen-families-separated-border-transcript.html.

213 "That's not the Kirstjen we know": Quoted in Joseph Guinto, "That's Not the Kirstjen We Know," *Politico*, July 2, 2018, https://www.politico.com/magazine/story/2018/07/02/kirstjen-nielsen-immigration-crisis-former-colleagues-218939.

213 "Nationally, with changes in policy": Interview, Adonia Simpson, October 16, 2018.

214 "volume of unheard cases jumped by 38 percent": TRAC Immigration, "Growth in Immigration Court Backlog Varies Markedly

by State," Syracuse University, https://trac.syr.edu/immigration/reports/526/.

214 "little chance of succeeding legally": Enrique Krauze, "Will Mexico Get Half of Its Territory Back?" *New York Times*, April 6, 2017.

215 "weep tears of blood in search of help": Quoted in Richard J. Smith, The Qing Dynasty and Traditional Chinese Culture (New York: Rowman & Littlefield, 2015), 61.

215 "At the end of the Ming, my grandfather": Quoted in Billé et al., *Frontier Encounters*, 38.

216 "prioritize investments that allow the organization": Government Accountability Office, "Southwest Border Security: CBP Is Evaluating Designs and Locations for Border Barriers but Is Proceeding Without Key Information," GAO-18-614 (July 2018), 24.

217 "I come from the Right": Interview, Alex Nowrasteh, April 6, 2018.

217 "le premier coup de pioche": "Le premier coup de Pioche aux fortifications à la Porte Clignancourt, Chaissagne-Royon," Agence Roi, May 5, 1919. Gallica digital library, https://gallica.bnf.fr/ark:/12148/btv1b53016224z.item.

218 "where the harvest was of broken bottles": Aristide Bruant, quoted in Luc Sante, *The Other Paris* (New York: Farrar, Straus and Giroux, 2015), 60.

219 "On the border it's so much more complicated": Interview, Roger Hodge, June 8, 2017.

219 "It's different than a fence in that it also has technology": Quoted in Jane C. Tim, "DHS Chief Marks First Section of Trump's Border Wall," NBC, October 26, 2018, https://www.nbcnews.com/politics/donald-trump/dhs-chief-marks-first-section-trump-s-border-wall-it-n924941.

219 "It's just a matter of what you call it": Quoted in Burgess Everett and Marianne Levine, "Senators Bicker Over Definition of Trump's Wall," *Politico*, December 6, 2018, https://www.politico.com/story/2018/12/06/congress-border-wall-trump-funding-government-shutdown-1046169.

220 "Nobody had alerted us to any change": Quoted in Roger Cohen, "Haphazardly, Berlin Wall Fell a Decade Ago," *New York Times*, November 9, 1999.

220 "I am going to end all controls": Quoted in Laurence Dodds, "Berlin Wall: How the Wall Came Down, As It Happened Twenty-Five Years Ago," *The Telegraph*, November 9, 2014.

221 "had just thrown a coat over her nightdress": Quoted in Tony Patterson, "Angela Merkel's Unlikely Journey from Communist East Germany to the Chancellorship," *The Independent*, November 17, 2015.

221 "one of the happiest moments of my life": "Merkel Pays Tribute to Courage of East Germans," Der *Spiegel* online, November 10, 2009, https://www.spiegel.de/international/germany/remembering-the-fall-of-the-berlin-wall-merkel-pays-tribute-to-courage-of-east-germans-a-660391.html.

221 "It just happened a couple weeks back": Interview, Agent Vincent Pirro, October 4, 2018.

221 "the 124 miles of new and improved fencing": Cited in Denise Lu, "The Border Wall: What Has Trump Built So Far?" *New York Times*, February 12, 2019, https://www.nytimes.com/interactive/2019/01/05/us/border-wall.html?action=click&module=Top%20Stories&pgtype=Homepage.

223 "8.8 percent, despite all the rearguard attacks": Cited in Bertha Coombs, "Rates of Uninsured in U.S. Remain at Historic Low," CNBC, September 13, 2018, https://www.cnbc.com/2018/09/12/rates-of-uninsured-in-us-hold-steady-at-historic-low-8point8-percent.html.

223 "All of the indicators are, 'Boy'": Amy Walter quoted in Peter Hamby, "Get Over Your Election-Needle PTSD: The Blue Wave Is Real, and It's a Monster," *Vanity Fair* online, September 12, 2018, https://www.vanityfair.com/news/2018/09/get-over-your-election-needle-ptsd-the-blue-wave-is-real-and-its-a-monster.

224 "that are bad in the medium and long term": Interview, Ahmed Moor, October 14, 2018.

225 "I said to them, 'What will you do to me if I pull this out?'": Interview, Bashar Masri, April 23, 2018.

226 "You have to look at the whole mission": Interview, Raul Grijalva, September 25, 2018.

227 "broke for Democratic candidates by 19 percent": Cited in Alec Tyson, "The 2018 Midterm Vote: Divisions by Race, Gender, Education", Pew Research Center, November 8, 2018, http://www.pew research.org/fact-tank/2018/11/08/the-2018-midterm-vote -divisions-by-race-gender-education/.

227 "raising $1 billion in private donations": Cited in Morgan Gstalter, "$20 Million in GoFundMe for Trump Border Wall to Be Refunded," *The Hill*, January 11, 2019, https://thehill.com/homenews /administration/424976-20-million-raised-in-gofundme-for-trump -border-wall-will-be-refunded.

227 "debate in private": Quoted in Marina Fang, "Trump Battles with Nancy Pelosi and Chuck Schumer Over Border Wall Financing," *Huffington Post*, December 11, 2018, https://www.huffingtonpost.com/entry /trump-pelosi-schumer-border-wall_us_5c0fefc2e4b00e17a5337320.

227 "at the request of Democrats": "Trump's Speech on Immigration and the Democratic Response," *New York Times*, January 8, 2019, https:// www.nytimes.com/2019/01/08/us/politics/trump-speech-transcript .html. Other members of the administration had already signaled the official retreat to fence-building, including Chief of Staff John Kelly, who admitted in December that the project "won't be a wall"; he was succeeded the following month by former OMB Director Mick Mulvaney, who had previously gone on record calling the whole wall idea "absurd . . . almost childish." Quoted in Tom Porter, "Trump Hits Back at Claim Concrete Wall Plan Abandoned," *Newsweek*, December 31, 2018, https://www.newsweek.com/trump-hits-back-claim -wall-plan-abandoned-and-reveals-itll-be-partly-see-1275686.

229 "It's like a manhood thing for him": Quoted in Mike DeBonis, "'It's like a manhood thing for him': Pelosi's Power Play with Trump Serves as Message to Opponents," *Washington Post*, December 11, 2018.

229 "A city will be well fortified which is surrounded by brave men": Quoted in Plutarch, *Plutarch's Lives Vol. 1*, trans. Bernadotte Perrin (New York: Macmillan, 1914), 267.